LYRICS AND LIES

Susan Reedy

Dedication

For our family

Chapter 1

Wednesday, December 16th 8:48 P.M.

Sims' Farm - Newport, Oklahoma

"...like a glimpse of Heaven from God above
Eyes wide opened, our path paved in love
If I ever get lost in this dream we're livin' in
one thought of you will lead me home again..."

Crinkled white pages fluttered in the night air. Tracy Sims clasped her journal and hugged it to her chest, shivering as her latest sentiment lingered in the air. The glow of the red and green Christmas lights strung across the front porch spilled into her eyes and as she glanced to the side, she met Jared Frazier's gaze.

"It came to me last night," she offered, shoving her journal and unfinished calculous aside. "After you left."

"Mmm," he nodded.

The porch light captured Tracy's hazel eyes just right – that kaleidoscope of denim blue, teal and amber – prisms of light that sparkled like Lake Murray at sunset. And that grin curling at the corner of her lips, her one girlish trait that never quite grew up. It had captured her daddy's heart since she was a baby, and now seventeen years later, rendered Jared speechless anytime it unfurled.

But Tracy heard him loud and clear. The love in his ebony eyes and the many ways he showed his love said more than any words could ever say. Securing her seatbelt as soon as she climbed in his truck, holding her close to his side while they tramped through the pasture, carrying her piggy-back after a rainstorm so her feet stayed dry, calling her just before bed every night so hers was the last voice he heard. Those were the simple things that made her feel so... *cherished.* That thought brought an easy smile. She stroked the hair from his eyes. "Known you most of my life and you still make my heart race."

Jared exhaled and stretched his legs, smoothing his hand along his thigh. Clumps of dried dirt crumbled from his work boots as he shifted his six-foot frame; he swept it from the step with his Packers ball cap.

"Just gettin' you back." He crammed his hat on her head and yanked the brim over her eyes. "Torturing me with that tight ass," he teased. Eyeing the dinner plate just behind her, he reached around and tugged it closer. "And these cookies!"

Tantalizing whiffs of chocolate chip cookies lifted on the air. Seizing another one from the plate, he popped a seventh into his mouth. Warm, melted chocolate smudged his fingers but instead of licking it away, he traced the gooey sweetness around the curvature of her lips. She steeled herself, stifling a smile as he completed his artwork. Without warning she lunged forward and kissed him, coating his own mouth with the rich, sticky ooze. Just as Tracy wound her arms around his neck to enjoy more of the taste, she sensed a movement from the living room window. Her muscles tensed as the sight of her uncle filled the window frame. *Denny Sims.* She cringed at his lanky frame, recounting his "just here for a visit" greeting earlier in the day. Her hazel eyes flared with anger as she remembered his last visit years before – the day of her grandfather's funeral. Correct that. The day *after* the funeral. Denny skipped his father's actual memorial service. What *memorialized* the event was the scene that played out in front of the courthouse as the police hauled her uncle away after the fool went ballistic in front of God and everybody during the reading of the will. Sims had not made the cut, so to speak, and once the executor announced the recipients of his father's inheritance, Denny chose to let the world see his rage for not having been included.

Nothing had changed. His coal black hair and unkempt beard still screamed *outlaw*. From beneath the brim of his weathered Stetson, two cold, sunken eyes bored into Tracy, leaving her to wonder what she had done in one afternoon's time to warrant his anger. She tore her eyes away and once the inside curtain fell free, she began to breathe again.

The warmth of Jared's palm brushed her cheek. As he stroked her face she noticed the tiny laugh lines around his eyes – *character lines*, her mother would have said. Just one of the many traits she loved about the boy she so adored. The words of her poem waltzed through her mind. *Glimpse of Heaven, path paved in love, livin' in a dream...* sure enough, thoughts of him brought her home again. She rose from the porch, dropped the journal to her side and took Jared's hand.

"Let's take a walk."

Jared laced his fingers through hers. Descending the porch, they fell into step – leaping the mound of gravel that lined the driveway as they negotiated a path to the edge of the hayfield - their private hideaway.

Tracy drew in the brisk air, clearing her mind of everything but Jared. Laughter sprinkled through the night, like the hit and miss traces of snow that had begun to fall. They rounded the hay shelter just beyond the reach of the security light beaming from the barn, then breathless, collapsed into the freshly-thrown straw scattered along the ground. Jared peered toward the house, then to the darkness of the pasture. Pressing his fingers to her mouth, he muffled her laughter. "Your dad'll kill me if he catches us out here!"

"Nah, he'll probably keep you alive and make you suffer!" she teased.

Deep, raspy breaths marked time with the rise and fall of her chest. Jared lifted her hand to his heart.

"Do you feel it?" He pushed the ball cap away to see her eyes. She nodded. Both hearts had slowed to one rhythm. She kissed him – losing herself in the moment as the frozen wheat crumbled beneath them. His strong arms swathed her in warmth -- like that cozy, down-feather quilt she disappeared into on cold, rainy days. His breath ebbed and flowed like a tide of soothing heat and with every release of air, Tracy drifted deeper and deeper into his hold.

Her hands migrated south into the back pockets of his frayed jeans. Her gentle squeeze made his muscles react and that same familiar longing pulsed within her. Their lips brushed together -- tender, sensual sweeps that fanned the flame. Feverish heat blurred her mind, but in the dim glow of the distant security light, her sights became suddenly focused. Maybe it was the fear her uncle provoked. Or maybe it was the excitement of Christmas, or the last semester of high school, or the stress of applying for college. Then again, maybe it was just the simple, warm assurance that she and Jared Frazier belonged together. While it was always assumed that their first time would be after marriage, something deep inside told her *the perfect time, the perfect place* was here and now.

"Daddy's out checking the cattle," she breathed against his ear.

"You sure?"

With a gentle tug she unsnapped his jeans, and at once their hands could not work fast enough. Jared stretched his long, tight-end arms around her, pushing her jacket aside and reaching underneath her hoodie to feel the warmth of her skin.

She cradled his head to her chest, feeling the steamy heat of his breath against her breast. Her body arched into him – perfectly. Trembling, she pulled his face close and kissed him, so deeply her senses swirled like the airy snow. Muscles tightened. The rise and fall of her chest quickened. Their minds and hands wandered in a drunken flurry as he tenderly began to lead them into undiscovered love.

But from across the road a dog's unruly howl shattered the silence. A porch light flared, splashing an arc of light across the front yard. The screech of the screen door wailed its warning, alerting they were no longer alone.

"Damn! It's your uncle."

In one fluid motion, he gripped Tracy's hands and yanked her to her feet - fastening, straightening, buttoning. Snatching her jacket from the ground, he froze. Listened.

Silence…

A peek around the hay bale confirmed her uncle was still patrolling the porch. The red glow of his cigarette shone through the darkness.

Jared exhaled his frustration. Tracy pressed her finger to his lips. "Tomorrow night," she vowed as she ran her hands up and down his arms to warm him.

His face glowed in the beam of the security light. She knew the look. The tiny gold flecks in his eyes had darkened as they always did when he grew serious. It had never failed to give away his mood. Carefree, indifferent – *amber gold.* Intent, somber – *chestnut brown.* And at the moment, even in the low light she could see his eyes were as dark as night. He leaned in with a kiss so familiar and comforting, yet in the mix of heated emotion and light snow flurries, more sensual than anything she could have ever dreamed.

"I'll be here," he breathed.

***

Nine miles to the east, U.S. Senator Matthew Hastings stared into the glow of the fireplace, strumming his fingers in steady rhythm of the *tick, tick, tick* of the mantle clock. His anxiety -- or the incessant barking of the dog next door -- had him on edge. Every shadow, every flicker of motion, every ordinary sound that echoed through the house triggered fear. With a slow unsteady breath, he brought the tumbler to his lips and felt the last of the bourbon burn the length of his throat. A long sigh accompanied his ease into the recliner. Unclasping his briefcase, he lifted the transcripts and studied his testimony notes one last time.

The clock chimed. Hastings stared at the ceiling, counting the strokes in anticipation of his business partners' arrival. But at the stroke of nine, the dog's high-pitched wail sliced the air. The agonizing whine echoed louder and louder and then, silence. Dropping the papers, Hastings rushed to the window to see the neighbor's property come alive – motion detectors sweeping white light across the side property. In a panic he sped a text to alert his partner David Frazier, CEO of Sutherant Petroleum. A movement from outside caught his eye. Ducking aside the curtain, he waited, searching the darkness. That same adrenalin rush he remembered from past surveillance missions raced again.

From behind, the deadbolt popped.

He held his breath. But when the muted beep of the front entry alarm sounded, he grew faint. The front door creaked open unleashing a flurry of sounds: incessant beeping, fingers tapping an alarm code, a snip of wire cutters releasing a cold, eerie end to all noise.

Hastings dove behind the sofa, measuring every distressing sound: the intruder's steady approach, the soft *whish, whish* sweep of cotton with each new step, the *tah, tah, tah* of the clock marking time, and the pounding of his pulse surging within.

A sudden flick of light flashed in the gold-plate engraving of the mantle clock. Hastings turned - directly into the aim of the assassin's gun. His limbs went numb - not in fear of the 9mm, but in sheer terror as he stared into the face of his former special-ops sergeant.

The assassin grinned and flipped a mock salute. *"Nu tradez un prieten.* Isn't that what you always told us, Colonel?"

Hastings blanched with the memory. *Never betray a friend.* The code. The man snatched Hastings' papers from the open briefcase and chucked them into the flames. Evidence. All that was left of Hasting's written testimony smoldered into ash. His last hope of justice spiraled into the air along with thoughts of his wife and children who were sleeping upstairs.

"Mack...please, I can explain... "

The invader had not come to listen. He was not there for an apology or for excuses. The dark fatigues, the gloved hands, the precision of every movement. Senator Baird Mackenzick was there for one reason: to eliminate the threat to his interests in Sutherant Petroleum.

Hastings glanced at the clock. Against his ear, he heard the faint *click* of the gun's safety. He closed his eyes, yielding to the protective memory of earlier years – before the rise of Sutherant Petroleum and before his first election. Life had been simpler then.

The silencer of the SIM Bauer 9mm pressed into the tender flesh of his left temple. He thought of his wife. One inaudible whisper brushed his lips.

"Claire"

Then Hastings drew his last breath.

***

Just to the west of Shiloh, the Newport Air Facility operated daily routes throughout the Southwest and occasionally catered to private flights coming in from greater distances. But when airport manager Hank Tisdale studied the Prince Air 200 corporate jet which had arrived an hour earlier with the pilot as the only occupant and no recorded flight plan, his curiosity piqued.

With every tightened bolt and every tweak to the control panel of the small Cresta 182 he had been restoring, the odd behavior of the Prince Air pilot rankled his mind. Paying cash for fuel, producing no identification when asked, and climbing into the black rented four-door Police Officer Waylon Vincent had left in the lot earlier in the day, all tangled into a knot of suspicion. It was enough to warrant a phone call to alert his friend, David Frazier, founder of Sutherant Petroleum.

"Like I said, Dave, it was over an hour ago. Late forties, light complexion, crew cut, muscled up. Flashed a wad of cash and took Vincent's car like he owned the place. Said he had business in Shiloh, but something about him just felt off. I know you've been tightening up security at Sutherant the past few days, so I thought..." Tisdale continued.

David Frazier did not need to hear more. It was what he had feared the past two days. Somehow, somewhere, someone had discovered their collaboration with the FBI. And if this phantom stranger had ties to Newport Police Chief

Waylon Vincent, Frazier knew he couldn't be trusted. Frazier disconnected and wheeled to the side of the highway. That's when he noticed the text message from his friend, Senator Matthew Hastings: *URGENT! CANCEL MEETING!*

Frantically, Frazier pressed Hastings' number. Five long, unanswered rings taunted him. He tried Hastings' business cellphone that was used for governmental business. Six more rings - unanswered. The torturous silence screamed out to him like a hurt child, and like a caring parent, his sixth sense kicked in, telling him to worry, telling him that all was not right. His chest tightened and in the darkness, he fumbled for his glasses. He tried a different number, that of his friend and company lawyer, Leonard Osteen, the fourth in the partnership that had been formed to confront the conspiracy. His pulse pounded stronger with each unheeded ring. No answer. He searched again and found Osteen's landline number. Three rings.

"Hello?"

"Oh, thank God, Sara, it's Dave. I need Leo. I can't reach him on his cell and I need to cancel our meeting."

Frazier paid no mind to the rest of the conversation as Sara explained that she thought her husband had left minutes ago. He barely heard her ramble as she made her way through the house to see if she could catch him. He disregarded her laughter when she joked about Leo getting lost in the neighborhood without his GPS. Frazier even failed to bend an ear when she invited his family for dinner later in the week. But as he heard her enter the garage, he pulled the phone closer. Her surprise to find her husband's car still there led to another string of chatter. But then he heard the scream -- a shrill, heart-wrenching surge of agony.

Between hysterics, he gathered details of the scene as she frantically detailed what she saw -- the raised garage door, a gray smoke rising rising from a metal garbage can, the noxious smell of burning trash, the twisted necktie slashed into her husband's neck. Frazier tasted bile a moment too late. Vomit spewed across the side panel and as he flung the door wide, his stomach lurched again. His mind went wild. *Ambushed in his own garage...burning what? Evidence? Files? Within minutes and one mile of Hastings' place where there had been no answer. Had Hastings been the first target?*

They say that when we face our most life-altering despair or fear, our spirit gains strength from some outside source – adrenalin, mind over matter, God's grace. It's what got him through the death of his infant daughter twelve years before. And now as Frazier listened to Sara's suffering, regret struck his soul and he felt that same weight of grief overcome him.

Before he gained composure, a jabbing pain shot through his chest and he bolted upright. *His own family!* Eyes shot to the dashboard clock – *9:08. Linda! Jared!* In a panic he swerved across traffic and braced his foot against the accelerator to race the nine miles back to Newport. His own home would be the assassin's next target.

On speed dial he reached Phil Murphy, the new head of security for Sutherant Petroleum. In rushed, staccato commands, Frazier set his escape into action, ordering Murphy to drop everything to get his family to safety.

Another frenzied call to Mark Sims, Sutherant's financial director and a key witness to the extortion, money-laundering, and drug trafficking. With a prayer on his lips, Frazier begged that he was not too late to warn his friend.

No answer.

Frazier struggled to type a text, hoping beyond hope he could reach Sims in time. But deep down, he knew his frantic prayers were too late.

***

From the distance of the pasture, Tracy heard the steady crunch of gravel and knew that her uncle had re-entered the yard. Car lights approached from the south. A dark four-door pulled into her drive and her uncle stepped from the shadows to meet the driver.

"Let's get out of here," Tracy urged, tugging at Jared's elbow.

Jared fastened her jacket. Since she had been diagnosed with juvenile diabetes at age thirteen he had never wavered in protecting her. "Warm enough?"

Her simple nod appeased him.

With a flashlight drawn from his coat pocket, Jared illumined the trail that bordered the hayfield and led Tracy deeper into the darkness. Light snowflakes began to mix with sleet and the brisk air stung their every breath. Tracy reached for a cottonwood branch and began to slice through the stubbly winter wheat, blazing a new trail toward the small grove of trees in the distance. Together, they slowed to a lover's pace, paying more attention to each other than to their surroundings. Tracy slid her arm around his waist. The woodsy scent from a recent high school bonfire lingered on his crimson letter jacket and she leaned against his shoulder, inhaling the rustic aroma.

"Cold out here tonight." Jared's lazy drawl skimmed the silence.

"It's perfect," she livened as they conquered the last few steps toward their destination, encouraged by the fact that once they made it through the two exams scheduled for the next day, Christmas break would follow and two whole weeks could be shared.

Jared helped her across what was left of the trickling stream that ran along the trail then lifted her to the massive tree root that jutted from the base of an ancient oak. Gawky branches and roots had knotted together like lovers, and as brutal west winds and the yearly rise of the creek prevented the mangled limbs from taking root, a suspended hammock of sorts had formed. Tracy's mom had lain many a picnic lunch in its shade over the years, and as she had died of cancer when Tracy was only twelve, Tracy's father, Mark Sims, frequented the special place to reflect on her memory.

"Hey, thanks again for last night. My birthday gets harder for Daddy every year. Glad you were there."

"Wouldn't miss it. Seventeen. Almost legal."

She flashed that grin. "I love my new journal. And the rose rock is beautiful."

A rose rock -- the combination of barite and iron found in the Central Oklahoma soil made for an abundance of the unique red-hued sandstone formations that became the state rock of Oklahoma in 1968. The "petal-like" layers overlap to form perfectly-shaped blossoms and the reddish color gives them a likeness of a perfect, crystalized rose.

"Found it down by the pond. Thought it'd remind you of Oklahoma when you got to be rich and famous."

"Yeah, right," Tracy chuckled as she stretched her hand across his thigh. "Like that'll ever happen. And I'll never forget home."

Jared twisted her way. "Marry me, T."

Shock paralyzed her. But then her face softened, reflecting on all the times he had said those very words in past months. Still, it always took her by surprise to hear him actually say it. "Soon as you ask my dad," she teased.

"Already did. We talk about it all the time," he confessed.

Tracy choked. "You and Daddy talk about us?"

"Unless he's yakkin' about fishin' or his work," he confirmed. "He could jaw all day about those computer programs he works on." Jared's face came alive. "Just last night he showed me his design for the new security system he installed. He loaded these killer security blocks for the new financial files he has on his computer. This thing's foolproof and nobody can break through without the right password and codes. Said I'm the only one who's seen it," Jared bragged.

"Did you know he's thinking about resigning from Sutherant?" Tracy tip-toed through the topic, knowing her dad had not announced it to Jared's father, David Frazier, the owner of the company.

"Yeah, he told me. Even hinted that if I didn't want to work for my dad, I could take over your farm."

"The farm? What did you say?"

"After I stopped laughing about the thought of working for my dad?"

Tracy sneered and punched his arm. "Your dad's not that bad, Jared." For years she had watched Jared's relationship with his father deteriorate and as the growth of Sutherant Petroleum had spiraled, the tenuous father-son bond had weakened. Worse still, the stress of constantly having to vie for his father's approval had at times placed a strain on Jared's relationship with Tracy. The added burden of feeling responsible for his infant sister's death twelve years before did not help matters. Alli had choked on a wheel from one of his toy cars. Although his parents reasoned that she had crawled into Jared's room while he was in the kitchen, Jared blamed himself for having left the toy within reach. Although Alli's death was obviously an accident, he never forgave himself and bore the guilt any time he looked into his father's eyes.

"So what did you tell him?" Tracy pressed.

Jared's voice softened. "Told him it was up to you." A clump of moss growing on the tree stump stole his attention, and as he poked at it with a stick Tracy waited. "I'm pretty simple, T. I don't have any huge plans to go out and conquer the world or anything. After graduation we can stay here if that's what you want."

Tracy drew a deep breath, smiled and brushed his cheek, but Denny Sims' harsh voice caught her off guard.

"NINE-FORTY! Time to come in!"

Tracy winced, gritting her teeth as she felt her uncle's reins tighten. She stiffened more when the visitor's car door slammed. Peering toward the house, she watched the brake lights flash when the stranger backed out of her driveway.

Jared braced to jump from the tree root, but Tracy stopped him.

"No, Jared, wait. Please."

He scooted closer. "What's wrong?"

A shrug. She shot a nervous glance toward her house as she tugged the cords of her jacket. Her feet knocked together - the cadence of a tightly wound clock. "Just stay 'til Daddy gets back."

She considered the reason for her suspicion – how she had walked into her bedroom to find her uncle closing one of her desk drawers. His lame excuse of "getting some ideas for Christmas" had infuriated her. And overhearing a phone call he had made earlier that afternoon was fresh on her mind. His words were clear - *to keep an eye on things – a lot of money at stake – as long as I need to stay.*

Jared followed her eyes and saw her uncle walking through the yard. "Why do you think he's here?" Jared wondered.

"He started calling three or four months ago. Got so bad Daddy considered changing our number. Denny's always been the moocher of the family so I assume it's about money. He says he's here while his girlfriend in Colorado is away on business. But get this. I walked in when he was talking to Daddy this afternoon. As soon as he saw me, he started whispering - trying to get Daddy to sign some kind of papers."

Jared shifted. "Papers?"

"Farm documents," Tracy explained. "Daddy got so mad he flung them across the table. Funny thing, later we were eating dinner and Daddy signed them, stuffed them back in the envelope and slapped them down beside Denny's plate. That's when you showed up and I came outside."

Tracy pitched a clump of moss toward a brush pile. A cold front settled overhead and the sudden drop in temperature made her shiver. The grating sound of Dennis Sims' gruff smoker's cough spurned evil thoughts of a massive heart attack.

The screen door creaked open then slammed shut as Sims stormed back into the house. The *whappp* reverberated in the air – marking his presence with an eerie permanence.

Tracy cocked her head and remembered Jared's own brief encounter with her uncle earlier in the night: the awkward hand-shake when they first, the brevity of words, and that sneer in her uncle's eyes when her dad walked Jared to the barn.

The screen door swung open again and her uncle's boots pounded the porch.

"Almost ten!" he yelled. "Come on in."

She could feel his beady eyes scan the property, searching for his prey.

"Be right there," Tracy hollered. More pounding echoed as he stomped back across the porch. He threw open the screen door; the slamming force riveted anger into the frame.

"We'd better go," Jared said.

Tracy pushed hard against his thigh.

"Jared..." For the briefest moment she was the small scared child from years ago – the girl who was afraid of the dark, of spiders, and of stepping on a crack in fear of breaking her mother's back. Then just as quickly that hypnotic grin unfolded. *Fear* was the last thing on her mind.

She locked her arms around his neck and pulled him close. This time, Jared did not resist. His lips conquered hers before she could finish her sentence. While their bodies collided in lustful motion, a harsh cold wind stirred above carrying a gentle, more respected voice.

"Traaacy – Jaaared..."

Her father this time. With the official curfew call, their lips parted. Tracy stroked her finger along his jawline and caught her breath. "We could always elope," she grinned.

"Ha! Don't tempt me."

Light snowflakes dotted Jared's brown hair and the awkward position of sitting on the tree root had caused his legs to stiffen. He kissed her again before helping her from his lap, and then with a labored sigh pushed himself from the tree suspension.

"AAHHHGG!" Jared bolted upright and dropped the flashlight to the ground. His lower body went rigid as he doubled over in pain. He grasped his leg and collapsed to the ground.

Tracy knew what was wrong. She had seen it all too often. She fell to her knees and squeezed pressure into his calf, kneading his muscles to relieve the pain of the leg cramps he had been so prone to during football season. She clenched her hands around his thigh, massaging deep into muscle as Jared groaned.

"Shhh, let me work it," she insisted.

His eyes blurred as he writhed in pain. She stroked his leg until moments later, his face relaxed and he slowly exhaled. Tracy swiped his forehead and steadied him against her.

"Better?"

He strained a nod and rolled to his side. He reached for the flashlight and the bright beam arced across the ground. Something shiny caught his eye. He focused and in a hollowed-out space just beneath the gangly tree root, he saw the flicker again. Fingering the tiny object, he raised it to the light. It was a sparkling, clear, cut stone.

"Whoa, is that a diamond?" Tracy gasped and turned it in the light.

Jared sat silent studying the tree.

"What's wrong?" Tracy watched his eyes shift between the ground and the tree.

"Ah, nothing." Jared scanned the tree root again then lifted the diamond.

"What are you thinking?"

"It's just something your dad said the other day while we were burning brush." His eyes drifted again to the base of the tree. "Just said there're all kinds of treasures on this land. Anyway - pretty, huh?" He rolled it in his hand then held it out to her. "Here…" He let it drop into her hand. "…to remind you."

"Remind me of what?" Tracy lifted the diamond and watched it sparkle.

"That you belong to me."

Tracy paused as the words settled. She met his gaze and saw the pooling darkness of his eyes. It was true. He had captured her heart years before – she did belong to him.

She smiled and hugged him close as together they shuffled through the field toward her house.

"Tomorrow night?" She whispered as they entered the yard.

He released her hand and tightened his arm around her waist. "Definitely."

From the distance, Mark Sims called out in mid-stride as he lumbered from the barn. "Hey, kids. Better call it a night. Getting' cold out here."

Sims' soiled farm jacket swallowed his weary frame and his hunched shoulders added the look of another hard-lived decade to his forty-six years. He stomped the manure from his work boots. With a lift of his brimmed hat, he pushed his damp, thinning hair back into place. He looked haggard and worn, like a 'player on the losing team' as Tracy's grandfather would have said. Her face softened as she watched his approach, noticing his slow unsteady gait.

A sudden movement from inside the house caught her eye. The edge of the curtain fell free just as her uncle's shadow passed by the window. A sharp pain flared and she realized she was grinding her teeth again.

"How're the cattle tonight, Mr. Sims?"

Tracy had always wondered why Jared didn't take her dad up on his offer to call him by his first name. Good manners – another thing she loved about Jared.

"Good, Jared. They're settled in the north hollow. How was school today?"

Sims shuffled toward Jared and as always, Tracy had to indulge their small-talk. But seeing her father's slow movement, she stepped in to give him a hug.

"Real good. Coach has us doing some easy weight training so I'm getting a breather and can focus on other things." Jared inadvertently glanced at Tracy.

"Well," Mark winked. "Staying focused is important." He cocked his head toward Tracy, swiping his finger down the bridge of her nose. "I know I don't need to remind you two that your *focus* needs to be on school more than anything else, right?" He smiled, but suddenly a hint of worry fell across his face as he read a missed message on his cell phone. He snapped it shut and the color drained from his face. "Did you notice who was in that car that pulled up?"

"Somebody Denny knew," Tracy answered. Her dad smoothed his hand across his brow. "What's wrong, Daddy?"

A swirl of cold wind lifted between them. She noticed the heaviness settle in his face and reflexively shifted her eyes back toward the curtain.

Mark grimaced. "Cold gets to me a little more than it used to. That's all." Tracy studied him, knowing the weather had nothing to do with her father's sudden change.

"Jared, I need a favor…" Sims' voice trailed away as he guided Jared deeper into the yard. Tracy kicked at the dirt and waited, watching her warm breaths invade the cold night air to pass the time. When the men returned, she heard the last of her father's sidebar.

"…best hurry since the weather's turning. And be sure to go the back way. Oh, and I finished up that last security block for the computer system at work today. Remember that series I showed you last night?"

Tracy rolled her eyes. Jared had spent more hours in front of computers with Mark Sims than Tracy cared to remember. As her dad showed Jared the internal systems of every computer he mastered, Jared was slowly gaining knowledge of the most expert computer techniques. Tracy sighed under her breath, wondering how much of her Christmas break would be spent watching the two of them hunched over a keyboard.

"Sure thing. So the codes worked like you had hoped, huh?" Jared asked.

Mark glanced toward the living room window. "Exactly like I showed you. Remember the sequence?"

Jared nodded, disinterested. "Umm, Mr. Sims, you know I'll be around over Christmas break. Let me know if you need some help feeding the cattle or cutting firewood or anything. I know it's tough between work and the farm."

Sims hesitated and while Jared didn't notice it, Tracy did. His evasion struck her hard, knowing that her dad had always welcomed Jared's help around the farm. And then it hit her. *Denny.* She whirled toward the house and felt her cheeks heat in anger.

"Yeah, we'll see." He jabbed a soft blow to Jared's shoulder and held his gaze for a moment. "Get on home, Son. Stay off the main road and steer clear of any cars. That four-wheeler is hard to see at night."

"Yes, Sir. I'll bring it back tomorrow night."

Mark hesitated and then nodded toward the house. "Come on, Trace. Let him get home."

Jared cuddled Tracy under his arm and walked her toward his truck to get his gloves. Just as he opened the driver's door, he noticed a pungent burnt oil smell. In the glow of the cab light, he spotted a shiny liquid underneath the cab.

"Son-of-a…!" He slammed his fist against the truck bed.

"What's wrong?" Tracy pressed.

"Damned thing's leakin' something! Smells like oil or brake fluid," he scowled, but softened as Tracy rubbed his back. "It'll wait 'til tomorrow. Your dad wants me to take your four-wheeler anyway. Wants me to tune it up before dove season kicks in," Jared snickered. "Just like your ol' man to pick the coldest night of the year for me to drive it home." He grabbed his gloves from the truck cab and tossed her his keys. "In case he needs to move it. Be sure and tell him it sprung a leak so he doesn't drive it."

The light snow had begun to accumulate in the grass so Jared clutched Tracy's hand and hurried her toward the porch. Her eyes fell.

"What?" he asked as he smoothed her long hair.

"Stay with me."

"Ha! I don't think your dad would go for that," he chuckled.

"Just a little longer."

"You need to get in out of the cold. Look, T., your uncle probably won't stay long. Besides, we have Christmas vacation coming up." He pressed his forehead to hers. "And our date tomorrow night." His kiss soothed her, but she felt a sudden shiver when he turned and rushed to the barn. Over his shoulder, he called out to her. "I love you, T.! See you in the morning."

He ducked into the barn and heard her reply those same special words. They warmed him like a cozy quilt and as he pulled her words around him, he began to count the hours until he could see her again. He popped the gear into neutral and backed the four-wheeler from the barn. Turning the key, its engine sputtered to life unexpectedly on the first attempt. Gas fumes violated the fresh air and as he straddled the seat, he noticed Tracy watching from her upstairs bedroom. The soft ceiling light spun around her hair like a halo and for a brief second, he held that vision – *his angel*. With one final wave he shifted the gear, accelerated, and disappeared into the cold, dark night.

Chapter 2

Four years later -- Monday midday

Lunchtime in downtown Newport created such a traffic frenzy that residents longed for the safe quiet streets of yesteryear. Not only were there very few decent restaurants to sit and have a quiet noon meal, but the local high school allowed open-campus lunch which afforded students the privilege of driving into town for their half-hour lunch period. The generally accepted rule was that if you happened out of your office during the latter part of the lunch hour, you had better be prepared to dodge careless teenage drivers and deviants who sometimes got their kicks by throwing full styrofoam cups of pop toward unsuspecting passersby.

Tracy Sims and her long-time friend, Lauren Mayfield, worked in research at the *Tribune,* the local newspaper that prided itself in providing all the important news, sports, and gossip for Newport and the surrounding area. Tracy worked a part-time freelance schedule which coincided nicely with her budding career as a song lyricist. Having gained the admiration of the staff, she was considered a lead writer and along with Lauren was handed the top leads at the newspaper.

Mondays and Wednesdays were usually hectic since they were the deadline days for the Tuesday/Thursday publications. But as the April weather was so tempting, Tracy and Lauren had chanced a quick getaway to the community park with their brown bag lunches, hoping to unwind from the stress of working under Stan Dothan, Editor-in-Chief of the newspaper.

"Hey, follow me for a second. There's Lowell. I want to see what he knows about all the FBI activity that's going on." Tracy hustled to corner the local sheriff. Her floral dress danced around her 5'7 frame as her light brown waves swung with every step. Lauren, whose new Italian stilettos were no match for Tracy's low-heeled flats, watched from a distance as Tracy nestled to Sheriff Lowell McClain's side and surrendered to his burly hug. As an old friend of her family, he held a special bond with Tracy, so Lauren allowed them a private moment before she entered the conversation.

"You two girls are gettin' prettier every day! I'd best keep a closer eye on those fellas."

Lowell McClain was a landmark in Newport, Oklahoma. Not only had his fifty-plus years of law enforcement earned him the respect of the county, his loyalty to the small town and his dedication to protecting the citizens made him everybody's friend. Whenever times got too hard, or at the first sign of bad weather, busted cattle fences, or minor fender-benders, McClain's was usually the first encouraging smile you'd see. And when harvest time came around, he rolled his sleeves up like everybody else and pulled an extra eight-hour shift to help bale a neighbor's hay crop.

"Now, what can I do for you ladies?" he asked as his glasses slid to the tip of his nose.

His overhanging belly had grown another inch in the night it seemed. His ruddy face brightened in their company, and as Tracy inched closer, his cheeks blushed slightly more than usual. Under different circumstances, Tracy would have enjoyed his company. But the mangled cigar protruding from his mouth reeked of bitter, decaying tobacco. She hoped she could withstand the stench long enough to get some answers.

"What's all the federal presence about, Lowell? Stan Dothan said something pretty big must be going on to have all these agents snooping around." Although she jogged four miles three times a week and was the picture of health, Tracy's shorter legs took two steps for his one as she scurried beside him. She was also hindered by the Oklahoma wind. It was a fight to keep her cotton dress at bay.

Lauren, model-slender and much too refined to chase down a story in her new teal Christian Duphrane suit, drifted closely behind. Her cropped auburn hair lifted in the breeze as she floated like a goddess toward the courthouse.

With a sudden spark rimming his tired eyes, Lowell spun around. "Now Tracy, you know I can't tell you that. Stick to the news that the town needs to know."

"Please, Lowell. Just give us something so we can know if it's worth pursuing." Sheriff McClain pivoted so abruptly Tracy fell against him.

"You need to stay away from this! Now Fraz...uh, nobody wants the *Tribune* snooping around their private business." He adjusted his footing for a possible escape, but Lauren blocked his way. Her looks could have stopped any man in his tracks, but with those *I dare you to move* piercing gray eyes, Lowell had no chance.

"Wait, Lowell, please," Tracy begged. "I don't understand. Who is this about?" She pinned him with her gaze and stood erect, determined to get her facts. Lowell bowed his back and shifted away from her drilling glare.

"This - is - not a story you want to involve yourself in Tracy." He wiped his brow and with a desperate turn shot a plea toward Lauren. "Girls, listen, some things are best left alone and this is one of them. Suther...uh, some of the businesses have private legal matters that don't need to be released to the public, so please, just pursue the stories that really matter."

Once off the main road, Tracy released Lauren's arm, shuffling along as the *tap, tuh-tap, tuh tap* cadence of her sandals mimicked the rhythm of the throbbing between her brows.

"I think we're due a long lunch after the hell we went through getting this edition out," Lauren encouraged. They spotted a park bench nestled under a redbud and after brushing the blossoms away, Lauren motioned for Tracy to take a seat. She collapsed onto the bench and fell into questions.

"What do you make of it? Why is Frazier back? Do you realize how long it's been?"

Lauren nodded. "I'll make some calls when we get back to the office. Grant Reynolds may just be a local cop, but he's got to have some knowledge of this. Besides, he owes me a favor. I've got to ask you, though. How do you feel about it? I mean, I know we searched non-stop those first couple of years, but are you still even interested in finding Jared or has it been too long?" Lauren studied Tracy's face then slid half of a tuna sandwich her way. "And if you don't want to talk about it, I understand."

Tracy leaned back into the bench, unconsciously twisting a napkin in her unsteady hands.

"We were so close, Lauren. You remember... inseparable," she huffed. She thought back, remembering her seventeenth birthday and the following night which, as dream-like as it had been had turned out to be the beginning of her worst nightmare. When Jared had not called that night and had not shown up at school for exams the next day, she knew something was wrong.

Tracy attempted to eat a little more but pushed the sandwich aside and let her head fall back against the bench. "Why did I have to push Lowell? I never would have known

Frazier was back. I never would have thought about ..." She shook her head, "No! I'm not even going there. I spent far too much time thinking about Jared Frazier and I'm not going to waste my time pining over some...*guy.*"

"So if he *did* show up – you wouldn't want to see him?" Tracy smoothed the crinkled napkin across her thigh.

"That was a long time ago. I'm sure he's moved on just like I have." She blotted her mouth then wadded the napkin and stuffed it in the bag. "But I know one thing. I'm going to find out why his dad is back. Hearing those allegations about Sutherant Petroleum makes me even more eager." She sat up tall and faced the sun, drawing new energy from the soothing heat.

"Then that's what we'll do. I just finished the state government piece I've been working on so I'm free to help. You can tackle Frazier and Sutherant, and I'll focus on the FBI. Maybe we can talk Stan into dumping some of the local interest stories on Jim Crenshaw. Lord knows he doesn't do a damned thing anyway." Just as Lauren rose from the bench, a cardinal swooped from the tree and knocked her off-balance. Tracy stifled a laugh.

"Careful, might be one of Jim's homing pigeons."

Lauren smirked then stuffed their trash into the bin. She grabbed Tracy's hand and led her along the azalea-lined pathway. A cloudless sky stretched from east to west and the smell of freshly mown grass rode on the breeze. Familiar sounds of Newport called out from ahead – the daily train from Chickasha whistling south of town, air compressor blasts from Peterson's Automotive, children's laughter and chatter from the nearby elementary playground. But with every recognizable sound, random memories of Jared crossed her mind.

A cool spring breeze tempted them to ditch their remaining shift at the *Tribune*, and most days they would have stretched the lunch hour into some kind of reporting foray. But the thought of investigating an apparent crime wave in their own home town drove them forward. To lessen the distance by three blocks, they cut through the parking lot of the Methodist church. Just as they turned to cross Main Street, a familiar black quad-cab wheeled into the parking lot and cruised to a stop.

"Well, look who's spying on you," Lauren razzed.

"Hold up a minute. Let me see what he wants."

Tracy smoothed her dress and shuffled over to greet Eric Williams, a computer technician with Sutherant Petroleum. His cool aqua eyes glistened as he watched Tracy approach, and when he leaned his arms over the door of his truck, Tracy's gaze wandered to his sexy smile. And then lower to that perfectly knotted tie and that burgundy shirt that gripped his taut, rippling muscles. She grinned, remembering their arm-in-arm stroll through the mall just days before when she picked out the ensemble at Halpern's Menswear. His spiked hair taunted her and she had to fight the urge to muss it like she had on their date the night before. He was twenty-eight, single, and the man most likely to be drooled over by women. To Tracy, he was one of the nicest guys she had ever known, and as her face brightened at his very presence, she could not deny that she was slowly falling in love with him.

"Hi, Eric," she said, inhaling his scent.

"Hey, Babe. Just coming back from lunch?" He tendered a friendly wave toward Lauren then settled his eyes on Tracy. Sitting in the truck cab, he towered over her. To close the distance, he shifted his arm over the door jam and rested his chin on his wrist. As he spoke, Tracy's eyes never left his face and suddenly, her whole world was inches before her.

"Yeah, we had to get out of the office for a while. How about you?" Her sun-kissed hair lifted in the breeze and as he swept it from her face, she smiled.

"Just got a burger – headin' back to work so I can get some things finished up. I've got to work late tonight and tomorrow, but I was hoping to see you Wednesday night. I could get tickets to the game. Or we could try out that new sushi place in the city."

Tracy grinned and slid her hand along the muscles of his arm.

"Or maybe just stay in," she grinned, suddenly wishing she could crawl into his lap and not go back to work.

His smile shot a warm current to her heart and as he caressed her hand, she entwined her fingers through his. "Even better," he winked. Their affection spoke volumes, and at the moment their gaze could not have been more sensual.

"See you Wednesday," Tracy whispered, backing away so he could leave. Without releasing her hand, he lured her back toward his door. He pressed his lips to hers and encouraged her closer. As if on a cloud, she floated to the running board, linking her arms fully around his neck. Forgetting post-lunch plans, she parted her lips and kissed him more deeply than either had intended. Added seconds became a long, passionate minute until in the distance, Lauren cleared her throat. Tracy roused, pressing her palm against Eric's cheek and kissing him again. He snickered under his breath as Tracy slung back her hair and craned her neck with a contented sigh.

A brief thought of Jared flashed through her mind as did his last promise: *I love you, T. See you in the morning.* That familiar voice was still so clear. But as a warm breath brushed her ear, she realized it was Eric's voice stirring the silence.

"Is that okay?" he asked.

"What?"

"If I call you after my meeting tonight."

She nodded then stepped from the running board, lifting her hand in a light wave as she cut across the lot. Eric shifted his truck into gear then drove away. Tracy gathered her thoughts and watched the dust trail scatter. Even before it cleared, Lauren's questions began to fly.

"Where the hell did that come from? Why haven't you told me you two had gotten that tight? And remind me, how did you meet Mr. Gorgeous anyway?"

"He used to work with my dad, and a few months ago he did some computer work for my uncle."

"Ol' Uncle Devil-eyes?"

"The same. And introducing me to Eric is about the only good thing he's ever done."

Tracy stepped into the crosswalk - alone. Glancing back, she saw Lauren perched beside a street sign, arms akimbo.

"Details!" Lauren demanded. "You're my best friend and you have obviously been keeping your sex life a secret," she laughed.

"Nothing to report," Tracy chuckled. "We've gone out to dinner a few times... to the movies, he helps me with the horses..."

Lauren narrowed her eyes.

Tracy threw her hands out. "We've been going out a few weeks now. We get together after work; we talk, he listens to my songs, we go for walks – just casual dating, okay?" Lauren glared, unconvinced. "What more can I say? He's great. Now he just pulled up and you no doubt heard the whole conversation, so you are officially informed."

Lauren grabbed her arm. "Tracy, that kiss was not 'casual' dating. It looks to me like you have fallen for this guy." Lauren urged.

"Why does it matter?" Tracy snapped. "Alright! Yes, I'm crazy about him. And yes, we're getting serious. Satisfied? It actually feels good to have someone in my life again."

Tracy bolted away, but with every step she took, she felt guilt weigh her down. Too much history had passed between them to ever be angry. Lauren, she knew, understood her pain. She had lost her father at an early age – heart attack when she was eight. Since then, and especially when Tracy's mother had died, both had clung together through every high and low life had dealt them.

Lauren watched Tracy walk away, recalling the four painful years she had spent waiting, literally hoping each new day would be the day Jared returned. "No wonder she never said anything about Eric," she mumbled to herself. In beginning to date Eric, Tracy had essentially accepted that Jared wasn't coming back.

Lauren raced to catch up and pulled Tracy to a stop. She gathered her into her arms and hugged her.

"Sorry," Lauren whispered.

"Me, too," Tracy rested her head against Lauren's shoulder as they moseyed on.

***

Sidling through the door of the *Tribune* office, Tracy and Lauren nestled into their side-by-side cubicles and busied themselves by organizing strategies to streamline their research. After reviewing what they had discovered in earlier searches, they decided to focus their efforts on past business practices and financiers of Sutherant Petroleum in hopes of finding a more solid lead regarding the FBI investigation. Additionally, by conducting more extensive research than she had in prior years, Tracy hoped to break through past roadblocks to finally discover the truth as to why the Frazier family had left Newport in the first place. Maybe then she could move on with her life.

Later in the day, just as Tracy was about to shut down her computer for the night, Lauren sent her an instant message: *Productive day?*

Tracy's response was immediate: *Very! Meet at my car in five. We need to talk.*

Lauren closed her laptop, stuffed it into her tote bag and became a blur of motion as she exited the door. Like locking onto the aroma of her grandmother's chicken and dumplings, Lauren smelled a story coming together and could not turn away.

Tracy logged out of her computer and placed some drafts on Dothan's desk. She noticed Lauren duck through the door, so waved a goodbye to her co-workers and sped to follow. Once she rounded the corner of the building, she spied Lauren leaning against her car.

"Sooo? What did you find?" Lauren lowered her bag from her shoulder.

Tracy flashed a playful grin. "Do you have plans tonight?"

"Nothing I can't change. Why?" Pressing her finger to her mouth, Tracy tapped her lip twice. Lauren chuckled. "Want me to come over to your place?"

Tracy shook her head. "No way! I was half serious when I told you I thought my uncle had the house bugged. Let's go out tonight – just the two of us. Are you up for a little adventure?"

"Absolutely!"

Chapter 3

Tracy followed Lauren to her house with plans to drop off her jeep. Once they pulled into the driveway, she gathered her research material, locked her yellow soft-top jeep, and then slid into the passenger side of Lauren's sleek five-speed. Lauren phoned her mother to cancel plans for dinner and as soon as the call ended, she peppered Tracy with questions.

"Okay, what's going on? Is this about Sutherant? Why all the secrecy?"

"I got Frazier's address," Tracy sang as she waved a pink sticky note in the air.

"How in the world?"

"It's all in who you know. Actually, I called Mary Luther over at the post office. I said I needed to get a package to Jared so she asked me if Mr. Frazier's temporary address would be good enough. She said he's – and I quote – 'no longer a resident but is occupying a company-owned house while he's in town' - babbled on about how Frazier has been in Newport for the past two months! She even whispered like she was supposed to be keeping it a secret."

"I don't get it. Where's his wife? Where's Jared?"

"I wish I knew. But according to Mary, he lives behind an electric fence with enough security to house inmates. Let's just head over and take a peek."

"That's fine. But fill me in on what you found today."

Tracy turned away. Her sudden silence left a chill in the air.

"I'll tell you what I know. But after tonight I want you off this project. I'll handle it myself and you can cover my other stories while I work through this."

"I'll decide that." Lauren was a year older and a year more senior at the *Tribune*; Tracy usually fell into step behind her, but not this time. The raw fear in Tracy's eyes stopped her cold.

"Do you remember that story Jim Crenshaw ran a couple of weeks ago about a pilot that got into an argument when he had to wait so long to get his plane serviced?" Tracy fixed her attention on the windshield.

"Vaguely, over here at the Newport airstrip, right?"

"His name was Clint Burris, some hotshot on the school board in Oklahoma City. He was upset because this scuffle broke out in the airport office and it delayed his refueling. Anyway, I was reading that story – you know, just poking around about Sutherant Petroleum's travel and shipping - and one story led to another."

"Okay…so?"

"There was a lot more to it than what went to print. One of the witness accounts was from a Mr. Thomas Renfro, a businessman from Kansas. He witnessed everything from a back corner of the office. But his interview was never used in the piece. That got me curious so I thought I'd ask Jim Crenshaw about it."

Tracy let her head fall against the seat.

"So what did he say?"

"He wasn't at his desk. Probably'd gone out for a smoke. But I was standing there and I noticed an icon on his computer screen. It was the Sutherant Petroleum logo. Before I could talk myself out of it, I downloaded the file to my jump drive."

Lauren muffled a laugh. "Tracy? -- Good job! Didn't know you had it in you, girlfriend." But Tracy was not smiling. She was trembling. "Wait a minute, why would Crenshaw have a computer file on Sutherant?"

Tracy shrugged. "That's what I was wondering. But don't say anything. You know how he is about his privacy."

Lauren locked her lips for show. "I sure don't want you getting into hot water with our big *award* winner. Lord knows anybody who has won a Pulitzer deserves his privacy. Jeez, he's been a pain in my ass since he won that thing three years ago." Lauren hunched her shoulders and sneered, mocking her most despised co-worker with an angry crease of her brow. "And don't be messing with my shot glass collection from all over the *la-tee-da* world," she barked. "That jerk probably never served in a single one of those military operations he brags about. God, I'd like to take one of those shot glasses and cram it up his ..."

"Okay, okay…just let me get back to the airport story. According to Renfro, Hank Tisdale, the airport manager confronted the Sutherant pilot because he spotted something in the plane he shouldn't have. Seems the Sutherant pilot was bringing 'suspicious cargo' through the airport."

"Drugs? That won't be hard to research."

"Wait, there's more. That's when the pilot shoved Tisdale and told him - and I'm quoting Jim's notes here –'My bosses will not be pleased with your service.' According to Renfro, Tisdale stuck his finger in the pilot's chest and told him that if any shipping violations were evident, Sutherant would be reported and grounded until an investigation was complete. He even stressed that Congressional ties wouldn't save Sutherant this time. That's evidently when Clint Burris wandered in to file a complaint about the fuel delay."

"So that business man, Renfro, was watching all this from the shadows?"

"Right – according to Jim's notes he was in the back corner and was never noticed. Even told Jim that Clint Burris pitched a fit and threatened to file a formal complaint with the FAA Office and with a U.S. Congressman he knew."

"Okay, so this is a customer service issue." Lauren pulled to the shoulder of the road and grabbed the directions.

"No, it's more than that. After Burris was finally cleared for re-fueling, Tisdale stepped out to help him. That's when the Sutherant pilot made a phone call, detailing the whole ordeal to whoever was on the line. When Tisdale came back in the office, the pilot left the room."

"So that's it?" Lauren questioned.

"No." Tracy lifted a copy of a newspaper article. "This is Jim's article. It ran in the *Tribune* two weeks ago, the first week of April. It was just a low-key commentary in the editorial section. Says that flight traffic through our tiny airstrip is growing and that the city needs to increase funding to better accommodate the clients. Anyway, it has a couple of nicey-nice quotes from Burris and Tisdale talking about the convenience of the airport and how strictly they follow FAA guidelines."

"Not quite the same report that Renfro gave. Did you find out why Jim nixed his comments?"

"No, but this past Friday Clint Burris got his name in print again – his obituary in the *Oklahoman Chronicle*."

"What?" Lauren reached for the article as Tracy pushed it toward her.

"He was killed in what the police say was a home invasion."

"Jeez, this should have made the news."

"Exactly. Grant Reynolds pulled up the police report and can't believe they called it a *home invasion*. He said it looked more like an execution. The house alarm had been dismantled and Burris was killed in the kitchen while his family was upstairs getting ready for bed. And another thing: nothing was stolen."

"They were keeping Burris quiet," Lauren guessed.

"Wait until you hear the rest. Grant called me back today and said yesterday afternoon Tisdale and his wife got a phone call just as they were getting back from the morning church service. They thought it was a hoax; caller simply said an explosive device had been hidden on one of the inbound planes due to arrive that afternoon. Tisdale went to the airport office to check on it."

Tracy referred to her notes.

"He called 911 from the airport at 1:15. Just as the dispatcher started her list of questions, the line went dead. Grant was dispatched and when he got there at 1:25, he found the phone line had been cut. Hank Tisdale was dead, apparently of a heart attack. They ordered an autopsy."

"Holy shit," breathed Lauren.

A dead hush fell over the car as Lauren digested the information. Tracy shivered then stuffed the papers into her briefcase.

"I know what you're thinking, Lauren. You're worried about me getting caught."

"No, I'm worried about you ending up like Burris and Tisdale. You've got quite a lead here, I just..."

"This is not about a lead. I know Jared Frazier. Four years ago he and his family disappeared – without a word or a hint as to where or why they were going. I don't know why he hasn't contacted me, but I know there's a reason. Now his dad is back – supposedly not wanting anyone to know. Today

I find all of this about his company. Do you really expect me to just ignore it?"

The low drone of the car engine filled the pause. Their heavy breathing exposed their nervousness.

"Tracy, with Frazier back in town it will be impossible to get information. He's going to be on high alert if his company is about to be investigated."

"I'll stay out of sight, remain anonymous. Plus, nothing would go through the *Tribune*," Tracy added. "No one would know." But Lauren's expression said she still was not convinced.

"Remember the rule" Lauren warned. "Know your surroundings before you're surrounded."

She adjusted her seatbelt and put the car into drive as Tracy directed the seven-mile route to Frazier's temporary address. Once she had merged onto the highway, Lauren followed Tracy's directions as she guided them north along Highway 14 until it intersected an unpaved county road.

"This is it," confirmed Tracy. "Mary Luther said the last couple of roads along the route aren't paved yet."

Lauren eased the car along the gravel road, slowing in sight of a massive twelve-thousand square-foot mansion overlooking the Canadian River. The ominous front entrance had been erected about fifty yards from the road and screamed 'Stay Away!' for all passersby. The usual signs of welcome were absent – no mailbox, no visible address, no marked driveway, and no landscaping. The newly poured black asphalt led to a secured gate which on closer look, was manned by a stocky, uniformed guard.

Perched high on the hill loomed the mansion, a gothic, overbearing monstrosity that seemed to mock the smaller ranch style homes across the river. Random trees surrounded the main house as if to camouflage the pomposity. While two lower-level rooms shone lights, the otherwise dark interior suggested little activity. To further hide a welcome, the first floor windows cowered behind steel security bars.

As they coasted in front of the property, Tracy studied the electric fence that lined the entire perimeter of the property. Every fifty feet or so metal placards had been hung to emphasize a warning that was emblazoned in bright red lettering:

Empire Protection, Inc.: High Voltage Area

"Are they keeping people in or out?" Tracy probed. Reflecting on her dad's involvement with Sutherant Petroleum and David Frazier's powerful reputation, her mind drifted to Jared, wondering what part his life played out in all of the overbearing security.

"Good question. Let's get out of here. This place scares the hell out of me."

Lauren sped to the end of a cul-de-sac at the bottom of a long declining slope that ended within feet of the riverbank. "Take note, Trace. Once you pass the front of Frazier's house, there's no way out but to turn around."

They made the turn in one circular loop and the view of the gloomy residence towering overhead made Tracy's stomach churn. Lauren down-shifted and accelerated to overcome the hill and just as the gated entrance came back into view, so did a heavily-tinted black sedan exiting the property.

"Keep going! Keep going! Don't let them see us!" Tracy ripped the seatbelt from her waist and bolted to the floor. "Get us out of here! If it's Frazier he'll recognize me."

Lauren crushed the accelerator, forcing her back tires into a screeching spin. With a glance in the rearview mirror, she saw the sedan wheel onto the road and bear down fast, moving steadily closer. She ground through gears, revving the engine to a whining roar. As she approached the intersecting secondary road, she ignored the stop sign, plodding her escape through the rural area. A snatched glimpse to the mirror confirmed the sedan was closing in without mercy.

"Stay down! They're right behind us." Lauren ordered as she downshifted, grinding gears and spraying gravel. Tracy panted, shrinking further into the floorboard. Overhead, Lauren bawled in hysterics, "I don't know what to do! They're right on my tail!"

"Head to the city. Just don't stop. I can't let Frazier see me."

Lauren urged the sports car forward, maneuvering backroads, fighting to get to the highway. The sedan closed in - enough that Lauren could see two male figures through the tinted windshield.

"Can you tell who it is?" Tracy wrenched the visor mirror, desperate to get a glimpse of their predators.

"There're two of them. The glass is too dark to see more. What the hell have you gotten us into?"

"Just get us out of here!"

Lauren raced the engine, straining the transmission and barely managing to navigate the unpaved, narrow roads. "Highway's up ahead. Hold on, this'll be close." She gathered speed, praying that southbound traffic would cooperate. Just as she careened the small knoll that intersected the highway, she saw a stretch of cars and a semi-truck barreling down fast.

"Oh, shit! Tracy, stay down!" The car fishtailed as she slammed on the brakes.

"What is it?" Tracy shouted.

"Traffic. Oh, God, they're right behind us. I'm gonna go for it. Hold on!"

Lauren glimpsed to her left, seeing a possible break in traffic. In a panic her eyes shot to the mirror just in time to see the sedan's passenger door open. A man stepped out. She strained to see his face, but the sunset's reflection blinded her. He moved from behind the door. That brief moment was all it took. She saw far more than she needed – the short black hair, the firm, chiseled face, the burgundy shirt and tie, and the stunned daze that washed over his face as he recognized her. Eric William's cold, piercing eyes were alarming enough. But when she saw his outstretched handgun pointed at her back window, she knew she had seen too much.

In slow, dreamlike motion, Lauren watched him lower the gun to his side. Unable to breathe, she stared, her pulse pounding through the death-grip on the steering wheel. Eric's glare locked on hers just as Tracy's cry shattered the air.

"LAUREN! What's happening?"

In a panic, Lauren's right foot slammed hard against the accelerator. Her left foot popped the clutch and with a lurch, the small sports car projectiled into the oncoming traffic. Tires spun in revolt - screeching along pavement as Lauren gunned the engine. She dodged oncoming cars, careening aimlessly through the chaos. A compact swerved to the right, breezing just inches from Lauren's back bumper. A pick-up skidded left, sliding sideways into the guardrail. Fiery flashes of metal shards spewed from beneath the truck bed, as metal scrapped metal. Unscathed, Lauren's five-speed spun to a stop in the median, only to launch into the other lane of highway traffic.

"Slow down!" Tracy warned.

Lauren ignored the command and barreled through traffic. Stunned drivers surrendered to the shoulder. Racing north and away from the wreckage, Lauren focused on the road ahead. She checked the mirror, fearing that the black sedan might still be in pursuit. Each breath was labored until seconds later, her pulse began to slow. The numb, bloodless fingers of her left hand clenched the steering wheel while she ground through gears with her right.

"Are they gone?" Tracy's timid voice revealed the frightened little girl she had become. Lauren steadied her gaze on the mirror without reply, staring blindly into the past as she watched for her pursuers.

"JEEZE, Lauren! Don't get us killed over this." Tracy strained to pull herself from the floorboard and settled into the seat. She watched as Lauren's grip of the wheel tightened and noticed the labored rise and fall of her chest. She heard a muffled prayer seep from Lauren's dry lips and finally, heard her barely audible whisper.

"We lost them."

Tracy bit her bottom lip, foregoing the tongue-lashing she had planned. She would never know just how close the pick-up had come to T-boning Lauren's sports car.

"Well, I'm starved. My treat since they probably got your tag number," Tracy laughed. But as she caught Lauren's eyes flick to the rearview mirror a fourth and fifth time, she realized a much deeper, unsettled fear had gripped her friend.

If I Had My Way

They say time will heal, I'll soon forget, and go on to better days
They say don't look back, just let it pass - start to live again.
But what if I can't breathe? And what if I can't find the strength
to rise?
They say to look ahead but what if I can't bear to open my eyes?
It's all wrong - when all I can see is that you're gone.

They say this broken heart will learn to love again
They say I'll meet someone new - just move on and then
Like a fairytale on the movie screen, it'll all turn out alright
My own 'happily ever after' – to get me through the night
But it's all wrong – how can it be right when you're gone?

If I had my way they wouldn't say a thing about getting over
you
No words of wisdom, "you'll make it through," or "here's what
I would do"
I know time won't heal this broken heart and my dreams will
never come true
But if I had a say, I'd have one more chance at loving you.

They say time will heal, I'll soon forget, and go on to better days
They say I have to let go, live again, just try and find a way
But they don't know that when you left the best part of me went
too
And if I had a say, I'd still be with you
We'd share one last dance and I'd have one more chance to say
how much I love you.
If I had a say, I'd still be there with you.

Chapter 4

The last remnants of the threatening thunderstorm were slowly passing through the area. Torrential April rains pounded the two-story farm house while howling winds slapped the window. An unwelcome chill settled in Tracy's bedroom and the passion she had savored on her date earlier in the evening had lost its warmth. Reaching for an afghan, she turned her attention to the new lyric she was pressed to deliver to her recording agent in Nashville.

Between the fury of the storm and the memory of the car chase two days before, she could not unwind. While Lauren had spoken very little of what had taken place in their getaway, she had offered more advice than Tracy was willing to hear. Frequent warnings to 'steer clear' of everything related to Sutherant Petroleum only motivated Tracy to dig a little deeper. And when Lauren cautioned that Eric Williams was an employee of Sutherant and pleaded with her to break ties, Tracy laughed and brushed the thought away, reminding herself that Eric was the most honest person she knew.

Even so, Lauren's apprehensions toward the Sutherant Petroleum conspiracy had escalated. Casual walks through town were laced with constant, over-the-shoulder glances. Personal conversations seemed short and one-sided. Lauren had all but abandoned her sports car and had opted to use her mother's minivan instead, in fear of being recognized. When Tracy suggested that it was probably safe to drive her own car again, Lauren merely shrugged and changed the subject.

In spite of the warnings from Sheriff McClain and Lauren, Tracy immersed herself in research and continually reviewed new discoveries that shed light on the unscrupulous business practices of Mr. Frazier and Company. The previous two days she had focused on perusing the news stories that had gone to print just prior to Jared's disappearance. But every paper trail dead ended in speculation and unfounded gossip. Still, she saw a clear pattern: for every illegal allegation or impropriety against Sutherant Petroleum there always seemed to be a political figure in the wings ready to wipe the slate clean.

She became aware that Sutherant Petroleum's pockets ran deeper than the oil surplus they controlled. And the company's influence stretched well beyond the U. S. borders. It was clear that the criminal activity surrounding Sutherant Petroleum had been the reason the Frazier family took flight so suddenly years before.

Minutes later, after strumming various chord combinations with little fulfillment, Tracy pushed her guitar aside and fell back against her pillow. The ceiling became her easel as in her mind she pictured all the corruption that Sutherant had set in motion. But as the jumbled images of cover-ups, money-laundering, and political kickbacks floated in the air, she found no rhyme or reason to any of it. Still, suspicions plagued her mind.

Her thoughts were also distracted by Eric. While their evening had ended on a very high note, earlier in their date she had sensed a tension between them. "Evasive" and "distant" were words that had crossed her mind during dinner. His mind was somewhere else. The way he continued to question what she had done two nights before almost made her wonder if he had grown jealous of her time with Lauren. But she would never disclose the truth of her run-in with Frazier's guards. Fortunately, her pat answer of 'had dinner in the city' seemed to pacify his curiosity. And when she cozied up next to him and whispered how much she had missed him all day, he left the subject of the previous night's activities far behind.

Replaying every detail of their date that evening, she thought of the touching words Eric had spoken when he took her home. *Since I met you, I look forward to each new day.* And as she thought of their last kiss and all he had come to mean to her, she closed her eyes and smiled, realizing his words applied to her as well.

Suddenly she was there again, two hours earlier in his apartment, cuddling together on the couch with a shared glass of wine as the storm raged outside. Reflecting on how close she had come to staying the night, she wondered how much longer she would be able to keep that promise to herself and "wait until marriage." Even so, as close as she had come to giving in, that last piece of her heart held out. Long remembered dating advice from her dad kept sounding in her mind. *When your heart is full of love, there'll be no room for doubt.* But as she smoothed her hand along her bedspread, it sparked again – that longing for something more.

She felt her guitar and remembered her deadline for composing her lyric. She played the first verse, singing the finished lines to herself. The more she sang the familiar words, the more she thought of Jared Frazier, the driving inspiration for many of her lyrics. Frustrated, she shoved her guitar away, wandering to the window to stare into the darkness as she had done so many nights in the past. Having given up on his actual return, she whispered a simple prayer for his safety then collapsed across the bed. Tears no longer came as they did those first two years. Still, she remembered. *Jared.* Even now as his name drifted so easily from her lips, she remembered their love. Promises and plans she'd never forgotten. A piece of her life she could never leave behind.

As the gaping hole in her heart widened, she wrenched the pillow to her chest and escaped into her dreams.

Sometime during the night the howl from a neighbor's dog startled her. She bolted upright, knowing the sound had not been dreamt. She rushed to the window and pushed back the curtain, catching a glimpse of a shadow beneath the security light just before it disappeared into the hayfield. Just like the night before - a presence in the hayfield across the road. She had not told the police or anyone else, fearful that she would have to confess her recent brush with Frazier's sedan. Instead, she reminded herself that the loaded shot gun was in the cabinet just outside her bedroom door.

Unable to fall back to sleep, she picked up her pencil and reworked the last stanza of her lyric. An hour later as she sketched in the final note changes, she strummed the melody on her guitar, pleased with how it had come together.

As was her routine, she went to her computer and typed the lyrics, downloading the guitar arrangement and piano accompaniment into her composition program to save as a back-up for her personal file. Retrieving her lyric jump drive, she saved the file. The handwritten lyric and music composition would be sent directly to her agent along with an encrypted computer disc of the recorded song.

As soon as it was light enough to call it morning, she gathered some clothes for work and turned to head to the shower. Drowsily, she removed her rings and necklace and as she placed them on her dresser, she noticed a new text message on her phone. *Eric.* She grinned. She tightened her arms around her stomach and drew a deep breath. She read the message again. *Can't wait to see you tonight.*

She smiled and felt her blood rush again, envisioning his morning routine - a pre-dawn three-mile jog then breakfast - bacon, fruit, and eggs every morning, so he had claimed. Eric made her feel so good inside and as she thought about him and all the special moments they had shared in the past weeks, she knew that he was slowly filling that emptiness she had known for so long.

After showering, she sat at her dresser, briefly pausing to straighten some of the scattered items. She stacked her journal and some unfinished song sheets into a pile and as she slid them to the corner, she accidentally jarred the rose rock that rested at the base of her mirror. It made her think of Jared again and her seventeenth birthday.

She brushed her fingers along the brittle edge of the crystal formation. A wave of sadness drained her heart – that acidic burning in her chest that had worn a hole since the day he disappeared. Her nerves tightened and she clenched her stomach. She wound her hand through her shirt to ease the tension and brushed the tiny diamond she had pierced into her naval. Memories flooded. Their hayfield, their walks, their tree... *her* diamond. *You belong to me.* Over four years later those words still entranced her.

She pulled her journal from the shelf and leafed through lyric after lyric of songs she had written about him, many of which had been recorded. Some had come to her as delicately as a feather floating in the breeze. Others, as anguishing as childbirth – a torturous ordeal of bringing new life into her lonely world. Over the years her music and lyrics had become a soft, velvety cushion, comforting the cruel blow of his absence. For so long she had tried to move on and put everything from her past behind her. But in the quietness of her room, there was no escape. His memory was everywhere.

She touched the rose rock and stroked the crystal petals again, remembering her last night with Jared and the dreams they had shared. But just as suddenly as those distant dreams floated across her mind, a distant clap of thunder shook her senseless – a harsh reminder to the reality that most childhood dreams never come true.

Young Hearts

Two hearts beating wild and free, joined in perfect harmony
Pounding through the winter night to wish upon a star so bright
Lovers swaying hand in hand - dancing toward their own dreamland
Whispered words and promises of a pure and simple kind of love
Like moon dust strewn across the sky, those dreams were cast aside
This bleeding heart was left to die from never hearing your good-bye
Praying for a way, to face another day
While left to weather winter's chill beside this lonely windowsill
To no longer pretend that our love didn't end

Can our dream be real or was it never really there? The life we always hoped to share?
Was it fate or is it just too late to whisper one last prayer?
Fantasies and fairy tales shared so long ago, where did they go? Or didn't you know
That two hearts bound in love can never be undone?
Young hearts joined in love will always beat as one.

Memories pass and pictures fade, still waiting for the kiss that never came
To see you leave without a trace, a broken heart to take your place
The words you said in the light of day forgotten somewhere along the way
Still, my heart beats on - singing you this lover's song
Strainin' to hear the words so clear as the music fades away.
Two hearts bound in love can never be undone.
Young hearts joined in love will always beat as one.

Chapter 5

Two weeks later, Wednesday evening

Newport, Oklahoma, (population 4,807). The old cliché applied to Newport – "if you blink when you drive through, you'll miss it." The one traffic light in town had been the point of origin for any driving directions offered to strangers, and as in most small towns, just driving down Main Street brought an onslaught of waves and honks from the various friends you were bound to see.

At one time, Jared Frazier had thrived on the attention of the community. Just over four years ago, many of the waves and honks had been directed right at him. After all, he was a hometown boy, a football standout, a member of the First Baptist Church, and steady boyfriend of Tracy Sims, perhaps the prettiest, most wholesome girl in town. Not to mention, his dad owned Sutherant Petroleum, the most lucrative petroleum company in the Midwest. At seventeen, Jared had seen it all. But now, having just turned twenty-two, he feared everything about Newport, and was doing everything in his power to keep from being seen.

As he eased from the car and faced the searing Oklahoma wind, the jagged metal rim of the driver's side door slammed against his shin. He pushed hard against the fury, protesting the door's force and unleashing his own emotional pain into the blow. The roar of the storm snatched up his angry curses, spitting back a gritty, hot dust into his searching eyes. Every spec of debris struck his skin with a piercing jab, pelting him over and over - punishment for leaving her so long ago. He shielded his eyes, pressing hard into his temples to allay the guilt.

Never should have left her, he thought for the billionth time, knowing that if it weren't for her he would never have come back.

Jared wiped the dust from his eyes and searched the house for some sign of welcome. But the blinding glare of the barn security light mocked him - an exposing beacon to remind him that he could not hide from his past. Even the dim glow of the porch light cast a condemning beam, leaving him to pass through the fire of his own private hell toward possible redemption. But forgiveness, he knew, would not come easily. First he had to make it through his worst fear - facing her again.

Too nervous to pull into her drive, Jared stashed the car beside a ditch just down the road. His six-foot three, two-hundred forty- pound physique dominated the small car. Yet, his manly frame looked worn, weakened, and as he wondered his next move, hesitant.

What he had planned was to merely approach Tracy's house, knock on the door, and see where it led. Simple enough. Still, it was rather late at night and the uncertainty of how she would react had him questioning his strategy. Then again, he didn't just risk his life and drive nine-hundred miles not to at least try to see her. So with all the determination he could muster, he swiped a hand through his wavy, windblown hair, smoothed his button-down and jeans, and started the long, redemptive walk up her gravel drive, swearing that if it was the last thing he did, he would make up for what he had put her through.

Turning his face into the howling winds, he labored toward the old farm house. A brief vision of his first date with Tracy flashed through his mind: a middle-school semi-formal dance. He chuckled to himself as he remembered: the boutonnière and corsage they had worn, that gorgeous blood red dress, and slow dancing together. He looked ahead and suddenly felt just as nervous heading toward her house as he had that night so long ago.

Reaching the clearing beyond the orchard, he stopped to gather his thoughts and to study the dated house that held so many memories from his past. The stark brightness streaming from the security light blinded him, preventing him from seeing more than the vague shape of the rustic house. But in his mind, he saw it clearly. The same dull, chipped white paint covered the two-story wooden frame. The creaky old porch swing where he had lazed away so many nights with Tracy. Ancient cottonwoods and the lone magnolia still towered over the north side of the house and just to the right stood the old decaying mailbox, leaning slightly askew from years of unyielding Oklahoma winds. A shooting pain gnawed at Jared's gut knowing he had not been allowed to send a single letter, a single note, a single word of his whereabouts. How many days had Tracy rushed to that mailbox only to find it empty? How many days lapsed before she stopped looking altogether?

Edging to the porch, a movement from inside told him someone was home. There was no need to knock; the beat of his imprisoned heart was loud enough for every person inside to hear his approach. Regardless, inch by inch, he made his way closer to the only girl he would ever love.

Glancing through the curtain sheers from beneath the porch rail, he peered into an empty room. Stretching to get a better view, he made out a figure standing in the living room doorway. He adjusted his eyes and at once, his breath caught. She was there.

"*Tracy,*" he sighed, watching as she illuminated the room like an angel.

Straining to see her, he stepped into the flowerbed and scooted along the base of the porch. Drawing closer to the rail, he saw her lift her guitar from the corner.

Her guitar. As long as Jared had known her, that old guitar was never too far away. He remembered how her grandfather had taught her to play. He held his breath and listened, struggling not to bolt through the door and grab her and shout how much he still loved her.

Just as the pulsing rhythms of her guitar began to hypnotize him, another person invaded the room. A man too tall and too slender to be her father. Tracy shoved her guitar aside as the man moved closer. She turned to leave, but he grabbed her arm and pulled her back. Jared bolted to his feet. "You son-of-a..." he choked, lunging for the window. But just as suddenly, he caught himself, pressing his hands to his head. Powerless, he paced while they carried on their private conversation. What else could he do? After all, it had been close to five years. She was twenty-one now and he hadn't exactly been in touch to keep the flame ignited. And that's when it hit him.

She had moved on.

"She's with somebody else," he exhaled.

The next few moments became a blur. Trying hard to focus, he saw her slip the guitar strap from her shoulder, clear some dishes from the table, and turn off some lights. The tune she had been playing consumed his mind, and he kept it there, hoping it would drown out the turmoil in his head. His body went rigid. He couldn't move. For so long he had dreamed of this moment and now a dark nightmare gripped his mind. As he watched her leave the room, he knew he was seeing a glimpse of what his life would be from that point on – *empty.*

The heat was relentless. His stomach turned and he started to heave. Maybe it was the smell of the rotten mulch he cowered in, or maybe it was the ruthless guilt poisoning his body, knowing it was his fault for losing her. Whatever the reason, it was all he could do to keep from vomiting. Peering inside, he saw that Tracy had left the darkened kitchen, and he assumed, had joined mystery man upstairs.

With no reason to stay, Jared fled into the darkness.

Once he reached his car, he looked back – one last glimpse at the only hope he had left.

That's when he saw it.

Two lights came on upstairs.

He remembered the layout of the house and knew that the upstairs bedrooms were on opposite sides of the house. Her father's bedroom was downstairs, just off the kitchen.

"Who was that guy she followed upstairs?" he whispered to the air. "And why the hell aren't they sharing a room?"

It didn't prove a thing. But it did stir his hope and made him curious enough to want to come back the next day.

***

After leaving Tracy's house, Jared opted to stay at a small motel outside of town, just to avoid those who would be looking for him. All night long, every memory of Tracy taunted his mind – her voice, the feel of her skin, the way her scent fogged his mind like a drug, how the very thought of her gave him life. Still, visions of that man blinded him with rage.

Tracy's live-in was really none of his business, but he would never forgive himself if he didn't at least try to see her. And if he just happened to kick the guy's ass in the process…well, that'd be a bonus. So with that in mind, he'd wait until morning and go back to her house, determined to at least talk with her before she slammed the door in his face.

Chapter 6

Thursday morning

To be on the safe side, Jared opted to leave the car just down the road from Tracy's property. Not only was he too nervous to approach her, but Lover Boy might be home and it would be easier to escape through the hayfield than to face murder charges. Running – one thing Jared Frazier had perfected in the past four years.

As Tracy's yard came into view, his stomach churned more with every step. Unable to tell if she was home, Jared paused a few yards from the porch to gather his nerve.

***

Inside the house, the scent of lavender and fresh air chased Tracy down the stairs. Bursting with energy from a good night's rest, an early morning jog, and a brisk shower, she felt especially free since she had taken the day off to run some errands. Scrunching her fingers through her damp hair, she bolted into the kitchen and grabbed an apple and some juice. But as she was closing the refrigerator, she stopped. Her heart fluttered as a strange sensation swept through her. She watched the apple roll across the cabinet and fall to the floor. As if controlled by that same force, she felt herself being drawn toward the front door.

***

Beyond that door, Jared took another step toward the porch, pausing as he heard a movement from inside. His breath caught and he waited, paralyzed with nervousness. Blood coursed through his veins and his chest strained with each frantic heartbeat.

***

Tracy's own heart drummed within her chest and her entire body began to shudder. Her mind swirled in confusion – half consumed with whatever force was compelling her to open that door and half overwrought in fear of the crushing disappointment of finding nothing there. But just as she clutched her fingers around the doorknob, a peace swept over her. She didn't know why. She didn't understand how. But as she closed her eyes it was as if an angel whispered the answer into her ear. A smile lifted and suddenly, her focus landed on one thought - *Jared*.

***

Outside, Jared wiped the sweat from his brow as he saw the front door ease open. The whining *creeeak* of the screen door sang through the silence. He searched the doorway and there she was – *Tracy*. Long, sun-kissed hair cascading across her shoulders, crimson Sooners tee shirt hugging the waist of her faded jeans, tattered low tops, unlaced with no socks. She was the embodiment of his favorite memory in life – all sweetened by the scent of wildflowers lifting in the air. In near disbelief, he stared. She was really there, more gorgeous than ever.

Tracy stood motionless, unable to speak, unable to breathe. As if her mind had faltered, she locked in a daze, absorbing every strand of Jared's being. Emotions raged -

confusing, raw, irrepressible emotions. Unsure whether to laugh or cry, whisper or yell, walk or run – she remained transfixed while memories flooded her mind. With each new thought, past feelings that had long since died suddenly found new life. But the Jared before her was no longer the wild-eyed, wiry boy of seventeen. He was a man - taller, broader, and older. And his face, while still perfect in her eyes, was worn and tired. Like her, he had aged far too quickly in the four years of painful separation.

Jared watched her face relax. Her hazel eyes, faintly blue in the morning light, began to glisten. Her lips trembled and opened to form a word, but closed again. He hesitated, and then, as if controlled by a higher power, took a bold step closer. Tracy's eyes softened and just as a smile began to curl, he saw her arms stretch toward him. He lunged forward, mounted the steps, and before his next breath, collapsed into her arms.

The strong, racing drum of her heart collided with his; she closed her eyes and gripped her arms around him, grateful that he was real, and safe, and back. She breathed in his intoxicating scent - Heaven could not have been sweeter – and then exhaled a slow, release of healing, as if exorcising all past heartache from her midst. With every gentle caress, Tracy's mind wandered farther away, floating on a teenage dream in the arms of her first love.

But suddenly, her mind awakened to the pain of all the lonely days and nights she had suffered. An angry wave slashed through her and she shuddered at how he had left her so alone. She shook her head and her dream shattered. Her soft green eyes ignited as she thrust hard against Jared's chest and cut short his embrace.

"No! I…Where…my God, I can't do this…" Fury flared in her eyes.

"T, I'm so sorry. I…"

"*Sorry?*" she choked. "*You're sorry?*"

"I know, T., Please…"

"Where have you been, Jared?" Tears spilled – pain-filled, suppressed tears, long overdue tears – aimed directly at Jared. Her hands drove into his chest, shoving hard to embed her anger. "You left me!" Extended fore-fingers jabbed in syllabic rhythm. "You - left - me!" Solitary pricks of anger lodged into his chest with each piercing word.

"Tracy…"

"Four years, Jared!" Her cries flowed. "Not even a goodbye. You just… disappeared."

Tracy looked past him into the yard. "Where is your car? How did you even get here? My God, where have you been?" Her voice crumbled into a whisper.

That's when it hit him – she too had aged. No longer the carefree, unblemished girl of seventeen. Now, a mature woman marked by time. Heartache always leaves a mark, and he had bruised her beyond repair.

"T, I'm trying to tell you."

"You never even called me. Not a single word. How could you just leave me like that?" She squeezed her arms to her chest and felt the all too familiar pain flare. "I don't know why you're here, but I can't do this again."

She turned away, but Jared restrained her from behind.

"Tracy – please, let me explain."

His unsteady voice fell against her ear. Tracy cringed with every thought of all the sleepless nights she had spent blaming herself for whatever had made him leave. And here he was – traipsing back onto her porch like nothing had happened. She felt her defenses bolster as he breathed against her skin. That perfect, indescribable peace he had always fostered had disappeared right along with him and in its place suspicion flooded her mind.

"Just listen and then if you want me to leave, I will." He lifted her chin, but when he saw anger straining her face, he had to close his eyes. "Can we maybe sit down?"

"No, Jared." Tracy crossed her arms across her breasts – a blanket to smother any fire that still lingered in her heart. "Just tell me why you left."

"Do you remember the last night I was here? Day after your birthday; we had been out in your yard."

"Of course, I remember. I've replayed it every single day since then trying to figure out what I said or did to make you leave." Fiery flames shot from her eyes.

"I replayed it, too. It's what kept me holding on these past years." She started to glance away but his words caught her. "We had a good time that night, huh?" Jared folded his hands over hers and slowly eased them from her chest.

"Yeah, we had a date planned for the next night as I remember," she snapped, quickly withdrawing her hands. "But that was a long time ago."

"Yeah, I know. Your dad had me take your four-wheeler home that night. I started out down the road and got to where the Whiton's property ends. I looked up and saw my dad – just standing there in the road. Told me just to leave your four-wheeler and get in the car."

She stared at the ground to avoid his hypnotic, ebony eyes – those eyes were a chasm she had fallen into before and she was not about to let that happen again.

"We couldn't even go by the house because something had happened at work and it was too dangerous to --"

"To say goodbye? Just a simple explanation of what was going on?"

A tear slipped down her cheek.

"Dad was in trouble at work. People were after him - some kind of hit men. He said we were being put into the witness protection program and we couldn't tell anybody what was happening. I fought like hell to get back to you, but he forced me into the car and we were racing down the road before I knew what was happening."

He reached out and touched her arm – a touch that sent warm, sensuous currents through her body. She pressed her hand to her stomach and as she grazed the diamond, she was suddenly there – at seventeen, on their last night together. She felt her knees go weak with the memory, but just as quickly braced herself and backed away.

"Anyway, his security guys had taken Mom in another car. She was supposed to meet us in northern Arkansas and then we were to meet up in a new town - somewhere nobody would find us. They gave us a new identity – a whole new life. That's what happened and we've been running ever since."

"Oh, come on, Jared. You couldn't write? You couldn't call? My God, I thought you were dead. Why didn't..."

"T, I wanted to. Dad said we couldn't make contact with anyone. If I had called, it would have put you in danger and the U.S. Marshalls..."

"Put me in danger?" She spun around. "Do you really think that would have mattered? You should have called. You should have found a way to tell me where you were." She pulled her hands away and thrust them deep into her pockets. "I needed you," she breathed as she turned away.

Jared shook his head. "If I had called you, they would have come after you. Your phone lines may have been tapped and these guys have killed to get to my family. I couldn't risk that."

Susan Reedy

He cradled her from behind and brushed his fingers along her arms. She fought to breathe as his warm hands skimmed across her skin.

"In the past couple of weeks some things have happened to make me think that my dad might be planning something here in Newport. That's one reason I'm here." Jared pressed his lips to her ear. "But the biggest reason I'm here is you. I never should have gotten in the car that night. I should have fought harder to stay with you." He stepped around to face her. "And I should have tried harder to get back to you."

She buried her face into her hands and tried to process his excuses. Closing her eyes, she savored his closeness, remembering that at one time, food, water, air were all secondary to her need for him.

But she still could not bring herself to face him.

"I love you, T. I never stopped loving you..." Those words floated straight to her heart – like a lullaby she had so longed to hear again. But the harsh reminder of their painful separation flashed its warning. *I can't go through that again.* Her pulse raced as she envisioned Eric, cherishing the trust and honesty she had found in him. Then she listened to Jared's vows – like a tug-of-war for her love, and she suddenly felt like the knotted, fraying rope being pulled apart.

With his most delicate touch, Jared turned her face back toward his then slid his hand to her hip. As their hands brushed together, he realized she was trembling. He pulled her hand to his chest and pressed it to his pounding heart.

"I heard your song," he whispered. Those words caught her breath and as she felt the steady unified beat of their hearts, suddenly, she knew. She knew the song, she knew the lyric, and as she felt the frantic cadence of his heart, knew why he was there. *Her answered prayer.* She had always thought that if God ever allowed this moment to actually

68

come, she would fly into Jared's arms with the kind of forgiveness that would never question his reason for leaving. But now that it was upon her she felt a dark curtain of doubt and mistrust shroud all the good memories of the past they shared.

"I know it's been a long time," he panted. "And hell, I know you've got somebody else living with you and I'm probably too late..."

She backed away. "How do you know someone's living here?"

"I was here last night." Tilting his head, he gestured toward the living room window. "So who the hell is he?" Jared urged.

"My uncle?"

Jared lowered his head.

"He moved in when... shortly after you left."

He walked to her side. "I want to tell you about myself and if you were involved with somebody..."

"You couldn't trust me?" She retreated to a porch chair and sat down.

"I trust you. But some of the things I want to tell you are only for you to hear. So who is he again, your mother's brother or your dad's? Wait a minute – your mom had a sister. She came to stay with you after your mom died."

"Aunt Jodie," she nodded.

His grin unfolded with another memory. "Remember that time she and your mom made ice cream?" He squatted beside her.

"Strawberry," she smiled.

Cautiously, Jared slipped his arm around her waist. "Didn't even use bowls. We all just grabbed a spoon and shared the bucket. God, your mom was always so good to me." Seeing her eyes shift to his hand, he nervously withdrew it. But a sudden chill made Tracy reach for his hand again, clinching it firmly to her lap.

"She loved you. She thought you were…" she hesitated and then went on to say, "the one."

Guilt flashed its ugly head. "T, I'm so sorry I haven't been here for you." He brushed a strand of hair from her eyes then shifted, taking the seat beside her. "I shouldn't have gone. You lost your mom then you got sick. God, I'm so sorry I left you."

His words seemed empty. Tracy stared off in the distance as another bitter memory came back to haunt her.

"I lost Daddy, too." Her voice cracked as she muttered the words it had once taken her months to be able to say.

Jared bolted upright in the chair. "What?"

"Right after you left – a couple of days later."

"Tracy, no…"

"Lost control down where the road goes out to Amberton. He was driving your old truck." She wrung her hands together and forced a smile. "Not what you would call a landmark week in my life. Losing you then losing Daddy at the same time."

Jared wrenched his gut and felt a sharp, piercing pain as his heart began to break a second time.

"He's buried beside Momma in Fairlawn Cemetery," she added, standing abruptly.

"God, I wish I could take it all back," he said, hugging her from behind. "I never should have left you."

The morning was creeping away but neither seemed to notice. As naturally as the Scissortails flittered from tree to tree, Tracy and Jared reminisced about old times and with each new turn, the wall between them seemed to crumble a bit more. So in the seclusion of her front porch, they shared the directions their lives had taken and in the course of the morning, Jared learned that she had graduated near the top of her class, had completed three years at the University of Oklahoma but was taking some time off to do some writing. She wrote song lyrics, as he had discovered on his own, and had made some pretty good money selling them to some up and coming artists. She still attended their same church and worked part-time down at the local newspaper. Friends from high school called from time to time, but the only close friendship she had maintained was with Lauren Mayfield, who had always been like a sister to both of them.

Tracy relayed that she had struggled physically the year her father died and had to be hospitalized, but her diabetes had been under control in the past three years. She loved cooking, horseback riding, and studying music, and as far as dating, (and Jared nearly lost it when she told him) she was involved with Eric Williams, a computer analyst with Sutherant Petroleum. He had worked with her dad and they had been dating steadily for the past three months.

"He's really been good for me, Jared. It's really helped having him around."

Tracy saw the pain in Jared's face and felt the emotional strain her words had caused. Suppressing the hurt, he closed his eyes and exhaled a slow, draining, breath. As she felt his hand slide away from her thigh, her heart sank - as if the movement of that hand carried the last of promised hopes and dreams away as well.

She remembered her loneliness, her endless days of waiting, and the unbearable feeling of rejection his leaving had caused. She knew she could never endure that pain again. But in the same way she remembered her many nights spent writing - her constant thoughts of Jared preserved into lyrics and how she had promised in so many songs that she would wait for him. She stretched her hand across her stomach and as her fingers grazed the tiny diamond, she remembered his parting words – *you belong to me.* He had been her life back then. He had been her one true love. Jared had been her everything. As she explored his cavernous eyes a part of her wished he still was.

"So how serious is it?" She heard the hitch in his voice and watched the remaining hope abandon his face.

Tracy took his hand, searching her heart for the right words.

"You have no idea how much I have dreamed of this moment – seeing you come back. Every night I sat at that window waiting, hoping, praying." She caressed his hand and saw the pain in his eyes. "Over four years of my life were spent holding onto the dream of you returning. But inside, the longer I waited, the more it felt like I was dying. It was like the biggest part of my life ended when you left. I don't think you'll ever know how hard it's been for me."

He looked away and pulled their entwined hands to his lips as Tracy continued. "When I met Eric, it was like that part of me came back to life. I realized I couldn't sit in an empty window and wait for a dream that would never come true. He's given me a reason to get up every day and these past months have been the only happy days of my life since you left."

Tracy thought of Eric and weighed the newness of their love against the unbreakable bond of love that she and Jared had once shared. She wondered if one day they too would share that inseparable kind of love. While Jared would always be her first love, she knew that did not always prove to be the best love.

"Please, just give me another chance," he begged.

As Tracy looked at him, she found herself flashing back to their last night together – the closeness, the honesty, the near surrender. She smiled and pushed the stray strands of hair from his eyes, wondering if Jared was the reason she had never fully committed to Eric. While there had been moments of near surrender, she had held fast on saving that special "first" experience for that one special someone and she still wasn't certain Eric was that man.

"We've both changed and we're not kids anymore. So can we just take some time to kind of get to know each other again? We owe it to ourselves to make sure we still feel the same way."

May was about the only time Jared had ever really liked being in Oklahoma. To look out and see the wheat just before harvest was always so gratifying. To hear the wind whistle through the fields put his mind at ease. But in Oklahoma, there's always a sense of urgency even in the most relaxed settings. As calm and serene as the gentle breeze blew today, without warning that same gentle breeze could turn into a wicked, black tornado, dropping out of the sky to destroy everything in its path. Or with a sudden change of heart, that gentle breeze could turn up the heat and sear Creation, scorching the land and rendering it useless. So as Jared sat thinking on these things, that same urgency reminded him that it would not be safe for either of them if he stayed much longer.

"Got any plans today?"

She shrugged and shook her head.

"Then could we maybe take a walk – get out of here for a while?" He had not felt safe since he had crossed the Oklahoma state line and to be exposed out on her front porch was too risky.

"Sounds nice."

His hand fit perfectly to hers, just as it always had – her right fingers clinging to his left thumb and his fingers wrapped tightly around her small hand. Together, they strolled through the yard and across the road that led to the hay field.

"So what's on your mind?"

Without thinking, Jared blurted out the one thing that had occupied his mind all morning. "I just think we better go out tonight – you know, date a little before we get married."

Tracy stopped.

"Married?" she choked on a laugh then seeing his nervousness realized he may have been serious. Her outstretched hand stopped him. "Look, Jared. I've got to be honest with you. I'm supposed to go out with Eric tonight. I need some time to work through this. But I want to be clear. I won't put myself through that kind of pain again. I'm glad you're here," she added, palming his cheek. "But it's not easy for me to just go back to how my life was over four years ago. Can we just see how it plays out and not rush things?"

"Nobody will ever love you as much as I do, Tracy. I just want a chance to prove that. But you need to know I ran a risk coming here and I'm afraid that it may put you in danger if anyone sees me. If my dad is involved in any of this..."

"What are you saying?"

"I want you back, T."

She glanced away, wavering in the suddenness of it all. "It's been so long since I've been called 'T.' When did you start that anyway?"

"First grade, Mrs. Brady's class."

"Oh, yeah, I used to sign my papers 'T. Sims.'"

"I copied your work when you weren't looking so I always thought 'T' was your name. It kind of stuck." His guilty grin tugged at her heart.

"Guess it's pointless to confess I knew you were cheating." She bumped him. "I never let anyone else call me that, you know." She reflected on the many things he knew about her. He was right. No one would ever love her like him. He stopped her and took her hands. "I'm not safe here and if anybody recognizes me it will pull you right into this." She stepped back from him. "There's something I need to know. You left your truck at our house the night you left. But the four-wheeler – you said you left it down at the end of the Whiton's turnoff." He nodded. "Then why was it in my barn the next morning?"

Jared shook his head, puzzled. "I don't know..."

"And after Daddy fixed the leak in your truck, I asked him if I could take it back to your house, just to see if there was a note, a clue – anything. He got really mad and told me not to go near there."

Jared's eyes glazed over.

"What is it?" Tracy urged.

"Your dad practically demanded I take the four-wheeler that night. Maybe he knew my family was leaving. I remember he kept telling me to go the back way. Maybe he knew those hitmen would be watching for my truck."

"So he was *afraid* for me to drive it?"

He shrugged. "Do you know what he was working on at Sutherant?"

She shook her head. "He never talked about Sutherant..." Tracy's eyes flared open with the realization. "Except when Denny brought it up. My uncle didn't even work for Sutherant, but he pushed Daddy about it all the time," she remembered. "Asked about mineral rights, oil, and even Daddy's computer."

"His computer?"

A single nod. "He wanted to see Dad's systems for navigating Sutherant work programs. He wouldn't stop. Daddy yelled and finally bolted out the door, almost in a panic. Just before he climbed into your truck, he hugged me and told me not to worry. Said he was going to put an end to it once and for all. I tried to stop him..." Tracy shook her head.

"Was there a police report? An insurance claim? Anything that showed what caused the crash?" Jared rushed.

"Denny took care of all that."

"You never saw an accident report?"

"Jared...they had to put me in the hospital. I couldn't eat. I got dehydrated and my blood sugar levels shot above 700 ...they said I almost went into a coma." She drew a deep breath then slowly exhaled. "He died two days after you disappeared. I couldn't get out of bed much less read about his death."

Jared's face went pale and he pulled her close. "I'm sorry, T. I didn't know. It's just that your uncle was set on me leaving the last night I was here and that leak seemed awfully suspicious after I saw him come outside so many times. "

Tracy nodded. "I remember that. It was brake fluid. Daddy said the plug was loose."

"It wasn't loose. Maybe it was *loosened.*" Tracy's face tensed as she recalled her uncle repeatedly walking into the yard that night.

"What if it is related? Not just this, but what if your dad or Sutherant is part of it, too?"

Far in the distance a tractor cranked to life and reflexively, Jared ducked her deeper into the hayfield. Tracy lowered her voice.

"I wasn't sure how I was going to tell you this, but I haven't exactly been sitting around twiddling my thumbs while you've been gone. A while back I spent a lot of time looking for you – trying to find out the reason you might have left Newport."

"Impossible since they made me change my name."

"That's why I concentrated on Sutherant. There is so much evidence of drug trafficking that the FBI opened an investigation. Your dad has been back here for a few weeks and…"

Jared raised his hand to stop her. "My dad is what?"

"He's here in Newport. Living over toward Hwy 14." She went on to explain the description of the house and her untimely visit to his house.

Jared kicked the ground, cursing. "He came back to the very place he said would never be safe for us again!"

Tracy saw his point. Mr. Frazier had warned his family that Newport was too dangerous. Yet here he was like in so many times in Jared's past – putting the business above all else.

***

So many memories came flooding back as they roamed the hay field. In the distance a covey of dove shot from the clearing and Jared went on alert, scanning the horizon in fear of being seen. He surveyed the new crop of wheat and his face strained. He crouched to the ground and his eyes filled with tears.

Tracy stooped beside him.

"I'm so sorry about your dad," his voice cracked. "Who planted the wheat?"

"Bill Campbell. He started leasing it three years ago. Bought most of the herd and is boarding Sugar Bee and Cimarron. I had to sell the rest of the horses, but I leased out the main pastures and equipment. My uncle, Denny, fought me, but I wasn't about to let the land go to waste."

Jared sneered. "Your uncle? What did he have to do with it?"

Tracy hesitated. "Daddy signed power of attorney over to him just before the accident," she sighed.

Jared balled his fist and stood.

"Don't ask me why because I have no idea. Denny tried to stop me from leasing the land, but as soon as I threatened to hire a lawyer, he backed down. I took Campbell's offer and it's brought in enough to pay the taxes and most of the bills."

"So your uncle's lived here the past four years?"

"Yep," she sighed. "Aside from an occasional trip to visit his girlfriend in Colorado, he's always here. The best part of my day is when I see him pulling out of the driveway."

"That bad, huh?"

She rolled her eyes. "I could swear he has me followed when I go out. I even caught him snooping in my bedroom the other night."

"What the hell was he doing in your bedroom?"

"Looking through my desk. Nearly lost it when I saw he had moved my guitar."

"You shouldn't stay here, T. When you put it all together..."

"That's what I'm trying to tell you. I found out some things about Sutherant that you need to hear."

With every shared detail of the disturbance at the airport and the FBI investigation into Sutherant Petroleum, Jared's shoulders sank more.

"Thomas Renfro, the businessman who had witnessed the altercation at the airport, requested to have his interview expunged from the report after the pilot was killed. And it was a good thing he did because a couple of weeks later,

Hank Tisdale, the airport manager was found dead at the airport."

"Hank's dead?"

"Supposedly of a heart attack. Only thing is the medical report just came back and it says he had enough potassium chloride in him to kill three people."

"Potassium chloride?"

"Yes, mixed with a bromide drug that caused paralysis. And what really got my interest is that the autopsy results were buried. The coroner insisted that he had returned the results to the police department within a week of the autopsy. Grant Reynolds - he's a cop now, by the way - is certain someone on the force deliberately hid them."

"What about the pilot?"

"Clint Burris – he was killed in his home. It was written up as a home invasion but the evidence showed differently – a single gunshot to the head, the alarm system had been disarmed, nothing stolen. Family was upstairs at the time and never heard a thing. Grant speculated there was no more than a ten minute window from the time the wife went upstairs to tuck her kids in and the time she came back downstairs and found him dead."

"Don't tell me she's a suspect," Jared asked.

"No, but Grant did some research and remembered another home invasion in Shiloh that was almost identical."

"When was that?"

"Four years ago - same scenario as in Burris' murder a few weeks ago. Disarmed alarm, single shot to the head, family upstairs, nothing stolen. And both murders had the look and feel of a professional execution-style assassination."

"And both filed as a typical home break-in, no doubt."

Tracy nodded. "But the real reason Grant is so concerned is that the victim from four years ago was a U.S. Senator from

Colorado who had a vacation home down on Lake Chickasha. You'd think the death of someone that important would have had the FBI swarming around here, but only a couple of agents came in. He's sending me copies of the case file as soon as he gets a chance to sneak them out."

"Tracy, you need to back off. This kind of story..."

"This isn't for a story, Jared. And I'm keeping my name out of it so I..."

"Dammit! Keeping your name out of it won't matter! I know the people behind this. I'm not going to lose you over this."

"Then that goes for you, too."

As soon as she said it, she knew her words were pointless. She knew the look in his eyes – that *'trust me'* look - even when the odds were so heavily stacked against him. Down by six, third and twenty-three on the fifty yard line with eight seconds left in the game – *trust me*. His game-winning Hail Mary catch still finds its way into conversation down at Sue's Coffee Shop.

Those 'trust me' eyes had gazed at her at so many times and she knew without question she would trust them again. As he explained how over four years ago his family had been forced into hiding, she listened. He relayed how his dad had been separated from them at times and how they had lived under different aliases – all in an effort to evade assumed assassins.

When urged, Jared went on to describe the various towns where his family had lived. He explained how over a year ago, they had made a final move – covertly this time as his father had begun to suspect his own employees. Using a new false identity arranged through a private lawyer who had no ties with the U.S. Marshalls or Sutherant Petroleum, they leased a small farm in Wyoming and had not disclosed their location to anyone. It had been their only months of peace.

The outdoors suited Jared well. He spent his weekends fishing and explained that he had taken some technical classes at a state college, had invested and done well in the stock market, and had become somewhat of an expert in various computer systems, thanks in large part to her dad. But lately, his time had been consumed in searching for answers regarding his father's business affairs. He shared that two weeks ago his mother had overheard a phone call between his dad and the lawyer he had hired. She became suspicious. Jared's own research in the past year had raised doubts about his father's innocence as well. For that reason, and because he could no longer stand being separated from Tracy, he decided to risk coming back to Newport.

Over the course of the morning, the closeness they had missed tempted them again. The four-year separation became less significant as they lost themselves in conversation and shared the secrets they had kept locked inside while being apart. As they relaxed under the shade of their old oak tree, every harbored pain, fear, and heartache spilled between them and with every released emotion, their physical distance disappeared.

"I have missed this so much – just having you here," Tracy shared as she draped her arm through his.

Jared noticed her smile before she looked away but all he could see was the damaged heart behind the smile. And it wasn't hard to see something was missing – her trust.

"I won't leave you again, T. Whatever it takes for me to prove that, I will."

As the morning passed, Jared seemed increasingly nervous. He worried that his departure from Wyoming had been discovered and that Newport would be the first place anyone would look. In his nervousness, little infrequent glances toward the road increased to longer stares in every direction. With every inattentive glance, Tracy became more infuriated.

"So level with me – what's next?" she snapped, a crimson heat rising in her cheeks. Releasing his hand, she stood, picked up a rock, and tossed it into the air. Catching it, she took aim and launched it into a mound of dirt in the distance. "I mean, do I just get this one day or are you staying the night or what?" She hurled another rock and it shattered its target. Jared got to his feet and as Tracy cocked back to throw again, he caught her wrist. Grasping her hand in mid-air, he spun her toward him, restraining her as she tried to break free.

"I was hoping you'd come with me."

That was a shock. His words floated to her heart and as they settled, the tight line of her upper lip softened. He loosened his grip and pressed close to her ear.

"I've been away from you too long, T. I know you have a lot of doubt, a lot of questions. I understand that. But if you can forget the past, I'm begging you to have me back. I'll take care of you. I can find a safe place for us. Just please don't make me leave here without you."

"Jared…" He pressed his finger to her lips.

"Trust me."

They kissed, tentatively at first, then more deeply, wanting so desperately for those walls between them to crumble. But no matter how tightly he clung to her, one thought kept rolling through her mind – the people she had loved the most had always left her. That distrust gave her the strength to push away.

They began the long stroll back toward her house.

When he reached the porch, Jared opened her door. "I need to take a drive over to Sutherant and at least pass by the place my dad is staying just so I can see for myself. Take this phone. I'm number one on speed dial. Don't call me from your own cell because they may be tracing your calls." Tracy nodded as he placed the phone in her hand. "And T., I had to change my name. I go by Jake Simmons now."

Tracy's heart raced, remembering the last time he had walked her to this very porch and said goodbye. She felt her body stiffen – wanting so badly for her childhood dream of "love ever after" to be with him. But she knew so much had changed in the four years he had been away. *She* had changed. And she had learned a great life lesson since that last time he was standing here: *guard your heart.*

So as Jared leaned in to kiss her again, she pushed against his chest, struggling from his hold. "Wait, Jared, please…I just need a little time."

He feathered his finger across her lip and nodded. "I'll be at the Clairmont Motel just outside of town," he smiled. "Jake Simmons…room 119 around back in case you change your mind."

She smiled and closed her eyes, knowing that if she kept looking at the long lost love of her life she would weaken to the point of accepting his invitation. But before she could respond, he had leapt from the porch and was sprinting toward the field where he had stashed his car. As she watched him run away, it took all of her strength not to follow.

Calling Out Your Name

Rounding every corner of places you may be

Tracing every step that led you far from me

Trying to remember, though memories slowly fade

Was I the one to blame when you left me here that day?

Did you hear my whispered prayers when I searched the endless night?

Or were you reaching for some distant dream you never seem to find?

Did you even look my way when I was calling out your name?

Just hold me in your dreams. I'm still calling out your name.

Still calling out your name.

Chapter 7

Thursday - early afternoon

Gazing from her porch, Tracy watched until the last of Jared's white shirt tail disappeared into the cover of trees. She stood in silence, save the soft *whirr* of the wind and the lonesome *kachug thup, kachug thup* of a hay-bailer churning up a field on a neighboring farm. With a mind-clearing breath of the lingering scent of Jared's cologne, she smiled. She scanned the endless fields stretching south and west and north – boundaries that had entrapped her in recent years. Like the jetliner streaking thirty-thousand feet overhead, she felt free, savoring the warmth of the afternoon sun splaying across her face. Her heart leapt at the very thought of Jared. She lifted her head to Heaven and exhaled – wishing she could see into the future.

With a turn, she darted upstairs and collapsed on her bed, half-laughing at the thought of how often in the past she had done the same – retreat to her bedroom to scratch down thoughts in her writing journal. As she stared at the ceiling of her room, her mind replayed every word, every action, and every touch from her morning. She pressed her fingers to her temples trying to slow her thoughts, but Jared's image swirled in dizzying motion – a montage of his smile, the cleft in his chin, the tiny scar above his right eye (his reminder not to ever challenge her to a grocery cart race), his strong arms, his eyes – deep pools of darkness that were forever imprinted in her mind. As the various images melded together, his calming voice sounded in her mind. *Date a little before we get married.* With a soft laugh, she rolled her eyes and pushed the thought away.

She jumped from the bed and grabbed her phone, eager to reach Lauren with news of his return. Just as she pressed the last number, she remembered Jared's warning – tapped phone lines, changed identities, hitmen. No one could know he was here. She disconnected and pushed the phone away.

An empty silence swelled around her. She stared through her window and shivered, suddenly so alone – separated from the world like a lost child. And like that lost child she turned to the one parental figure she counted on - the one person she could trust not to put Jared in danger. Remembering not to use her own phone, she picked up Jared's cell and pressed her aunt's number.

"…so yes, it's been a crazy morning to say the least. But Jodie, there's something I need to know. Tell me what you remember about Denny."

"Aside from the fact that I've never seen him sober and I can't stand the sight of him?" Tracy suppressed a laugh just as her aunt plunged into an overdue venting of her feelings for Dennis Sims. Years of painful secrets came to light – most piercing, the harsh discloser of her uncle's attempt to draw a loan against her mother's life insurance policy within a week of her death.

"I'm sorry to unload on you, Sweetie, but you're older now and I think it's time you know the truth about that uncle of yours." Tracy grabbed a notepad and pen. "The drinking was bad enough, but it was his anger that put so much stress on your dad. He always held such a grudge about Mark inheriting the farm. He wanted control. He thrived on control."

Jodie's choice of words hit Tracy hard. *Control.* Her stomach churned as she considered his tight rein. All the out-of-state college applications – all seemingly denied. Information requested from Columbia, NYU and Juilliard that had never been answered. Two years later she decided to move into an apartment with Lauren, but the lease application was denied. Denny had put a freeze on her bank account on the basis that he could not protect her if she weren't on the farm.

"But why did Dad give him custody of me? He always said you and Kevin would take care of me if anything ever happened to him."

"The will said nothing about your uncle having guardianship. I tried to contest it, but he threatened me with a restraining order."

"But I've seen the paperwork. Denny showed me the signed power of attorney and --"

"No, check the original will. That power of attorney was signed the week of your dad's death. Find the will Mark had drawn up when your mom first got sick. It will give you some answers."

One half-hour later Tracy ended the call. She glanced at the clock – *2:36.*

She grabbed her purse thinking ahead to the bank, her lawyer's office, and the post office. As she darted to her jeep, she added one more stop to her mental list of all the places she needed to go before her date with Eric – City Hall to see Sheriff Lowell McClain.

***

In a daze, Jared made the long drive back to the motel. For the first time in years he could breathe without that damn knot of guilt in his chest. But looking out on either side of the road to the oil derricks slowly pumping in lazy rhythm, he was reminded that the peaceful serenity of the landscape held a hidden danger. What might look like a passive, country town was a formidable trap just waiting to snare him.

He had left the confines of a life in hiding to come back to Newport. Now there was the looming threat that U.S. Marshalls or Sutherant Petroleum security would converge and take him back. But his greater fear? The assassins who had forced his family into hiding. By now they would have found out he had surfaced and would no doubt seek revenge for his father's involvement years before. He did not know these trackers and did know when they might strike. What he did know was that Newport, Oklahoma was the first place they would come to find him.

Between the stress of learning of Sutherant's criminal involvement and the death of Mark Sims, he had started to feel queasy. It was well past three and as he drove the last few miles toward the motel, he concentrated on what he had seen at the Sutherant office and at his dad's guarded residence. But the news that weighed most heavily on his mind was what he had discovered when he stopped by the Hendricks-Bates Attorneys-at-Law office. And that news, he knew, had changed his life forever.

Traversing the back roads until safely out of town, Jared proceeded to the motel then continued a little further down the highway so he could stop in a drive-thru for a burger. He whirled into the restaurant lot hoping for a quick exchange. Grabbing his red ball cap from the glove box, he tugged it low over his forehead. After ordering, he pulled forward and paid for his food and just as the girl turned away from the window, he caught a glimpse of a customer at the inside counter – staring directly at him.

Jared shielded his face; seconds later he peeked through loose fingers to scan the counter. Finding it empty he assumed the man had taken a seat. But when Jared proceeded toward the exit, he saw the man rounding the corner of the building and running straight toward him. A handgun flashed in his hand.

Jared floored the accelerator narrowly missing the man who stumbled around a picnic table and collapsed to the ground beneath the jungle gym. Jared raced on, careening onto the highway, swerving into the median. Heading south, Jared gunned it, spraying gravel into a dust cloud behind him.

Several hundred yards down the road, he slammed on the brakes, swerving to a reckless stop. White-knuckling the wheel, he considered his options. Behind him – a nightmarish armed voyeur. Up ahead – the safety of the motel.

Fight or flight? It was not in his nature to flee.

In a sudden frenzy he spun the car around and flattened the accelerator, leaving two tread marks embedded in the hot oil of the pavement. Once in sight of the restaurant, he slowed, wheeling into the obscurity of a parking lot across the street. From the shadows of the vacant building, he watched and waited.

Within minutes he was rewarded. The man, tall and lean, exited, tugging his necktie loose with one hand and wrenching a cell phone to his ear with the other. As he climbed into the pale yellow four-door, Jared noted every detail – the tinted windows, the dented back bumper, and as the car barreled onto the northbound lane of the highway, the Sutherant Petroleum parking pass in the upper left corner of the windshield.

Sensing a snare, Jared stuffed his second burger into his mouth. Thoughts of Tracy swayed the balance. Nothing was more important than her, so in the quiet loneliness that settled all around him, he made a vow to spend the rest of his life protecting her. So he eased back onto the highway and merged into the southbound lane, hell-bent on getting to the safety of the motel.

Chapter 8

Afternoon had passed far too quickly. Not only was Sheriff McClain out-of-pocket in the next town over, but the lawyer Tracy had needed to question was detained by a client. In the meantime she busied herself tweaking some lyric submissions and analyzing the most recent research on the Sutherant investigation she had just received from Grant Reynolds.

Eric had texted her to confirm their date and as she tried to decide what to wear, her stomach roiled as she thought of Jared. "God, why did you have to come back?" she exhaled, staring aimlessly into her closet. Because here she was, getting ready for a date with Eric, a guy who was there, and trustworthy, and wonderful, and so good to her. So why could she not stop thinking about Jared? "Who am I kidding? I haven't stopped thinking about you since our first kiss in middle school." Truthfully, she had to admit that her feelings for Jared had never made much sense at all. She and Jared just always seemed to... *belong*. And while the biggest part of her was mad as hell that he had never bothered to call during those long four years, the quieter, more reasonable part of her understood. "He was protecting me."

Just knowing that he *wanted* to come back to her seemed enough.

As she pulled an emerald-green dress from its hanger, thoughts of breaking up with Eric rattled around her mind. How could she possibly tell him it was over when just that morning she had wanted it to last forever? Still, the past four years had proven that a life without Jared was like a song with no soul. It just left her empty.

Just when she pulled the dress over her head, a cell phone vibrated. *Jared,* she brightened. But her shoulders fell when she realized it was her own cell phone. She recognized Eric's number and felt a twinge of regret.

"Hi, Eric."

"Hey, Beautiful." Hearing his deep velvety voice brought an unexpected smile.

"How was work today?" She led.

"It was okay. Thinking of you was the best part of it."

Tracy pressed her hand to her stomach, straining to ease the tension she felt inside.

"When are you coming over?"

"When can you be ready?"

"By the time you get here."

She finished dressing then headed downstairs. Her phone vibrated again, this time, from the new phone. She checked the screen and on seeing *Jake Simpson*, her heart leapt.

"Jared!" she beamed.

"God, it's good to hear your voice."

Chills swept across her skin. "It's good to hear yours, too." She swallowed, feeling her heart pound with that same intensity she had always felt whenever Jared was near.

"Got lucky today. Dad was having some kind of a pow-wow at his house. I cut through a pasture around back and had a good view from the tree line. Got some license plate numbers I was hoping you could trace so we can see who these guys are."

"Sure, Grant can look them up." Tracy started writing as he recited the numbers.

"Okay, a silver Limited Navigation - Oklahoma GWR-568, a black SUV - Arkansas IHJ-935, a black sedan - Oklahoma SED-496, and a black pick-up - Oklahoma SLN-227 that I spotted behind the property in the woods. If you can get those traced for me, when we get together I'll fill you in on what I overheard." He exaggerated a long sigh. "So – still going through with that date tonight?"

Glancing once more at the numbers on the piece of paper, she folded it and crammed it into her pocket. "Jared, please don't..."

"I know, I know. Will you call me tomorrow?" His voice cracked.

In that moment she wished she could rewind her life to the first time Eric asked her out. Maybe a different answer might have made things easier now. "How about tonight when I get home?" She picked up the rose rock and tried to remember a time in her life that did not include Jared. A flurry of memories took her through the years. She vaguely remembered her dad removing the training wheels from her bicycle and Jared was nowhere in sight.

"Even better."

His voice was like a soft pillow against her ear. She sat down at the bottom of the stairs and pressed her face to the phone, recalling his warm lips against hers just hours before. She shook her head, wondering why she had pushed him away when she had dreamed of kissing him again for so long.

"I wish I was there with you now," she admitted, surprised at her sudden honesty. Truth be told, she wished she could skip the next tragic scene of 'old flame -vs-boyfriend' and move on to the 'happily ever after' finale. If only she knew who was scripted to be her leading man in the final scene.

"Yeah, it's driving me crazy knowing you're only a mile away."

"Don't know what I can do about that," she toyed.

"You could marry me."

Tracy swallowed. Her thoughts scattered as his words elbowed their way around her mind.

"Still there?" he asked.

"I'm here - just don't know what to say."

"Four years ago you said 'yes.'"

"A lot can change in four years."

"Do you still love me? Has that changed?" he pressed.

"Jared, please…"

"I don't want an answer right now. I'll ask again - when the time is right."

"Then I'll give you my answer…when the time is right. But right now, I need to go."

As if scripted she heard tires on gravel and knew Eric had arrived. She inhaled and stood up abruptly.

"I'll call you later."

She disconnected, glanced in the mirror to smooth her lip gloss, then twisted her hair into a bun. With a second thought, she let it fall free to her shoulders. The pretty, yet not too revealing green dress seemed to be a good choice.

His truck door slammed. Was it from nervousness or had her heart always raced like this when Eric came around? Whatever the reason, she felt an unexpected tingle race up her spine. Before he was able to knock, she opened the door, mentally reminding herself not to say anything about Jared. But before she realized it, he gathered her into his arms and pressed his lips to hers in such a way that she found it hard to move. She hesitated, but as his hands drifted down her back and to her hips, she was soon as lost in the passion as he was. She wrapped her arms around his neck and as he smothered her in the warm, slow kiss, her head began to swim. His touch was exhilarating. And as he pressed her against the wall and began to slide his hands up and down her body – *Oh, no... Focus, Tracy – Focus!*

She gathered her senses and suddenly Jared's image raced to the forefront of her mind; lowering her hands to Eric's chest, she pushed firmly to break his hold.

"Eric, wait." Clutching his hand, she led him through the door and onto the front porch, hoping the change in venue might help her concentrate on keeping things light.

"What's wrong?" Tracy squeezed his hand, knowing she owed him the truth. She had to be honest about her feelings.

"Nothing. You just caught me off guard."

She twined her fingers through his and then led him toward the center of the porch. Turning toward the yard, she glued to a random object in her line of vision, hoping it would help stabilize her emotions. Desperate eyes locked onto his truck then wandered to the license plate. She vaguely heard Eric mumble about the restaurant, but she wasn't listening. She was reading the numbers of the black quad-cab pick-up. *S-L-N-2-2-7 Oh, God. He was there today! Just like Lauren warned – he's part of the corruption at Sutherant.* A slow anger began to boil as she read. *S-L-N-2-2-7 - the black Oklahoma pick-up.* Her breath lodged in her chest – unable to exhale for fear of repeating the sequence aloud. She felt her face burn and Lauren's other warning shot like an arrow through her senses. *Know your surroundings before you're surrounded. Don't trust anyone at Sutherant.*

"Tracy?" Eric playfully waved his hand in front of her eyes. "Traacyyy? Is everything okay? Where'd you go?"

Snapping out of the daze, she faced him.

Eric laughed at her wooziness.

"So where do you want to go eat? What's wrong with you tonight?"

Tracy found her voice and raised some questions of her own. "Oh, I was just thinking. Tell me, what did you do at work today? Anything interesting happen?"

"Same old thing. I sat behind my desk and crunched numbers all day." Tracy searched his eyes, but saw only the same ocean of blue honesty she had grown to love in past weeks.

"Hmm. It was such a nice day - you weren't able to get out this afternoon?" Tracy asked, giving him a second chance to tell the truth about being at the Sutherant mansion.

"Worked straight through until I called you. Pretty boring guy, huh?" Tracy forced a smile and felt the reporter in her come out. She needed answers.

"Eric, I need to ask you something." He looked her way. "You used to work with my dad. What was your relationship with him? Were you close or just co-workers or…?"

Eric crossed his arms and relaxed against the porch rail. "I like to think we were pretty close," he told her. "We spent a lot of time together while he taught me the ropes. Why?"

"What was he like at work?"

"He was great. Taught me everything I know - most honest guy I ever knew – next to my dad anyway." They both smiled knowing that Eric's father was a Baptist preacher. "I don't think I've ever seen anybody hold their temper like he did," he chuckled. "Whenever he didn't like how things were handled, he had this rule to always wait until he got behind closed doors to vent his anger – which usually was right at me."

"What kind of things made him mad?"

"Well, whenever somebody didn't go 'by the book' and follow protocol."

"Professionally or personally?"

"Both, I guess. Sutherant started to invest into more than just oil; your dad advised against it, but they didn't listen. He couldn't stand how money blinded them to everything else – even ethics."

Tracy turned away and let her eyes wander the wheat fields, wondering if Eric's own ethics were still intact.

"Did Daddy ever mention Jared Frazier, the owner's son?"

"Yeah, that name came up." Eric reached his arms around Tracy's waist. "Now, why all the sudden interest?"

Tracy studied Eric's face but found it hard to believe he could be involved in anything dishonest. She assumed that his reason for being at Frazier's house was legitimate. And hopefully, this lie he was hiding behind was justified.

"You know what I was thinking about a minute ago?" She brushed her fingers along his cheek. "Seeing you at Daddy's funeral. I never told you about it, but one of the things I always remembered was that you cried. It always meant a lot to me." Eric pursed his lips. "I mean, all of his friends were sad, but you…when I saw you crying it really touched me. So, tell me something. Did you ever hear details about Daddy's death? Do you know what happened?"

He shrugged. "They said he died instantly."

Tracy shook her head and placed her hand on his chest. "No, I mean the cause of the crash. He was driving Jared Frazier's truck and I just can't help but think…" She waved her hand through the air. "I just need to know what happened. I'm beginning to doubt his death was an accident."

"I always wondered about that."

His response shocked her and he must've seen it in her eyes.

"Sutherant was...*diversifying*," he continued. "A couple of business partners talked Frazier into a stock option deal and before he and your dad realized it, a group of investors had pooled enough money and power to practically take over the company. Started tapping into more than just oil production. Your dad was pretty vocal about his distrust of the new partners."

After three months of dating, Tracy had come to know his body language. She noticed his constant popping of knuckles and his averted eyes. She could tell he was nervous – he was holding something back.

"And now? Is the company still involved in those things?"

"Somewhat. But it's my job and I try and stay focused."

"Well, do me a favor. When you start to question things, think of my dad and remember what happened to him."

Her mind had become a senseless maze and the more she chased the truth, the more confused she became. Why was Eric lying about being at Frazier's? Why was he there in the first place? What kind of work did he actually do for Sutherant? Why exactly was Mr. Frazier back in town?

"Tracy, what is it? Is everything okay?"

She cleared her throat, forgoing the further work-related questions. A bigger issue was at hand – honesty. And she wasn't sure how Eric would react to it. But as she watched his eyes shift in nervousness and thought of the various times he purposely evaded her questions about Sutherant, the many nights he had said he had to work late came to mind. She had passed by Sutherant on many of those occasions and had not seen his truck in the lot. Was that the reason she had never been able to fully commit to him? That uncertainty suddenly made it imperative for her to ease out of the hold of Eric Williams. And while it had taken her all day to realize it, and even though part of her still needed time to work through the past, deep in her heart she knew Jared Frazier would always and forevermore be the one true love of her life.

"No, it's not. I don't really know how to say this..."

His smile faded and he stepped back toward the porch rail. Tracy's throat tightened and as she fought to find the right words to say, tears began to burn her eyes.

"What is it?" He gripped her hands and their eyes locked into a warm gaze – softening as the silence lingered. She buried her head into his chest to hide the pain because she had not realized until that moment how much she really loved him. She squeezed Eric's hands and kissed them.

"Years ago I fell in love with that boy my dad talked about. We dated through junior high and high school and then he moved away. We lost touch for a while, but we never forgot each other."

Eric slid his hands to her hips to pull her closer. "Tracy, don't...please."

"As much as I've come to love you, I can't get over the fact that I still have feelings for him too. I thought that I could move on and felt that maybe time would help me forget him, but I can't. And I can't control how I feel."

A cold silence invaded the porch. Birds retreated to distant trees. The wind paused to listen. Tractors and cars on nearby farms seemed to cut their engines out of respect of imminent death. Even her pounding heart seemed to stall.

Eric stood silent.

"Eric, I love you and I can't tell you what these past months have meant to me. But you deserve someone who can love you with their whole heart. And I don't think I can."

His arms dropped to his side. Tracy gripped his hands. His face paled and his eyes shifted in every direction, as if searching for a thread of hope. The emotion welled in his eyes and when Tracy saw his pain, her own tears spilled over.

"I'm sorry." She pressed her palm to his cheek, but Eric stepped back for distance. His eyes lost their warmth and focus.

Tracy wrenched her stomach. She hated the battle going on in heart – torn between Eric's apparent dishonesty and her hesitance to trust in Jared.

"I don't understand," he stammered, pivoting to face her. "Did this guy just call you up out of the blue? You just suddenly realized you're still in love with him?" The cool blue eyes came alive with fire.

"I don't know. Maybe I never stopped loving him. I just felt that before things got more serious between us--" She stopped short. "I don't want to hurt you, Eric, but I'm trying to be..."

"Look, just don't. Don't say anymore. I just hope he's worth it." He balled his fists and pushed past her.

"Eric, please..." She reached for him but he backed away.

"I mean if he's come back for you, I just hope you know it won't be easy. This could get dangerous and..."

His words trailed away but his threatening tone was loud and clear. She made deliberate steps toward him, defensively clenching her own fists at her side. "What are you saying?"

Eric wavered. Like a frenzied animal, he paced across the porch. But just as suddenly his face softened.

"Nothing. I better go." He turned toward the steps then stopped. "I'm sorry. It's just that I really thought things were going so great and now..."

"I know, Eric. Believe me, if I had seen this coming, I never would have wasted your time or..."

"Wasted my time?" Eric sneered. "Tracy, I love you." He pulled her into his arms; her knees weakened and she collapsed into his chest. He stroked her hair and steadied her as she cried into his shirt.

"I love you, too." She pushed away from him. *But I'm still in love with Jared*, echoed in her mind. He brushed his hand along her cheek then leaned to kiss her. With nothing more to say, they separated and he walked away.

Moving inside and closing the door behind her, she watched him leave. Her mind strayed to the memory of when they had met months earlier and skipped like a stone through the stages of their love. He had rescued her from the worst pain she had ever known, and in the midst, she had come to love him deeply.

Unable to move, she fought to breathe. Her chest tightened and she felt the last of her strength surrender to that enveloping sadness of parting ways that only lovers fully know. She gripped the window curtain, holding helplessly as part of her heart tore away. But as she watched his truck power down the drive, that Oklahoma tag flashed again - like a gaudy neon sign reminding her that maybe Eric was not as honest as she had thought. Her face drained of color as she released the curtain and turned away.

***

Eric Williams' black quad-cab slung gravel and dust into a swirling cloud as he tore along one county road to the next in his attempt to get away. His goal of putting quick miles between himself and the Sims' farm blinded him with rage, and he didn't care how many speed or driving violations he incurred. The more Tracy's words burned in his mind, the more he found himself losing control. He barely heard his phone ring over the pounding in his head.

"Eric Williams," he strained.

"Jared Frazier is back in town. Larry Nelson spotted him at a restaurant just west of here. Get over to my house and watch out for him," Dennis Sims barked.

"Get somebody else. I'm not with Tracy anymore."

Sims hesitated. "Is that so?" He shook a cigarette from his crumpled pack. "Then I guess you'll be free to keep an eye out for Frazier then."

"It's *not* my job."

"Your job is to do what I say. *Your job* is to find Jared Frazier."

Eric swerved to a stop at the side of the road. "Let me ask you something, Sims. What caused your brother's crash? Was it really an accident or just some part of a plan?"

Sims chuckled. "Maybe *he* wasn't doing *his* job. Maybe if he'd done what he was supposed to, Jared Frazier would be dead and we wouldn't be wasting our time now."

"You son of a bitch!" Eric tensed. Every encounter with Dennis Sims was a piercing reminder of all that he had sacrificed for Sutherant.

"Let's put it this way, Williams. How important is that family of yours down in Texas?"

Eric's head fell against the headrest and his knuckles tightened around the steering wheel. He did not need a reminder to think of his family. Fear and anger of what might happen to them because of his involvement with Sutherant kept them on his mind.

"By the way," Sims interrupted his rage. "Used your truck today," he snickered. "Found your spare key in Tracy's things. Good to know *something* good came from your relationship."

"Whatever, Sims," Eric scowled. "I've got things to do."

"No, what you need to do is patch things up with Tracy so you can watch out for Frazier's boy and..."

Eric threw his phone onto the dash then slumped over the steering wheel to gather his thoughts. Visions of the crash scene where Mark Sims had been killed – a nightmare he had been spared, but even the details he had heard from Sheriff McLain had haunted him the past four years. Hearing Tracy's questions and doubt stirred old memories of the events leading up to that tragic night. It had begun with his sister's referral which landed him an internship and entry-level position in the finance division under Mark Sims. Working alongside Mark Sims and David Frazier as they discovered the government-supported corruption had been rewarding. And once the investigation began, he did his part in secretly gathering financial records, photos, audiotape, and testimonials – all carefully stored in the impenetrable computer program that Mark Sims had designed. Then came the accident. Remembering the effects of the crash scene turned his stomach. He lunged from the cab of his truck. Bile rose in his chest and he bent forward to calm his mind.

"Come on...hold it together!" he gasped as he leaned back against the cab door. He tugged his collar and finger-combed his hair, but no amount of straightening helped. The side view mirror didn't lie. The truth of his shattered life stared back.

Eric Williams had never planned on falling into the trap of the Sutherant crime ring five years before. He never planned on Mark Sims dying before passing on the computer codes and passwords to all the hidden secrets of Sutherant Petroleum. And he certainly never planned on falling in love with Tracy Sims.

He climbed back into the truck and threw it into gear. As much as he wanted to be free of the Sutherant corruption, he knew his one chance to simply walk away had come and gone years before. Now there was only one way out. Not even Jared Frazier's sudden return would keep him from taking it.

Chapter 9

Thursday – Early evening

Flipping through the satellite channels as she sprawled across the couch, Tracy couldn't escape reruns of the scene that had played out just minutes before with Eric. She mindlessly caught spurts of the Sports Network,, a food competition, and a trivia game show, desperate to unwind. But television offered little hope. She needed Jared.

She pressed the speed dial for the fifth time in ten minutes and when he still didn't answer, she rolled her eyes and reached for an outdated copy of *Newswire*. After scanning an article on global warming, she tried a sixth time.

"Hey, T."

"Jared, you're there."

"Yeah, I was in the shower. Early date, huh?" Jared wound a towel around his waist then plopped to the bed.

"You could say that." Tracy kicked her feet up on the couch and cuddled with a pillow, envisioning the steam rising from Jared's naked body.

"Did you have a good time?"

"We just talked..." she rambled.

"Care to tell me what was said?"

"Told him that I needed some time – it's just that I never had a chance to get over you, Jared, and now that I know you're okay, I just need to, I don't know, analyze things."

Jared cleared his throat. "Okay, that's fair. So did you kiss him?"

No response.

"Tracy?"

"You know I haven't asked you about all your past girlfriends, Jared."

"What girlfriends? Kind of hard to date other girls when all I thought about was you."

Tracy paused as his words sank in. She smiled - an easy, genuine heartfelt smile that seemed to calm all her nerves into one warm reservoir of contentment. "Wow, wasn't expecting that."

"There's lots about me that may surprise you, T. I'm just asking that you forgive me for leaving you and give me a chance to make it up to you."

Tracy sighed. "I'm working through it, Jay. I just need time to let all of this sink in. But let me tell you what I saw today. It's what made my talk with Eric a bit easier. His license plate number."

"Oh, really?"

"Yep. S-L-N-2-2-7...The black quad-cab. I gave him every opportunity to tell me he was at your dad's, but he said he was in the office all day. What was that meeting about anyway?"

"Bunch of suits talking about Sutherant's cargo and shipping. Congressman Taylor was there. Sounds like he wants to switch exports to the Savannah branch and imports to Galveston. I want you to read through these notes, but it sounds like they have a list of Washington elites who are supporting them financially. I wrote some of the names down and thought you could look into it."

"Lauren would be the one for that. Political scandals are her forte. She'll probably know every name on your list. So what about your dad? Was he there?"

"Yeah, it was all I could do to keep from jumping that wall and kickin' his ass. I can't believe he came back here without telling us."

Jared paused. "There's something else, T. I didn't say anything earlier, but one of the reasons I came back was to see Thad Hendricks, the lawyer who was trying to find me. He left several messages on an old cell phone I thought had been deactivated. My mom found it in a desk drawer a couple of weeks ago. When she charged it she found his messages. Anyway, he's been looking for me for the past year."

"Past year?"

"I don't really know how to say this, but he told me some news about your dad. It seems he named me executor of his will." He hesitated. "He left me your farm, T."

Tracy stood up and walked to the window, speechless.

"I mentioned the power of attorney so Hendricks did a search and couldn't find a thing. He said it probably wasn't legal."

"Not legal?"

"There was a clause in the will; the power of attorney was worthless after your dad's death. Hendricks has been trying to track me down so he could carry out the reading of the will. Evidently, my part as executor became effective last May when I turned twenty-one. I know it doesn't make sense, but…"

"It makes perfect sense, Jared. To keep Denny from getting it. If Daddy had put it in my name, Denny would have wound up with everything. Since you weren't here, Denny was able to enforce the power of attorney."

The kitchen phone rang.

"Somebody is calling on the home line," Tracy said. "I'll call you right back."

"Wait, Tracy, there's more..." but it was too late. She had already disconnected and was bolting toward the kitchen.

***

"Hello?"

"Thought maybe you had gone out." Her uncle's voice grated every nerve in Tracy's body.

"I'm here," she sighed, reaching for a glass from the cabinet.

"I talked to Eric. He's pretty upset."

As she filled the glass with tap water, she could almost feel his reins tighten around her. Jodie's word came to mind. *Control.*

"He was fine when he left here. Now, if that's all you..."

"No, that's not all. Get ready to go out to dinner."

She took a long drink, feeling the angry heat rise in her ears. Anger for how he ordered her around. Anger for allowing him to do it.

"I can't. Not tonight."

"Meant to ask you. Do you have a red ball cap?"

Tracy rolled her eyes. "I have no idea."

"I'm on my way. Be ready to go."

Sims disconnected.

"That jerk!" Tracy fumed. She slammed the glass down, hung up the phone, then made a frantic turn and darted upstairs, shutting the bedroom door behind her. Like a caged cat she went on the prowl, seething at the thought of the bogus power of attorney. "I WILL NOT sit back and take this!" It enraged her to think her uncle might end up with everything if she ever left the farm. The thought of him looking through her past, handling her personal belongings, touching the various items her parents had meant for her. "Daddy, why did you sign it?" she wondered aloud.

Anger hit her from every angle. She spun in circles trying to get her bearings. Swaying from side to side, she stared aimlessly around her room. Her eyes fell on furniture, pictures of friends, college textbooks, CDs, make-up and jewelry - insignificant objects that had accumulated over the years. As far as Denny knew, this was all she had. What could he possibly be after?

Bank accounts? He would never have access to them. Her music career? She had carefully hidden that from him for the past three years. Her jeep? Her guitar? Her computer? Nothing would be worth Denny's attention. Why had he stayed there watching over her for so long?

That's when her eyes fell on the rose rock. "Jared," she thought aloud.

Scattered scenes from the past few years flashed through her mind. Denny's infernal questions, his daily patrol of the mailbox, screening phone calls, and using his private investigator to "help find Jared" so she could have some kind of closure. Her heart raced as the theory took form. She reached for her phone, pressing the speed dial for Jared.

"...the timing of it all – his arriving that week four years ago, the power of attorney, your leaving, Daddy's death. Even when Jodie wanted custody of me after Daddy died, Denny stood in her way."

"Why?"

"Because of you, Jared. You said it yourself. Why were the people who are after you so sure you would come back to Newport?"

"Because you're here..."

"Exactly. Maybe Denny kept me here to draw you back." A cold silence fell over the room.

"And somebody has been watching the house."

"What do you mean?"

"The past few days. The other night I heard a dog barking and when I looked outside, I saw a man out in the pasture."

"Tracy, you're not safe here."

She didn't hear him. Her attention had gone to her front yard. Denny's truck had pulled up. "He's here! Oh God, Denny just got home."

"Where is he?" Jared's voice cracked.

"He's right outside. He wants me to go to dinner."

"No! Don't leave!" He grabbed his duffle bag and began packing.

Tracy panicked as Jared drilled her with questions. Her eyes swept the room. *BAM!* The downstairs door slammed. The sounds she most hated carried through the house – his raspy cough, the scuff of his worn boots, the *clunk* of keys as he flung them on the hall table. She kicked off her shoes and dove into her bed, wrenching the covers to her chin.

"Jay?" she sighed into the phone. "He's coming upstairs. Don't hang up," she whispered. She pulled the comforter over her head – a lame attempt to drown out the sound of his heavy boots punishing the stairs. The house rumbled with the weight of his presence. Her door flung open, slamming against the wall.

"You're not ready!" Denny's gruff voice made her cringe. Sinking deeper into the bed did not mask the familiar reek of liquor that carried with his every breath. Only this time, it wasn't beer. Proof was the half-empty bottle of Tennessee bourbon dangling from his hand. In the other was a cigarette, its hot ashes falling free to the floor.

"I'm feeling sick," she rasped.

She caught a glimpse as his tall, lean frame staggered against the door jam. His grayish skin, scarred with pot marks and sun blotches, was leather-tough - far too aged for his fifty-two years. But his keen, steely eyes saw everything – her fear, her anxiety, her lies.

"Too bad."

His icy tone and dirty boots scuffing across the hardwood floor paralyzed her.

"Aw, Hell! I'm goin' back to town," he slurred.

He tripped against a chair and a pile of books crashed to the floor as he tried to catch himself. Tracy peeked over the covers and saw her closet door swing open. He thumbed through her clothes then turned to her desk, shuffling papers and receipts. He crammed one piece of paper into the pocket of his flannel shirt. That's when she saw it. A gun tucked into the back of his jeans.

"Friend of mine ran into your old flame today." Denny's words stifled the air. "Didya know he was back?"

"No," she managed.

"Really? I would've thought you'd be the first to know." Denny paused in the doorway. "We'll talk about it later. My friend's watching things while I'm gone. He'll tell me if you suddenly get better."

Her heart leapt, ceasing to beat as she counted every descending step. Once the heavy boots cleared the porch she lifted the phone.

"He's been drinking," she panted. "He's got a gun and somebody saw you today."

"I heard. Just tell me what he's doing." Jared threw a wad of cash and his room key onto the table in his motel room then snatched his bags, kicking the door closed behind him.

Tracy glanced from the corner of her window. "He's talking to some guy sitting in a car."

"What guy? What's the car look like?" Jared rushed.

"Four doors...ugly faded yellow with brown trim."

"Damn! The guy from town." Jared started his car and peeled out of the motel parking lot. "Listen, T. I shouldn't have come back here. They'll pull you into this and I can't stay here to protect you. I'm so sorry, T., but I promise, I'll find a way to contact you."

"Jared!" she snapped. "You're not leaving me again!"

"I can't stay! You have no idea what these people are capable of and..."

"Stop it! You can't just come back here after four years and walk away again." She glanced out the window once more and with one look at Denny her decision was made. "I'm going with you. And I know what I'm leaving behind. What hurts is that *he'll* end up with everything."

"Then hurry. Pack some clothes. Get your insulin and any medical records you need to keep. Just take what you need; we can pick up more once we're out of Oklahoma. I'm on my way."

Tracy snatched two duffle bags from underneath her bed and stuffed insulin, test strips, and diabetic supplies into side pockets. Jeans, shorts, shirts, and shoes were tossed into the second bag. Between the terror of what was ahead and the frenzy of deciding what to take and what to leave behind, she began to cry.

"I'm not ready for this..." The simple plea passed her lips before she could catch it.

Opening a drawer she found a small picture of her mom and dad from years before. Tucked beside it was her mother's wedding band. In one hurried motion she slipped it onto her finger. Her hand instinctively went to her chest, ensuring her favorite locket was clasped securely around her neck. It was her last birthday gift from her dad just before he died.

The more she looked around, the more she wanted to take. She grabbed old journals, her laptop, some old floppy discs and hand-written lyrics, her phone charger, stuffing them all in a separate, waterproof bag. Just before sealing it, she grasped her most vital writing component – her lyric flash drive. It held the only record of every piece she had ever written. She guarded it with her life and cursed herself for not having made an additional back-up drive. She slipped it onto the chain of her necklace and tucked it under her shirt. Her digital music player, the rose rock Jared had given her, a favorite blanket and pillow, a small bag of make-up, and a first aid kit rounded out what belongings she could not leave behind.

Her guitar stood in the corner. Locked in a gaze she stood frozen, half expecting the old keepsake to jump into her arms. She reached down and strummed her fingers across the strings, cherishing the rich, flawless sound of the old mahogany heirloom. Visions of past recitals, talent shows and midnight serenades stirred her heart. She withdrew her hand and felt the sting of tears as she turned for the door, knowing it would be too cumbersome to take along. Pushing it and all the other non-essentials aside, she choked back tears, but Jared's ringtone brought a sudden smile.

"Hey," she stood, swallowing her emotions.

"Do you have everything?"

"I think so. Clothes, medicine, journals ..."

"Grab a small picture of yourself in case I need it for a new ID." Jared went on to remind her of her passport, birth certificate, and credit cards which she retrieved from the lock box in her closet. She half-laughed when she threw an old blonde wig in the bag, thinking it might come in handy if she needed a quick disguise.

"Okay, that's it, I guess."

"Don't forget your guitar."

From across the room, she glanced at her "old faithful" and smiled.

"It won't be in the way?"

"We'll make room. Don't leave it."

She dropped her bags and reached for the one keepsake that meant so much to her. With a turn as natural as breathing, she flung the strap over her shoulder and as the guitar settled against her back, she grabbed the rest of her bulk and raced downstairs to wait for her next instructions.

Priceless Treasure

Tiny locket worn for luck, faded pictures in a book

Classic albums in a dusty case, money in a hiding place

Hand-me-downs, hometown pride - friends and family by your side

Holy Bible - pages worn, faded jeans – frayed and torn

Collections we forgot about, keepsakes we can't live without

Trinkets of silver, rings of gold, fragile heirlooms – growing old

Childhood dreams stored away, shoved aside for a rainy day

Precious memories of years gone by, priceless treasures of my life

Like the air I breathe, you're my greatest need

My priceless treasure, my everything.

Your love will always be the most precious gift to me.

I treasure your love; it's always been your love.

Chapter 10

Thursday - dusk

Bill Campbell's family had farmed in Newport for over sixty years. His place ran adjacent to the south of the Sims' farm and as Bill had three sons, the beautiful farm would in no doubt be maintained for several more generations. His white Charolais and Texas Longhorn herds had been the pride of Newport cattle, and on his west pasture, Bill raised some of the most beautiful Quarter Horses in the state.

The one depreciation of the Campbell farm was that his favored four-hundred-acre tract of premium wheat was separated from the rest of his property. One lone hundred-acre clearing, the original plot of Sims' fourteen-hundred acre farm, lie directly across the road from Sims' house and cut a pie-shaped wedge into Campbell's esteemed three-thousand acre spread. What's more, Sims' frontal property encompassed the only natural spring in the area and produced a year-round water supply to supplement the drought-susceptible ponds that Campbell's cattle required. Over the years Mark Sims had generously allowed Campbell use of the water supply during drought conditions. But when it came to selling, Mark had refused one purchase offer after another, reasoning that his father's dying request was to keep the family farm intact.

Jared thought on these things as he crouched behind a stack of hay bales in that very field. While Tracy had agreed to lease the hundred-acre tract to Campbell after her father's death, he knew that like her father, she would never sell. And now that Jared had legally been named the proprietor of the farm, he would make certain that it remained in Tracy's possession – especially after learning of its true value in his meeting with Hendricks earlier in the day.

As he took one final glance around the pasture and across the road to Tracy's house, scenes from their childhood crossed his mind. He saw Tracy's life play out before him – church activities, school dances, and the football games where she had always worn his extra jersey. He remembered falling in love with her, long before he gathered the nerve to actually ask her out. The late night phone calls that were always so hard to end, sunset walks around the farm, and every kiss they had ever shared. He snickered to himself when he remembered all the nights they had snuck to this very field to be alone and "cat around" as Tracy put it. So many memories from his youth floated across his mind and as he thought about it, he realized their central theme – *Tracy*. She was the best part of his life.

But as he leaned to his left, he saw the parking decal on the windshield of the stranger's car, remembering the other part of his childhood - Sutherant Petroleum. Long-repressed thoughts of his father shot through his mind and he shivered as memories of detachment and domination cast a darker shadow over his past life.

A sudden bawl from a lone calf carried on the wind and at once, he was on alert. Somewhere in the distance a car door slammed. He hesitated but saw nothing and the lookout had not changed positions.

The heat started to ease, and while true sundown was still an hour away, the long afternoon shadows blanketed the field to Jared's advantage. The path to the barn was just shady enough to provide cover. Still, an easy escape out the back door was not possible. The guard was positioned perfectly to see both the front and back yards. He would be on their trail before they even reached their car. Jared needed a diversion.

A memory of Mark Sims gave him an idea. He crouched low to the ground and sprinted to the barn. Inching the door open, he slithered inside and snatched the few items needed to enact his plan. With a prayer, he made his frantic way to the rear of Tracy's house knowing that at any moment Sims' truck could come tearing down the gravel road and spoil everything.

***

Inside, Tracy paced the hallway. With every other turn she darted to the window. Keeping one eye on the driver of the car and one eye on the road, she waited for Jared's call.

With a sudden thought, she raced back upstairs to grab another duffle bag from the top of her closet. She packed more items that she did not want to leave in her uncle's hands – old family photos, her mother's jewelry, the family Bible. Her eyes burned as she looked around. Stored memories were all she would have left of her childhood and her parents once she closed the door. Tears came without warning.

She thought of her father, his anger after Jared's disappearance, his death. For years she had hidden her suspicions – so afraid to question the police. Why had he left the house so quickly? Why had he signed most everything over to her uncle just one day before?

A blaring rap song from her old cell phone broke her concentration. She recognized the ringtone right away – Lauren. She hesitated, knowing the danger of saying too much, but eager to confide in the one friend she could trust.

"Lauren, I've got a lot to tell you so listen fast."

With an abbreviated run-down of her day, Tracy covered Jared's return, her final date with Eric, the license tag mystery, her uncle's deception, and the fact that she had packed and was about to leave Newport. When the last words spilled out, her other cell phone buzzed. The caller ID flashed. *Jake Simpson.*

"Wait! Tracy," Lauren interrupted. "It's about Jared. Grant needs to get word to him."

Tracy bolted to the window.

"They know he's here. Sutherant is spreading word that Jared's wanted by the FBI, throwing around warnings like *armed and dangerous* and all kinds of other lies. They ordered their security to shoot him on sight."

Tracy collapsed to the side of the bed and pressed the phone to her lips. Her head began to swim as she caught Lauren's final words.

"...they know his car so stay off the main roads."

"Lauren, I... please, tell Dothan –"

"I'll tell him. I'm here if you need me - money, a place to stay – anything." "

"Lauren...." There was so much Tracy wanted to say but in the rush, she could not find the words. She cleared her throat, but words never came.

"I love you, Trace."

Tracy disconnected. Like turning into a sudden cold winter wind, she fought to breathe. She lifted her phone and called the only other person she knew she could trust.

"Sheriff McClain here."

"Lowell, it's Tracy. I need your help."

"Yeah, I got your note. So Jared's back?"

"And now the FBI has a warrant to arrest him."

"There's something you need to know," McClain said.

McClain paced the floor of his office, passing the various commendations and plaques that lined the paneled walls. He paused and traced his finger across the engraving of one award that had at one time been his point of pride:

Fifty years of Community Service – Alton L. McClain.

The words culled out his guilt like a serrated knife.

"Two nights before your dad died I made a terrible mistake - a mistake I have had to live with for years. Your dad and David Frazier were helping me get evidence on some fraudulent Sutherant investors. I confided in my deputy, Waylon Vincent. Turns out he was part of the corruption and got a warning out to his buddies before your dad and Frazier could turn over the evidence."

Tracy's mind ran wild, reviewing all the recent corruption she had recently uncovered.

"Because of me, two good friends were killed that week. And your dad, well, I wish I could change all that happened."

"But Lowell…"

"I can't do anything about the past. But I can damn sure keep it from happening again. Now, you and Jared sit tight. I'm on my way."

The sudden click left a cold finality in the air. Tracy slid her own phone to her pocket just as she heard Jared's ringtone from the other.

"Jay…"

"T. Where were you? I've been calling."

"Sutherant's security knows you're here! They plan to kill you! Lowell McClain just told me the police are in on it. He's on his way over here."

Shock immobilized Jared. But, the past four years had taught him one valuable lesson. To trust his instincts.

"Are you there?"

"Yeah. Get your things and meet me at your back door. Be ready to run. And T., make sure you have everything you plan to keep. I'm not leaving anything behind for your uncle."

"But McClain wants –"

"Now, T.! We're leaving!"

Trust me. She didn't have to hear the words to know who she should believe. So with one final look around at her past life, Tracy steadied her bags and teetered down the stairs. She secured her guitar in its case then rushed to the front door to steal a glance at the lookout. Still there. She opened the back door and spotted Jared hunkered down waist-high, scrambling under the weight of his supplies. His loose shirt tail whisked in the air. For a moment he looked like the same boy who had run the path years before. Then she saw his frantic eyes and the urgency became real.

Breathe, just breathe, she told herself.

Tracy drew a long, soothing breath then rushed toward Jared. She took no notice of the gas can and leather bag dropping from his hands; as her own bags and guitar fell freely to the ground, she rushed into his arms wanting only to touch him and absorb him and hold him to know that he was really there.

Jared cradled her like a child, swaying gently from side to side, unleashing all his emotions into one desperate kiss. From there he breathed one word into her ear.

"Ready?"

Just one word – a simple word that meant so much. And her answer would set all else in motion - sacrifice, danger, uncertainty. Her answer, she knew, would mean committing to a future with Jared. And with that one decision in the balance, she had to push her apprehensions aside.

"Ready!"

Jared lowered her to the ground. "Wait here."

He flung open the back door, raced to the kitchen, turned on the gas from the stove and the heater, unlocked and slightly opened the front screen door, then returned to where she stood.

"Okay, this is it. Are you sure there's nothing left here you want to keep?"

"I'm sure." Tracy closed her eyes. "He can have what's left."

"Then stay low and when I say, run to that tree. I'll be right behind you."

***

From the side of the porch, Jared drew in a long, steady breath trying to prolong his last moment as a free man. He focused his eyes and then bolted toward the rear of the parked car. He slid to the ground out of sight of the rearview mirror. Scanning the area, he uncapped the gas can and set it beside the car. Crawling underneath the car, he located the smooth surface of the fuel tank. Grasping the screwdriver he had carried from the barn, he forced two abrupt upward thrusts into the tank, freeing a steady flow of gas into the street. The lookout stirred and as the driver-side door opened, Jared grabbed the small gas can, tilted it forward, and poured gas in a steady stream as he hustled across the yard. The dampened path of gas trailed behind him. He reached the porch and flung the screen door off its hinges, then heard an outburst of profanity.

Jared burst through the house sloshing the remaining gas along the floors, then ran out the back door and rushed to the bag to grab the flare and striker. Glancing back through the open front door, he saw the lookout struggle from underneath the back of his car.

"RUN!" Jared yelled.

Tracy seized her bags and dug her heels into the dirt that led into the wheat field. Jared watched the man stumble toward the house and once he was clear of any danger, Jared struck the flare, took aim, and let it take flight through the interior of the house, out the open front door, and to the gas-soaked car beyond. The gas fumes ignited in a deafening *WHOOSH*, hurling car metal and glass into a plume of fire. The helpless driver dove for cover, scrambling along the ground toward safety as the stream of gas ignited.

Shielding his eyes from the blast, Jared whirled around, slung the spent flare to the ground, and grabbed the guitar and duffle bag. He raced toward Tracy. Knowing the second explosion would be more fierce, he tackled her to the ground just as the gas stove ignited, incinerating her house in a deafening burst of flames.

Jared heaved Tracy to her feet and hoisted her baggage into his arms. He dragged her through the knee-deep wheat field, blocking her view as her possessions and memories disintegrated. Reaching the cover of the tree line, she collapsed to the side of Jared's car. He stumbled to her side, fighting for air as he yanked the door handle. Struggling to his knees, he lifted Tracy into the car and reached to fasten her seatbelt.

"You're bleeding," she gasped, swiping the blood oozing from his hairline.

"We've gotta get out of here," he panted.

That's when he heard the click of death and all else came to a mortifying halt.

His body tensed and one look into Tracy's frightened eyes told him she had heard it too. They turned to face the source - a 9mm automatic targeted on Jared's head.

"ERIC, NO!" Tracy scrambled from the car. Eric steadied his aim as Jared raised his hands to the air.

"Please," Tracy struggled to shield Jared. "Don't hurt him."

Her cries were muffled, drowned by fear. One hundred yards away the sound of a fiery explosion rocked the ground, knocking Tracy off-balance. Jared lunged to catch her.

"I'm sorry, T.," he whispered. She heard the despair in his voice and sensed his surrender.

"NO, Jared!" Bolting from his hold she clawed her way toward Eric – blind to danger and unaware that the gun was now lowered to his side.

"I trusted you!" she wailed, pounding her fists into Eric's chest.

Furious tears blurred her vision. But even in the confusing haze, her mind focused on two clear memories: the quad-cab license plate and Lauren's warning about Eric Williams. He flinched and with more force than intended, shoved her into Jared.

"They'll never let you get away, Frazier. You're interfering with their plan."

Tracy flailed her arms, bent on striking Eric again. She did not hear Jared's reproach as he restrained her from behind. Struggling in his grip, her angry sobs slowly tempered when she realized Eric's gun had been holstered.

"I can probably buy you a couple of hours," Eric offered as he flung a Sutherant Petroleum business card toward Jared. "Don't use the work number, use my cell."

Eric took Tracy's arm and pulled her aside. Her sneer followed his every move.

"I never meant to hurt you, Tracy. And you were right. Sutherant is in trouble. Your uncle has been using it as a front for shipping contraband. He was blackmailing your dad and forced him to sign power of attorney over to him." Eric looked at Jared. "He had no choice. He was trying to protect you both. And now that you've surfaced," he nodded toward

Jared, "you're a threat to everyone who is working with Sims."

Jared lunged forward. "I have nothing to do with--"

"You have everything to do with it! You're the only one who has seen the computer system Mark designed. And Tracy, your uncle knows Mark gave you the password."

"Dad never told me a password! I told Denny a long time ago I didn't..."

Tracy froze.

She wiped her forehead and whirled toward Jared. "My God...Jared... Denny brought one of the computer techs to look at Dad's computer – right after Daddy died. I remember they kept asking about codes and sequences."

"To see what you knew," Jared confirmed.

Two horrific explosions thundered in the distance as the propane tank and her jeep ignited.

"Get out of here!" Eric stressed, swiping the sweat from his forehead.

"But they need to know we aren't part of this." Tracy advanced. "We'll tell them – "

"No! Listen to me! Half of Congress is on their payroll. They're even tied to the Gangpaeh, Korean mafia. Why do you think I'm still here? I can't escape this but you can."

Tracy's attention volleyed between Eric and Jared. That's when she felt Eric's hand brush her lower back.

"Look," Eric continued. "It's all locked in your dad's computer. He was that good, Tracy. I've worked non-stop trying to reconstruct his research, but ..."

"Is that what happened to my dad? Was he killed for what he knew?"

"He had some serious evidence that would have implicated them all. The FBI couldn't afford to let it out.

These people – the same ones you are so ready to confront – found out about it and know what that information is worth."

"So they killed Daddy to hide the evidence?"

He shrugged. "What they didn't know was that Mark had transferred most of the liquid assets of the company into a hidden account. Plus, Mark discovered their plan to trade military weapons for a shipment coming from South Africa. He intercepted the shipment and was planning to use it against them. But he was killed before he could tell me where it was."

Eric pursed his lips and turned to Jared.

"Frazier, they know Mark shared his computer codes with you. They'll do whatever it takes to keep you from accessing it. But," Eric exhaled, "as much as they want to keep you from finding Mark's files, they still need you to access his computer so they can get to the company funds. That's why they've kept a close watch on you, Tracy." He motioned toward Jared. "They knew he'd eventually come back here."

Eric took Tracy's hand. With his free hand he lifted her necklace. A smile lifted. "Your dad had me help make this." He lowered his voice. "Tracy, I love you. I'm here for you."

Far in the distance, sirens blared. Jared shot a nervous glance toward the house. Turning back, he saw that Tracy and Eric were locked in their own gaze.

She wrapped her arms around Eric's waist and hugged him. Every muscle in Jared's body tensed. "Thank you," She kissed his cheek and slid her mouth to his ear. "For everything," she whispered. She pulled herself away and without looking back, eased into the car.

Jared knelt down and buckled her seatbelt. Tracy's own body tensed as the truth of the last four years became clear.

Betrayal. Corruption. Lies.

But in the midst of all the painful deceit, she saw the one good part of her life. *Jared.* Despite all that had happened, he had been true to her. As if all the love she had ever felt for him was screaming to be freed, Tracy held his face and kissed him, pouring herself into him – telling him not to worry, not to wonder, not to ever doubt her love. "I love you, Jay. I always have."

As small and powerless as her voice sounded, the words captured him. But even as he folded into the security her soft arms, Eric's words of warning sliced the air.

"Hurry! They're coming!"

Jared glanced to the destruction behind them. With a jerk, he bolted around the car, plowed in, turned the key, threw it into gear, and steered clear of the fiery scene. Careening through the pasture, the eight-cylinder held its own as the distance between them and the blazing house widened.

"My God! The house is gone!" Tears welled in Tracy's eyes as her home smoldered into flames. An uncontrollable tremor raked her body. There was no turning back – too many lies had cemented their fate and like a dirty blemish, their involvement could no longer be wiped clean. Even the bitter saliva she tried to force down tasted vile.

"Are you okay, T.? Did you get hurt?"

She shook her head. "Seeing that gun pointed at you – my God, Jared, I can't even..." Her voice trailed. She thought of Lauren and wished she could have seen her one last time. Eric crossed her mind and her heart ached, wondering what danger he had put himself in by helping them. Pulling his card from the console, she slipped it into the corner of her purse.

Reaching Main Street, Tracy saw the familiar scenes of her life stream past outside the window; she sat powerless, unable to keep the memories at bay: the church where she and

Jared had both been baptized, the football field, the Railway Cafe where she and her dad had shared chicken fried steak on their weekly "date" night, the Boomer drive-in, the *Tribune* office, the road to Lauren's house. She swallowed the lump in her throat and wondered if they would ever call this place *home* again.

From her left, she caught bits and pieces of Jared's mumbled plan: to get to Arkansas... swap rental cars in Fort Smith... use cash - no credit cards...leftover snacks from the motel...get clothes and supplies along the way... meet his friend in Georgia. Thoughts ricocheted through her mind like the pinball down at Ridman's Pool Hall. And with every thought came every reminder of what she was leaving behind.

Jared caressed her thigh. Tracy buried her face into the crux of his shoulder. The rhythmic motion of his massage eased slowly upward. She felt his muscles tighten and understood, feeling the same longing, the same need. With a twist she pulled his arm around her to keep him focused. She swiped the dust from her face with the back of her hand. "So how much trouble are we in? Is that man dead?"

"No, he got out of the car. But I expect we've moved to the top of your uncle's most wanted list. And God, T., I'm sorry about your house."

Her face was cold, expressionless. "Couldn't help it."

"Still, that was your home." He rubbed Tracy's shoulder but she shoved him away.

"*Home?* Ha! It's been more like a prison than a home! God, I wish you could see how much I needed you."

Jared stared into the distance. Each angry blow of her words was a chisel chipping away the hurt that had mounted between them.

"Can you even imagine what I went through? You - my *best* friend, just disappeared without a word. And two days later Daddy died." She thrust the bag she had been holding to the floorboard. "Lauren said I was so messed up at the funeral that I was crying out for you instead of Daddy," she sighed. "I thought you were dead. And as strong as I am," she chortled, "I had a few Juliet moments, believe me!" She turned away and choked back tears.

Jared's eyes strained to focus on traffic. The steady *padump, padump, padump* of the tire rotation filled the space of the otherwise dead silence.

"That's when I started writing...and researching," she continued. "And with every piece of information I found, I went from thinking you were dead to knowing you were alive – wondering why you wouldn't call me."

Jared's face twitched.

"Look Jared, I just want you to understand why I'm here. You said you were given a new identity after you left. That's what I want, a new life – away from Sutherant, away from Denny. I just want to erase my past and start over." She looked his way. "With you."

With the skyline of Oklahoma City rising in the distance, Jared accelerated and merged onto I-35.

The black sedan did the same.

***

As the final glimmers of sun stretched behind them, the miles between their past and present gradually became a forgotten void.

"So do you have any ideas for your new identity?" Jared asked, miles later.

A shrug. "Haven't really thought about it."

"How about we go by Mr. and Mrs. Jake Simmons for now? At least until it's safe."

Tracy relaxed her head on his shoulder. "For now."

Suddenly, they were young again. Teenagers - innocent, and free, on their own without a care in the world. Just for tonight, they could forget about the world and let all the spontaneous desires of when they were seventeen go free.

.

Chapter 11

Luck was in Eric Williams' corner, so it seemed. The two-hour delay he had offered had conveniently turned into a four-hour head start for Jared and Tracy. Chalk that up to Dennis Sims' affection for hard liquor. After Jared's rental had sped away, Eric drove straight to Sims' favorite watering-hole. As luck would have it, predictable Sims had left his keys in the ignition of his pickup truck. And as luck would have it, Eric noticed the perfect break in traffic that allowed him to move Sims' truck to a back alley without being seen. When Vincent sent his men on a wild goose chase in search of Sims, two hours were wasted, giving Sims plenty of time to quench his thirst. But Eric knew it would take more than a stupid prank to protect his interests and get Dennis Sims out of his way. So he waited.

***

As soon as the first warning that the lookout, Larry Nelson "had some trouble over at the Sims' place" breached Chief Vincent's secured line, a small band of the Newport Police Department went into action. With barricades erected to block every route leading to the Sims' farm, Vincent's chosen few took control. An immediate order was passed to prevent locals from coming within a mile of the explosion. So as the house was allowed to smolder, Chief Vincent hurled his "keep the area secured until further notice" command with authority. Even the county police and the sheriff's office from the next town over were kept behind safety barriers. As a result, no fire fighters or other officials were waved through until Vincent's own personal investigation had been completed. Analyzing the situation, he placed a call to his point of contact at the *Tribune* office.

"Crenshaw, Sims won't answer his phone. Find him and get him over here," he ordered.

Jim Crenshaw leaned around his cubicle to scan the few co-workers who were still on the clock trying to meet a deadline. He locked his file folders into his desk drawer and saved the byline draft he had just begun. *Tribune* business always took a backseat to Sutherant Petroleum business, and since kickbacks from Sutherant accounted for twice his annual income, he made it a point to be available when needed.

***

Back at the Sims' farm, Chief Waylon Vincent wiped his eyes to relieve the irritation of the foul, smoke-filled air. He spat into the wind and glared at Larry Nelson, who lingered near a rock pile beside the barn. Still blotting his brow in reaction to the near-death scare he had just faced, Nelson worried the dirt with the heel of his boot - a frightened child awaiting punishment.

Within the hour, Jim Crenshaw powered through the barricade at the helm of Dennis Sims' Silveranado. Sims crouched in the passenger seat, slightly inebriated and furious that Jared Frazier and his niece had managed to escape. As the truck skidded to a stop out of earshot of the other officers, Chief Vincent approached the passenger door and thrust a thumb over his shoulder in the direction of the barn.

"Nelson said Frazier had the house all rigged to blow. Just in case there's any evidence in there you don't want to be found, I'm lettin' her burn down before we remove the barricades," Vincent hissed.

"You've got some clean-up to take care of before those firetrucks come in." Sims took a drag from his cigarette then nodded toward Larry Nelson. "You know what to do. While you're at it, keep an eye on David Frazier. I used Eric Williams' truck to get on the property today and heard their plans. Looks like Frazier's got some new friends with mighty deep pockets. Worries me when he calls his little secret meetings. And with his son on the lam..." Sims pushed himself up in the seat and belched – 100-proof lethal.

"If that boy had been stopped years ago like you wanted, we wouldn't be in this mess now. He's damned lucky he's made it all these years without a bullet," added Vincent.

The eerie yellow glow of the dashboard lights reflected in Sims' eyes.

"His luck's about to run out. Once he gives me those codes he's done. " Sims flicked his cigarette out the window.

"Any idea where they're heading?" asked Vincent.

Sims gazed through the windshield to the lights of Oklahoma City far in the distance. His hand fell to the small satellite tracking monitor positioned securely at his side. Most would have never given the device notice since Mark Sims had designed it to look like a typical GPS system. Fortunately, Sims' partner had run a surveillance camera line into his brother's home office and was able to observe the final tests of the monitor. Why Mark Sims felt the need to track anyone's movement, Dennis would never know. But the device was a god-send for tracking down his niece and her long-lost boyfriend. "East," he muttered.

"You okay to drive?"

Sims sneered at him then heaved the passenger door open and bulldozed his way around the truck, jerking Crenshaw from the driver's seat. "You keep this out of the press! And clean this place up." Sims settled behind the wheel and motioned toward the barn where Nelson waited. "No loose ends." The dash board clock read nine-twenty. Sims spat toward the smoldering fire and revved the engine. "What a fuckin' mess." With a turn of the wheel, he disappeared behind a red spray of dust as he raced toward Highway 37. A ghostly cloud ascended in a sickening plume of debris and ashes.

Vincent brushed the grime from his uniform, wondering how Dennis Sims had managed to manipulate some of the most powerful men in Washington into throwing their support toward their covert enterprise. But with one turn of his head he understood. The rolling fields of wheat that blanketing the rivers of oil deep beneath Sims' hayfields defined power and wealth. Vincent's attention migrated to Larry Nelson. With a nod toward Jim Crenshaw, that next order of duty was carried out.

***

A half-hour earlier while moving Dennis Sims' truck, Eric Williams' checking the gas gauge had been more of an afterthought. He had reasoned that with less than a quarter-tank, Sims could not make chase without refueling. As luck would have it, Eric was right. So after obscurely following Sims from the fire scene to the service center just east of town, Eric parked in back and waited until Sims walked inside to pay for gas. Once clear, Eric crept from the side of the building to Sims' truck and saw the opportunity he needed. While pretending to check the oil in Sims' diesel, he punctured a hole in the radiator. Sims returned with purchases in tow: a six-pack of beer, a carton of cigarettes, and two beef sticks, totally unaware of Eric's ploy.

Thirty miles down the road, Eric's luck struck again. From a safe distance, he watched as steam spewed from underneath the hood of Sims' V-8, stranding him on the side of the interstate in the middle of Nowhere, Oklahoma.

Chapter 12

Thursday - late evening

The softness of Jared's arm and the sweet scent of his cologne could have easily enticed Tracy to doze off, but she was too anxious to sleep. It was just after ten and as they made their way into Fort Smith, Arkansas, Jared drove through town in search of the rental car company where he planned to change out vehicles. Miles back, Tracy had plugged in her digital player and every once in a while had played one of her original songs that had been recorded by some relatively well-known artist. She never told Jared he had been listening to some of her songs.

"Where are we heading anyway?" she asked in between bites of a granola bar.

"Georgia. I have a friend there who works with the U. S. Marshal Service. He helped with my relocation. Plus, he knows Sutherant and will be able to get us out of this mess. After that, anywhere you think we can lay low for a few days. There's the map."

She unfolded the map and her first thought was to see her Aunt Jodie. That made her think about her mom and dad and the home she no longer had. Her mind naturally veered back to Oklahoma. Before she could turn away he saw the sadness in her eyes.

"Hey, you okay?"

"It was just this morning that you came walking up to my porch. Four years since I've seen you. Now here we are," she half-laughed, "Mr. and Mrs. Jake Simmons."

"*Hmph*, and I've got you running from *goons* on your wedding night," Jared scoffed.

She shook her head, dismissing his concern.

"One day you'll have that big wedding you've always dreamed about."

"Doesn't matter," she rolled her head toward her window. "I mean, I've thought about it... wondering what our wedding night might have been like," she blushed. She glanced over the awkward pause. "By the way, Eric and I never..." A shy smile reached her eyes.

Jared's face softened. He draped his arm around her and squeezed her to his side. "I told you a long time ago that I'd wait as long as you needed."

Her eyes volleyed between the windshield and his face, analyzing his words.

"I meant it when I said there were never any other girls, T."

For a moment she stared blankly, allowing the full meaning of his words to settle. *He kept his promise.* And there it was...that smile of hers – just peeking up at him in pure love.

She jabbed her elbow in his ribs. "Maybe you'll be my first one day."

Jared's soft laugh was like a perfect chord on her guitar. "Maybe so, Mrs. Simmons."

Chapter 13

Sims reasoned that the only good thing about being stranded on I-40 waiting for the wrecker was that the beer was still cold. As he paced along the shoulder of the interstate, he looked at the time and tensed, knowing it would be too late at night to get his truck repaired. It would be well into the morning before he could get back on the road again.

Just as he was slamming back the third can, his cell phone buzzed. "Yeah."

"Do you have any idea where he is?" The caller barked.

"He surfaced in Newport, just like we expected. I'm tracking them now - near Arkansas."

"How the hell did he get away?"

"You tell me. You taught him everything he knows."

A beat of silence stiffened the air.

"Here's the situation..." The man's voice was cold and threatening. "We're getting a lot of pressure from the top to close everything down. That bunch from Korea is demented and with Internal Affairs involved we'll all go down if that information leaks out. Just tell me you have a plan to get him into the computer system to clear our names 'cause if IA gets to him first..."

"I have a plan. And it's not just about clearing our names. That fortune's been sitting there for close to five years and --"

"Don't screw this up. I need him contained."

"If you hadn't slipped up and scared his dad into hiding a year ago we wouldn't be dealing with this now." That long, uncomfortable silence pulled up a chair. "Maybe it's time you remember who started this operation in the first place. Without my property you have no oil and no trade with Soon's partners. And without my help you'll never find where that shipment was stashed." Sims stared into the darkness to the east.

There was an abrupt disconnection. Dennis Sims' gaze fell to the metal box securely at his side. He flipped the power switch and the screen illuminated into an array of green and yellow lines – a maze of countless possible routes of travel. The electronics began to calibrate, analyzing his prey's location in northwestern Arkansas.

"Five to six hours – easy drive tomorrow," he mumbled. With another flip of the switch, the screen went dark. He chuckled at the irony as he remembered the day he *procured* it, knowing Mark Sims had designed the device to ensure his daughter's safety. *Ha!*

Sims' hand went to his hip and as he adjusted his Creseda .45-caliber, his own plan formulated in his mind. *His* plan was simple. Place a gun to Tracy's head and Frazier, Jr. would have no choice but to break the computer codes and enact any order Sims demanded: to transfer Sutherant Petroleum's remaining money into one untraceable account, to delete every incriminating computer file that existed, to negate Mark Sims' will by signing ownership of the family farm and all mineral rights over to him, the rightful heir. Two quick gunshots later, Frazier and his niece would be out of the way and Sims would be well on his way to positioning himself as the key controller of America's oil industry.

With the twitch of his finger, a spray of white foam splattered across his hand. He gulped half the brew, swiped his hand across his mouth, and then slid his phone from his pocket.

"Hey, Babe – up for a little adventure?"

Several hundred miles away in Charlton, Colorado, Selena Salgado opened her closet door and grabbed her duffle bag. Weeks had passed since Sims' last visit and an invitation for a weekend rendezvous was enough to spark her interest.

"Business or pleasure?"

"Hon, if you head out now, we can take care of business and the rest of our lives will be pleasure. How's that sound?"

"On my way."

Chapter 14

The neon lights of the rental car building threw brilliant colors across the hood of the car, dancing in a frenzied rhythm to the beat of highway traffic. It was after ten and surprisingly, several customers were still in line to arrange transportation. As Tracy gathered trash and empty water bottles from the car, she watched Jared scan the parking lot with a cautious eye cocked in every direction.

"What is it?" Tracy followed his line of sight.

"Three cameras on the parking lot, another one inside the office." He pulled a ball cap lower across his eyes before starting toward the building. "Stay here. Keep your head down. No telling who's watching. With all that happened at your house, they'll use every source they can to find us."

Jared took his place in the rental car line and overheard the agent announce the next departure of the airport-bound shuttle. It would take extra time but going to the airport to rent a different vehicle from a different rental company would confuse the paper trail they were leaving behind. He paid with cash and flashed a fake driver's license he had tucked away and then hurried back to Tracy carrying their receipt and a map of the state of Arkansas.

When the airport shuttle arrived, they found their way down the aisle as the driver stowed their bags in the rear compartment. Realizing they were the only two passengers, Jared relaxed and for the first time in hours, lowered his guard. He plopped into one of the rear seats and without warning, pulled Tracy onto his lap. His kiss was eager, desperate. Between the four long years he had waited to hold her again and the torturous hours he had spent apart from her that afternoon, he could no longer refrain. He drew her closer and as Tracy folded herself against him, she moaned with pleasure as his tongue claimed hers.

When the driver boarded and dimmed the lights, Jared cupped her hips and tightened his arms around her. He buried his head into the softness of her chest, tugging the top of her blouse lower to smooth kisses along her breast. Breathing became secondary to tasting the sweetness of her flesh. The more he feathered his lips across her skin, the more she responded. Like the needle of a compass pointing due north, she was drawn to him - her center, her energy, her life.

All too soon, the driver announced the stop for airport passengers. Deliciously dizzy from the sudden rush, Jared gripped her shoulders and rested his forehead to hers.

"Brings back good memories, T.," he whispered.

That old familiar tingle spread across her skin. "Great memories" she grinned.

Ducking under the doorway of the shuttle, he jumped down the stairs then turned to catch her as she fell into his arms. Their easy laughter paved the way as they wandered to the rear of the shuttle to retrieve their bags. Tracy hesitated as he gathered their luggage. The loose button-down shirt hid his chest, but every flexing motion of his bold gait called out to her like a Pied Piper's melody and she felt her body awaken, so willing to follow his seductive lead.

She quickly fell into step with the steady pounding rhythm of the song blaring through her ear buds, and as she mumbled the sensual lyric under her breath, her eyes danced with his every move. The verse spun through her mind.

"Have I told you how gorgeous you are?" she whispered as she hustled to his side and yanked her ear buds away.

Jared chuckled. "You go for the fugitive type, huh?"

"You're starting to grow on me," she flirted.

Reaching the airport entrance, they shuffled through the revolving door just ahead of the young business man behind them, made a deliberate turn to the left and walked a few doors down to the next bay of rental car services. Heads tilted in conversation, they headed to a bay of phones and called to request transportation to a new rental car company. After making arrangements, they made their way toward the exit and found the ground transportation area. This time, several passengers were boarding the shuttle so they settled for the first two empty seats they could find.

Once they were on their way, it seemed the driver set his aim for the deepest pot holes and the sharpest curves. Hand in hand, they exaggerated the frequent jolts and turns, playfully bumping against each other. An older lady smiled, watching them flirt and caress each other with an unhindered affection. Tracy grinned in her direction and it crossed her mind that her own mother would have been about the same age had she lived. In the same thought the burning reality set in that she and Jared were on their own. They had no family and no home left in Oklahoma. The dark realization settled as a shadow crossed her line of sight. Her heart leapt, and while it was only the shadow from an overpass above the shuttle, it left her with a sudden feeling of isolation.

A young man a few seats down looked her way and smiled. He lifted his phone to type a text, and as Tracy noticed his wedding ring, her thoughts rolled to Jared. All uneasiness fell away.

"What kind of car are we getting?" Tracy's soft whisper tickled his ear and was so sensual Jared's breath caught.

"What kind do you want?"

The car was not important to Tracy at the moment, but having his face so close to hers caused her to reach up and kiss him. It may have embarrassed him since there were other passengers watching, but she didn't care. Unexpectedly, Jared ran his hand through her hair and drew her closer, deepening their kiss without regard to others. When he lifted his head, he paused an inch from Tracy's face.

"I love you, Mrs. Simmons."

She had told herself to take this slowly, to not rush back into his arms too quickly, to make sure she could trust him with her heart. But each new minute in his presence brought back the assurance that he was still the same Jared she had always loved. The pop deva had it right, she determined, as the verse and beat of the earlier tune resounded in her mind. *Her heart did skip a beat anytime she was with Jared.* Sure enough, as soon as she looked back into his dauntless eyes, her breath caught again. An easy smile spread across her face.

"And I love you, Mr. Simmons."

***

The rental car transaction was easy and within a few minutes they were accelerating down the road in lavish, four-door silver Ultrex GS. Having just crossed the Arkansas state line prior to exchanging cars, they set out toward Greer's Ferry Lake. Jared was familiar with the area and knew the secluded state park would be the last place anyone would look. He also knew there would be plenty of nondescript motels along the way when they got too tired to drive. Plus, the nice, quiet drive through the Ozark Mountains would give him a good chance to relay the events of his afternoon.

"I knew better than to drive in front of Dad's house, so I parked in a field and snuck around back where they were meeting. I didn't think much of it until I heard what Eric had to say. Now it all seems to fit."

"What do you mean?"

"Looked like a political convention there were so many brown-nosers. Congressman Taylor was there from D.C., and I counted about seven other suits hovering around him. I need to find out who they are."

"Lauren's working on it. She and Grant are keeping track of whoever's coming and going. I never knew how influential some of our lowly state politicians can be. Did you know that Congressman Davidson heads a subcommittee that oversees the management of all of our deep-water ports?"

"Davidson?"

"They study groundwater resources and decide on trade routes and shipping requirements from various ports. You said you overheard something about Sutherant moving operations to the Savannah and Galveston branches."

Jared nodded. "They said Galveston was a problem - too many security concerns with the Mexican border. He seemed pretty determined to use the Savannah port because they would have military protection."

"What would Sutherant be shipping that would require military protection?" Tracy questioned. "And why are our politicians and FBI meeting in your dad's backyard?"

"It's obviously bigger than oil. And it's definitely more wide-spread than Oklahoma."

"You say your dad was leading the meeting?" Tracy untangled her digital player and plugged it into the charger.

"It was hard to watch him. I just couldn't stop thinking about all the times he warned me to stay away from Newport, and then he came back like it was nothing."

Tracy looked away. The relocation of Jared's family even years later unsettled her. The facts were not adding up.

"Why would it be safe for him and not for us?" Jared asked. "Is he hiding something? Is he having an affair?"

Tracy shrugged. She remembered Lowell McClain's last words: he and Frazier were working to gather evidence against Sutherant. A nervous tremor shot along her spine as she realized Jared was right – this was so much bigger than oil.

"Well, I'm going to get to the bottom of all of this," Jared continued. "My friend in Atlanta was helping arrange my dad's security up until a little over a year ago. He'll know what's going on."

***

They had been driving for miles. As they conquered one Arkansas foothill after another, Tracy began to feel light-headed and knew her blood sugar was going low. She unbuckled and leaned over the seat to rummage through the snacks. She grabbed two granola bars and a bottle of juice, offering Jared a drink as she turned around.

By midnight a light rain had started to fall. The gentle motion and rhythmic whirr of the wiper blades was hypnotic, and as it was getting late, Jared started looking for a place to stay for the night. They had entered a national forest and were near the lake but had not seen a motel for miles; it was beginning to look like he had made a mistake in not stopping sooner. The few cars they had noticed minutes before had turned off the highway miles back in the more populated areas of town.

The lone exception followed obscurely in the distance.

After driving several more miles in what appeared to be a dense jungle of trees, Tracy sensed Jared was getting agitated for bringing them to the middle of nowhere. But as she stared into the thick, empty darkness, all she could think was how totally dependent they were on each other now. And how very alone. How ironic it was that four short years ago they would have given anything to have this kind of privacy, this opportunity to be together without fear of being caught. And now, here they were - side by side and miles away from any intrusion. But the fact remained – the four year separation could not be forgotten and she wasn't sure if he could be trusted not to leave again. All night she had told herself that it was too soon. How could he expect her to just rekindle a flame from so long ago? But when she glanced his way and was suddenly transfixed by the way the dashboard lights reflected in his loving, brown eyes, how could she not trust him? And when she saw the way his rock firm muscles seemed to flex with every movement, taunting her each time his hand smoothed across her thigh, how could she not at least be open to the idea of accepting Jared back into her life?

"Jared, pull over!"

Jared slammed on the brakes. "What's wrong?"

Tracy had long forgotten about a motel, a bed, or anything of comfort. All that mattered was that he had suddenly reappeared back into her life and she needed to somehow get to know him again. "Just pull over. It's late and you're tired."

"Tracy, it's the middle of nowhere."

"There - up ahead. See that turnout? Just pull off there."

She bit her lip as what had sounded like a good idea in her mind suddenly felt like a cheap, flimsy ploy to get Jared into the back seat. She tried to focus, tried to concentrate on protecting herself to avoid getting hurt again. But random movie scenes sparked to life in her mind - images of hot, sweaty bodies tangled in knotted sheets. Then her thoughts flashed to steamy romance novel passages – *shades* of every thought she had ever had of Jared. And as she listened, even the soft love song playing on the radio made her body ache. She looked at Jared and wondered how their love story would unfold. She trembled with nervous energy, certain their version would be more erotic than any fictional passage she had ever read. But not tonight. Too much chaos was rambling through her mind to ever appreciate that *first time* she had waited so long to share with Jared.

"Please don't tell me you're thinking of sleeping in the car." Jared's voice broke her thoughts. He slowed the car and glanced in the mirror, seeing nothing but cold, unfriendly darkness.

"I'm thinking we are both exhausted and that if we don't pull over, these dark, curvy roads will be the end of us." She turned in her seat and took his hand. "Can we just stop for a bit? Everything has just happened so fast and I think we need to just get some rest so we can clear our minds."

"Here? In the middle of nowhere?" His aggravation drove a wedge through the peace until he caught a glimpse of her face in the faint moonlight. The dimples at the corners of her mouth and the tiny creases around her eyes disarmed him. He could not resist pulling to the side of the road.

Their company did the same.

"See, this is nice. And as I remember, you were always kind of partial to getting me alone in the dark woods at night." Tracy's heart lunged as the thought draped around her - spending the night with Jared in a rainy, secluded forest in the back seat of a rented silver Ultrex GS. This was the most romantic paradise she could have ever imagined.

Jared slid the gear shift into park then hesitated, looking through the windshield into the darkness. A long moment passed. Tracy reached toward the ignition and turned the key. As the engine died, a hush spilled over the car. And then silence – a stillness broken only by the soft melodic lullaby of raindrops sprinkling through the trees, splaying and sashaying across the windshield. The last glow of the automatic lights faded into total darkness. Tracy laced her fingers through his and felt his pulse quicken. She rested her head to his shoulder and whispered.

"Do you remember how we used to sneak out behind the hay bales?"

He snickered and squeezed her hand.

"It was simple, you know? Unplanned, spontaneous - we just went for it without a care in the world." She turned his way. " I'd like to make you a deal, Jared Frazier. I need a night like that tonight. I need to remember you the way I knew you then, just innocent teenage love. I'm not quite ready to…well, can we just make tonight an easy --"

He pressed his finger to her lips then swallowed her in his arms, kissing her so tenderly she felt his every tremor, his every timid breath, his every touch. "I told you I'll wait until you're ready. But can we at least sleep in the back seat where there's more room?"

All at once he was guiding her over the seat. In an excited rush, she wrestled her guitar to the front seat, tossing duffle bags and snacks to the floorboard. In the darkness she heard Jared strain to heave his six-foot plus frame over the seat. With a laugh she reached for him and pulled him limb by limb into her embrace.

Soft, sporadic giggles sprinkled the silence like the gentle patter of rain tickling the hood of the car. When she looked up, their eyes met – his face so peaceful in the dim light. She touched his bristly cheek then kissed the corners of his mouth – tiny, soft, gentle sweeps of love to reassure herself he was really there. She draped her arms around him and felt the tension ease from his shoulders. Lying back into the seat, she pulled him closer, feeling the fullness of him against her. Warm kisses fell along the soft curve of her neck and as he wrapped his arms around her to keep her warm throughout the night, she felt safe, and loved, and whole.

Now and Forever

When you found your way to me, I gave my heart to you
All the desires deep within my soul came alive and then I knew
My life is nothing without you – I've known it for some time
You're the part of me I was hoping to find. Now you're forever mine
For now and forever you're a part of me
And the best part of me is you
For now and forever one life to share
As I give my life to you
No matter what the future brings, I'll be there by your side
To hold you, keep you safe and warm, to know you're always mine
As we share life's dance and take a chance on this love that's meant to be
We'll hear our song and sing along to this lover's melody.
For now and forever you're a part of me
And the best part of me is you
For now and forever one life to share,
My life is complete with you
Now and forever you're a part of me
For now and forever with you

Chapter 15

Friday morning

It was well into the night before the light rain finally subsided. Tracy and Jared never noticed. Nor did they notice the dark-tinted sedan positioned seventy yards away that had been lurking in the cover of trees all through the night. Truth is, as soon as Tracy's head curled into the crook of Jared's arm, they both had fallen fast asleep.

The gray early morning dawn had just begun to seep through the evergreens. Cool pre-dawn temperatures had spread a layer of condensation on the car windows. Jared pulled his jacket from the floorboard and draped it over Tracy's legs then adjusted the blanket to cover her shoulders, amazed at how deeply she was sleeping. Before he woke her, he crushed his face into her hair and inhaled, clinging to every intimate detail – her delicate skin, her scent, the soft purr of her shallow breathing, the way she whispered in her sleep – all the small things about her he had never known.

Things he had not been able to see in the darkness were now more visible in the gray morning light. Her body was perfect, still as toned and firm as he had always remembered, but sprinkled across her skin were the tiny bruises he knew so well – constant reminders of her diabetes. He lifted her shirt and smoothed his hand along her stomach, gently brushing each tiny bruise where her insulin pump injections had been.

Hesitating at her naval, he saw that it was pierced. He had felt it in the night and now noticed she wore a small diamond which glimmered in the soft morning light. A small computer jump drive and a silver music clef locket lay swirled around her neck. Remembering that her dad had given her the locket for her seventeenth birthday, he straightened it, soaking in the warmth of her soft skin. She stirred and stretched her leg from underneath his jacket. On the outer side of her right ankle he noticed a small, scripted tattoo - a treble clef and four quarter notes on a bar of music. "T., through and through," he smiled, so proud of how openly she expressed her passion for music.

He craned his neck and noticed the lake in the distance just beyond the tree line. Light fog blanketed the serene, dark water. A heron perching high on a limb swooped to the surface of the glassy pool. As it rose again, a tiny ripple swelled along the surface. It soared high into the air with its breakfast in tow. A sudden chill tingled along Jared's spine as he watched the scene. Stolen innocence. The kill took him back to their plight. He stroked Tracy's hair and she began to rouse.

"God, you're beautiful!" he whispered as he kissed her mussed hair. Even at her worst, Tracy was striking. No cover-page model had ever looked sexier.

She stretched her arms above her head and yawned as he streamed his fingers along her spine, snickering as he watched her wipe the drool from the corner of her mouth. Still floating in her most recent dream, Tracy arched into him, feeling the familiar fever rise as she reflected on the familiarity of his touch and his scent, and his wonderful passion as they kissed the night before. Adjusting to see him better, Tracy propped up on her elbows and tugged the blanket more completely over the two of them. She swirled her fingers through his chest hairs, kissing and caressing his firm abdomen and the tautness of his muscles.

"Thank you," she whispered, hoping he could sense how much he meant to her.

Jared pressed his finger to her lips and traced her smile. "You're welcome." He smoothed his hand across her stomach and brushed the diamond in her naval. "Where did you get this?"

"From you."

He looked more closely. "You kept it?"

She nodded. "To remember you."

Turning over on her side she nestled into his chest to catch the last moments of sleep before the sun made its appearance. An hour later Jared and Tracy were roused by the whirring sound of the slow-passing car. Startled by the early-morning park visitors, they bolted from the seat, scrambled to gather their senses, and then remembered their flight from Newport. After hurdling the front seat, they made their way to the park's bathhouse where they freshened up and changed clothes in the small restroom. Minutes later, they strolled back to the car never noticing the lone black sedan parked in the far corner of the lot.

"So where to?" Tracy wondered as she snuggled to his side.

"Memphis." Jared said as he helped her into the car.

"Memphis! I work there sometimes." Jared closed the door and ran around to climb in behind the wheel. Tracy grabbed two bottles of juice and a pack of peanut butter crackers from the stash and offered some to Jared.

"You never told me that. What kind of work?" He eased along the narrow road that would lead them from the park.

"I have a contract with a music company there. Oh, and a bank account if you need me to get some money out."

"A music contract?"

"Yeah, it's my main account. Any royalties I get are directly deposited there. And yesterday I went ahead and withdrew what was left in my account in Newport. I just had a feeling you might need some cash since you were hiding out."

"Good thinking. How much do you have with you?"

"Twenty-eight thousand." The car tires hit gravel as Jared swerved to the side of the road and back. Tracy white-knuckled the dashboard, straining to hold on until he had control.

"Twenty-eight...Geez, T.! Where the hell did you get that kind of money?"

Tracy loosened her grip, sneering at him as he steadied the speed of the car. She wiped the juice from the seat and shook her head, swallowing the heated words that had come to mind.

"I – write – songs!" She enunciated, glaring at him as she grabbed a handful of napkins to blot the juice from her jeans.

"Right. Any more secrets you want to tell me?"

"Well, I guess you should know I have an account in Jacksonville, too. And Nashville."

"Damn, Tracy, what kind of songs?"

She shrugged. "Sometimes about you." She looked down and twisted the cracker package in her hands.

"About me, huh? About what a jerk I was or what?"

"Yep," she teased. "Aunt Jodie got me hooked up with a band from Jacksonville. Their first two singles were of my lyrics. Then I started setting the lyrics to music and they have bought them ever since. Same thing happened with a band in Nashville. They recorded 'Young Hearts' - the one you heard. And by the way, Denny doesn't have a clue about it. So, take what you need."

She withdrew an envelope from her duffle bag and shoved it toward Jared.

"How about if you pay for a hotel tonight? We can't use credit cards so the cash will help." He pushed the envelope back her way. "Now, why don't you sing me one of those songs?"

Her face lit up as she unlatched her seatbelt, bent over the seat, and unlocked her guitar case. Gazing through the back window, she noticed the dark, ominous rainclouds settling on the Oklahoma horizon. She shuddered as she thought of the chaos of leaving home the night before. But as she felt Jared massage her bare foot, sweeter memories of the night before made her smile. She lifted her guitar over the seat, pausing at his neck.

"I hope you know how much I love you," she breathed as she kissed his ear.

"I've waited a long time to hear you say it again."

With every passing mile her melodies lightened their spirits, pushing the threat of approaching danger and the ominous clouds of Oklahoma deeper into the western horizon. Up ahead, the soothing strokes of sunlight danced lazily across their path, drawing them in to the slower, more relaxed tempo of the South.

Chapter 16

"You mean to tell me I have to wait around here for another five hours to get my truck fixed? Where the hell is the part coming from – Detroit?" Dennis Sims, irritably sober, sneered through narrowed eyes at the embroidered name tag on the mechanic's work shirt. "At Your Service, Nate," he read aloud.

Winslow, Oklahoma, inconveniently located off the beaten path for car repair, relied on surrounding larger towns for various deliveries. As Sims had been unable to get a straight answer for the timing of his truck repair, he paced through the repair bay, leering at Nate with every turn. He eyed his watch – 8:25.

The young mechanic swiped his grimy hands across his pants as he inventoried mufflers and oil filters. He had not even clocked in for work and was already having to deal with an irate customer. It was not his problem that the man was supposed to have been in central Arkansas the night before. Neither was it his problem that a busted radiator had delayed the man's urgent business. And it certainly was not his problem that the truck part could not be delivered until noon.

"You say there was a hole in the radiator casing?"

"Yes sir, 'bout the size of a pen." Nate clicked his ball point for reference. "Looks like somethin' punched clear through it."

Sims spat then placed the one phone call he did not want to have to make.

"There's been a delay," he groaned into the phone. "I'll catch up with them tonight."

There was a long pause followed by a one word response and an abrupt disconnection. "Unacceptable."

Chapter 17

Friday - mid-morning

While writers, reporters, and editors of the *Tribune* newspaper office usually did not start arriving until closer to ten on weekday mornings, this particular Friday morning, the morning after perhaps the "hottest news day of the year" as the staff had humorously labeled the previous night's event, had become an exception. Phones in the *Tribune* office had not stopped ringing since Stan Dothan had opened the doors at just past six that morning. When news of the "fatal bombing" and Tracy Sims' "violent kidnapping" had begun to spread the night before, he had mandated an early workday for every available employee.

Lauren's desk was in disarray; strewn with notes, phone messages, and un-read memos just ready to be compiled into the biggest news story of her short career. Still, she put everything on hold, waiting until she could locate her primary source.

As she pressed Tracy's speed dial for the hundredth time in two hours, she discreetly listened in on other conversations among her co-workers. Rumors whisked through the air - lover's revenge, mental breakdown, armed kidnapping. But Lauren dismissed each rumor with a laugh knowing that Tracy must have had a good reason for whatever had happened over at the Sims' farm.

"Okay, let me have your attention everybody." When Stan Dothan addressed the entire staff, eager ears lifted. "Everybody's heard the news by now. Tracy's house went up in an explosion last night. Looks like the police are trying to pin it on Jared Frazier, a good kid who lived here back four, five years ago."

Lauren clung to every word of Dothan's speech, personalizing every word.

"We're going to hear lots of rumors 'bout this. But if you ladies don't mind, I'll go ahead and speak my mind. That story the police are spreading is a crock of day old shit. They can lie and plant all the evidence they want, but Jared Frazier no more kidnapped Tracy than I did.

"A guy named Larry Nelson was found dead out there and from what I hear, they're trying to stick Jared with that too. If Jared was involved, it had to be self-defense or accidental. So before anything goes to print, there damn well better be some truth to it."

Lauren scanned the room and when her attention landed back on Dothan, he winked at her, his reminder that she was like a daughter to him. "Tracy's a part of our team so let's make sure we treat this situation with some integrity. And somebody please get to the bottom of who is spreading these lies!"

Dothan stepped aside and as everyone returned to their desks, motioned for Lauren to come into his office.

"I'm stepping out on a limb here and what I am about to say stays here." His voice was a tired, muffled whisper. He closed the door then took a seat.

"Sure, Stan. What's up?"

"We have us a mole here and I need you to find out who it is."

"By 'mole' you mean…"

"I mean someone in this office is sabotaging the news. They're sitting on information to keep it from being printed. I'm getting word from some of the employees that they've had information deleted from their computers, notes and leads missing from their desks, and even a case of a stolen tablet." Lauren shook her head in disbelief. "And whoever it is may be trying to frame Jared Frazier. Find out who it is."

"Of course, Stan. I'll get right on it."

"And one other thing. When Tracy calls in, better not say anything. That mole has some big ears and I have a feeling we need to keep Tracy and Jared's whereabouts quiet. If they're in trouble, we need to help 'em all we can."

"Okay, I'll let you know as soon as I hear from her." Lauren reached for the door but hesitated. "Stan, did you know Mr. Frazier is back in town?"

"I heard that, yes."

"Doesn't it seem a little strange that the FBI agents have been here two weeks and have yet to pay us a visit – the only news source in town?"

Stan snickered. "Look, I know where you're going with this and you've got to let it go. Sutherant's not about to let a reporter from the *Tribune* blow their cover. Let the FBI finish their investigation. When they're done you'll have the story."

"Tracy and Jared are my best friends, Stan. They're family. The hell with 'blowing Sutherant's cover' and I don't give a flip about the FBI." Stan sat back in his chair. "And by the way, the last thing Tracy said was that she was sorry for having to leave without saying goodbye."

Stan's face relaxed.

"You let her know I'm here if they need anything. I mean that."

Lauren walked back to her desk and tried Tracy's number again. Before she could pull her phone to her ear, a shadow darkened her cubicle.

"Hello, Lauren."

The deep, baritone voice crept toward her like a dreaded nightmare. The phone slipped through her fingers as Eric Williams' piercing blue gaze paralyzed her. Her last vision of that face triggered fear and for a moment, she forgot to breathe. The memory of staring across the barrel of his gun still had that power over her.

"Let's grab some coffee." The intensity of his stare and his rigid, domineering stature made Lauren cower. "Please," he added as he extended his hand.

Lauren swallowed, conscious of the audible *gulp* she could not suppress. She forced herself to stand but refused his assistance. He stepped aside as she bolted past him toward the door. From the adjacent cubicle Jim Crenshaw swiveled in his chair, eyeing their every move. Lauren scanned the room and found Stan Dothan watching closely from a distance. When her eyes flashed fear, he pushed from his desk and swung open his office door.

"Lauren?" Dothan asked, peering over his glasses.

She threw a wave then strode through the front door. Once on the sidewalk she drove her finger into Eric's chest to stop his advance.

"No need for coffee, Eric. Just tell me whatever it is you came to say."

He stepped back and Lauren studied his eyes. The gray iciness warmed to the gorgeous deep blue shade that Tracy had once described in detail over margaritas. They really were as blue as the Caribbean. *Hypnotic.* Just as Tracy had said.

"Come on Lauren, just so I can explain things," he motioned toward the diner. "Please."

His voice was like aged brandy – potent and smooth.

"Lead the way," she waved. "I think I'm due an explanation."

When they approached the café entrance, he opened the door and chose a vacant booth in the corner. He folded his frame into the leather then motioned to Naomi, a waitress they both knew.

"Two coffees," he mouthed over his shoulder, lifting two fingers in the air.

He swept his hand through his coal black hair then unbuttoned his shirt sleeves, rolling them casually toward the bulging peaks of his upper arms. Lauren pried her eyes away.

"Thanks for coming. I've wanted to talk with you but never found the right time. After last night, I knew I needed to make the time."

"What's on your mind, Eric? Start with how you felt when you were aiming that gun at me."

Eric winced, noticing the way her auburn hair whipped with every angry turn of her head. "You're just like Tracy," he grinned. "You both speak your mind."

"Yeah? Just not well enough to report you to the police."

Eric leaned across the table and lowered his voice.

"I was just doing my job. I had no idea it was you. Frazier insists on his privacy and when you sped past the house, we thought you were someone else." He hesitated then scanned the customers. "Look, Lauren. I'm really sorry. And what happened at Tracy's last night had nothing to do with me. As a matter of fact – and this can't go any further – I helped them get away. Jared is in a lot of danger and…"

"Yes, I know. 'Shoot to kill' I believe is how your company put it. Eric, how can you be a part of something like that? If Tracy had known…"

"I know - if Tracy had known, things would have been different."

"Of course things would have been different! I never would have let her go out with you to begin with."

Even as her words were slicing through the air, Lauren saw she had cut him deeply.

"Does it make any difference that I'm only staying with Sutherant to help with the investigation?" he asked.

"Is that true? Is that the reason you are working for them?"

"You have my word."

Lauren rolled her eyes and snorted. "Right now that's not worth much."

Her throat tightened as the words hung in the air. She tried to inhale the painful jab, but it was too late. She could see the hurtful shame in his face.

The waitress approached and placed two cups of coffee and creamer on the table.

"Thanks, Naomi." Eric smiled.

"You bet," she chirped. "Y'all gonna eat?"

Eric glanced at Lauren and she shook her head.

"This'll be it, thanks," Eric said. He slid a cup toward Lauren. As she reached for it, she unintentionally touched his hand. In the awkwardness, she pulled it away too quickly, nearly spilling the coffee.

"Sorry," she said, concealing an embarrassed smile. "And I shouldn't have said that."

"Look Lauren, I don't blame you a bit for how you feel. But I'm trying to make things right. I just want to be able to talk with you and I'd like to know that I can count on you to keep me informed about Tracy."

She shook her head. "That's not going to happen, Eric. Jared's back and I won't let you interfere…"

"No, that's not what I mean. I know she's with him now. I just want to stay in contact with her until…" Eric caught himself. He inhaled to gather his thoughts then added, "I want to keep in touch with her about a project her dad and I had been working on."

"A project? Her dad died over four years ago. How could you still be working on a project?"

"I'm hoping she can help with the final touches. Anyway, I'd appreciate it if you would pass on my apology to her about that night and just let me know when she comes back to town."

"I never told her about that night. She was crouched in the floorboard and didn't see a thing," Lauren reached for the sugar. When she looked up again, she saw that he was smiling at her. "What?"

"I can usually read people and you just shocked the hell out of me. Kind of figured you as the *informant*-type. Plus, I never realized how pretty you are."

She choked on a laugh and covered her mouth. "Think that's my cue to change the subject," she diverted, taking a sip of her coffee. "There's something I need to know. Tell me what you were meeting about at David Frazier's house yesterday afternoon." She watched confusion twist his face. "Don't deny it. Grant ran the truck tags and I know you were there."

"There's nothing to deny. I wasn't there," he asserted.

Then his eyes grew nervous.

"Wait!" he remembered. "Sims said he took my truck while I was at work."

Lauren settled back into the booth and noticed his body tense in anger.

"That son-of-a..." Eric swiped a hand through his hair. "That was a private meeting. Frazier was preparing to testify against a couple of state senators. Sims wasn't even...Damn! He had no business being there. He must have slipped through security."

His hands were so tightly clenched around his coffee cup she was afraid it would break. Suddenly, her hands floated to his, wrapping around them with an unplanned tenderness.

"It's okay. I just needed to know..." she started.

He loosened his grip of the mug but before she could pull away a second time, his hands folded over hers. As natural as breathing, their fingers laced together and before she could pattern a reaction, he leaned closer. "Lauren, you have to believe me. I have nothing to do with all this mess. Yes, I work for Sutherant. But you've got to understand that there are people above Frazier...pressuring him. There's so much more to..."

"I believe you."

I believe you. Just hearing those words made Eric pause.

Lauren stiffened as he caressed her hands. Strangely, she could not bring herself to release his hold. To avoid his gaze she glanced to the clock above his head, chuckling under her breath.

"What?" he asked.

"Been with you fifteen minutes – it's not gonna work, Eric. Don't think I'm going to fall under your seductive spell and do whatever the hell it is you want me to do." She slipped her hands from his and leaned back into the booth.

"There's no *seductive spell,* Lauren. I don't want anything but to find Tracy and Jared so maybe they can help with some information. Besides, I can't help it if we have some sort of...what? Chemistry?"

She exhaled, settling her hands into her lap with a gentle laugh. He tried to hide a frown and began to snicker himself. The conversation turned more casual. They enjoyed a second cup of coffee and fell into an easy, unhurried rhythm of sharing more about each other than anything else. Lauren looked at the clock again and saw that another half hour had passed.

"This has been nice, Eric," she breathed, pulling her purse over her shoulder and sliding from the booth. "But I better get back to work. We're trying to decide what to print about last night and we don't really have a lot to go on."

Eric threw some cash on the table then pushed to his feet. "Meet me after work and I'll tell you what I know. How's that sound?"

She smirked. "Sounds like you are every bit the silver-tongued talker I thought you were." She halted and spun to face him. "Listen, Tracy's my best friend...and this..." she waved her hand between them.

He mimicked her motion. "*This* -- is us working together to get her out of trouble. Let me help you figure all this out. Besides," he reached for her hand, "there's that chemistry thing we need to resolve."

His smile was contagious. Lauren shook her head and warned herself as she reasoned her reply. A gleam sparked in her eye – that innate reaction whenever a bright idea struck her mind. Maybe it *was* in her best interest to keep him close at hand. Besides, she was a reporter and she knew how valuable a source could be.

"I get off at five," she relented.

"Perfect."

In a daze she hustled toward the office. Her heart pounded as she strode through the door to the privacy of her desk. She flashed a wave and a smile to Stan Dothan and out of habit scanned the room in search of Jim Crenshaw, wondering what kind of gossip he was stirring. But all she saw was his empty desk and dark computer screen. Turning back to the growing mound of notes piled on her desk, she set her focus on creating some sense of order to the chaos of the night before but found it impossible to concentrate. Her mind had taken flight. It was a million miles away – lost in thoughts of Eric Williams.

Chapter 18

Dennis Sims paced the floor of the customer service lounge of the Ace Automotive Repair in Winslow, Oklahoma. The call he had received some three hours before confirmed that his bad luck had followed his trail as his girlfriend, Selena Salgado, had been delayed on I-40 near Clinton, Oklahoma because of a tractor-trailer collision. Eight cups of coffee and a pack of cigarettes had not improved his mood. He pounded his frustration with every step – hammering a rolled-up issue of a fishing magazine against his right thigh. Keeping one eye on his truck suspended high on the repair bay lift and one eye on the pre-recorded Championship Rodeo Finals airing on the local station, he cursed his bad luck and Jared Frazier, swearing that by nightfall both would be nothing more than a memory.

With every passing minute, he envisioned the flashing red indicator on the GPS device moving farther and farther east across the highlighted map of Arkansas. A quick glance toward the dusty wall clock surged his anger. "Twelve o'clock! What the hell is taking so…"

The vibration of his cell phone broke his thoughts.

"Sims here."

"I'm flying to Memphis. Keep me posted with their location." The voice – edgy and demeaning – magnified Sims' rage. The burn in Sims' gut flamed anew. Five seconds later, he was doubled over cradling a strained hand, groaning in pain. The only good thing about the hole in the wall of the customer service lounge was that it didn't draw as much attention as the "This is Redneck Country!" banner that was mounted beside it.

Chapter 19

Morning travels through northern Arkansas proved to be a calming release as pink dogwoods and redbuds welcomed Tracy and Jared into the rolling foothills of the Ozarks. As they entered Little Rock, Jared suggested stopping at a local mall before heading to Memphis for the night.

"Twenty-seven messages," Tracy moaned as she checked her phone while Jared pulled into the parking lot. "Nineteen from Lauren, one from Stan Dothan and seven that I don't even recognize. I really don't want to rehash all that happened in Newport last night. I'll just text Lauren and tell her we're okay and that I'll call from the hotel tonight."

"And then shut your phone off. They may be tracking us."

After a hurried shopping spree for some additional clothes and toiletries to get them through the week, they shared a quick lunch in the food court. Jared devoured the last of his sandwich then helped her from her chair to escort her to a day spa he had spotted earlier. He pressed two fifty-dollar bills into her palm and encouraged her to enjoy herself while he picked up a few more things in the mall.

"Off to buy some sordid disguises, no doubt," Tracy teased.

"Something like that."

Clenching his hand, Tracy hesitated and held his gaze. Her grip tightened. "I'm afraid to let you go."

He nodded. "I expect by next week you'll be so tired of me you'll..."

She reached up and kissed him – so deeply he forgot his next words. Passersby brushed around them with a smile until Tracy pushed away.

"I will never get tired of you, Jake Simpson," she whispered.

***

Four stores and an hour later, Jared stopped in a sitting area to repack his new purchases. He smirked as he opened the fake facial hair and hair dye he had purchased to amuse her, but suddenly grew anxious when he considered that the disguise might actually be needed at some point. Pushing the thought away, he ripped the new flashlight from its package, inserted the batteries then slid it into the larger bag. With plenty of time before meeting her, he opened the two new cell phones and programmed both of their new numbers on speed dial.

Slow minutes passed and sitting on the hard bench aggravated the crick in his shoulder. The thought of snuggling with Tracy all night in the backseat brought a quick smile, but a twinge of pain reminded him of his next order of business – hotel reservations.

After a lengthy conversation with the concierge as he made plans for the night, he shut off his phone and retrieved the final item he had purchased. His breath hitched as he lifted the lid of the velvet-lined box. The 1.7-carat marquis diamond solitaire sparkled beneath the accent lights, and he exhaled, confident that he had made a good choice. Tracy, he knew, had been cheated out of way too much in her life, and he intended to make it up to her in every way that he could. If only he could be sure she would accept it.

"She must be one special lady." Jared jerked around, startled from the sudden scare. "Sorry, man," the stranger continued, gripping Jared's shoulder. "Didn't mean to spook you. Good choice." He pointed at the ring and hunched over the bench to see a little better.

Just an ordinary guy – a bit frumpy, slightly over the top with the coat and tie on such a warm day. His smile was disarming, but as Jared settled back and snapped the lid of the jewelry case, a long forgotten childhood memory filled his mind.

Age five - lost at the zoo. After tense minutes of searching, his mom had found him sitting by a water fountain talking to two teenagers. Jared never forgot the sheer terror on his mom's face – or the tears that pooled in her eyes as she kept repeating that infernal warning that even now was pounding in his ears. Don't talk to strangers. Don't talk to strangers.

And here he sat, face to face with a man who flashed *danger* like a neon sign.

"Thanks. She is very special," he managed.

Eager to get back to Tracy, Jared hurried through the crowd, checking over his shoulder to make sure the man didn't follow. As he rounded the corner, he stopped cold when he saw Tracy - the clarity in a kaleidoscope of color as countless people streamed by. Everything else became a blur. Everything but her freshly styled hair, polished nails, and those hazel eyes that reached deep into his soul. *Stunning!*

He closed the distance in two strides and opened his arms. "Tracy…" He kissed her before she could respond, oblivious to the young businessman leaning over the rail of the nearby fountain. "You're gorgeous!"

She breathed him in – one long thrilling draw of her favorite scent – the intoxicating aroma that marked Jared - fresh spring air, Ardente cologne, and Oklahoma roots. Her laughter spilled over as he twirled her around, and as he swung her back into his arms, she froze. Her face had gone pale. He wrenched her to his chest, sensing her alarm.

"T.? What is it?"

"That man - over by the fountain," she whispered. "He was on the airport shuttle last night."

Jared searched the fountain but saw no one. A young girl and her mother were tossing pennies into the water, but no one else was near. Tracy pushed away to look again. But it was too late. Jared had snatched their packages and was hustling them as one toward the exit.

Passersby became a blur as he whisked her by one store front then another. Bolting through the exit, they broke into a run toward the car. Jared hustled her toward the driver's side, hovering like a protective bodyguard. He tossed the packages toward the backseat then fell in beside her, slamming the door and breathlessly scanning the distance to see if anyone had followed. Seconds passed. No one in sight.

"The last shuttle we caught at the airport," she gasped, "to the right of the older lady. I know it's him. He was texting just before we stopped."

"Shhh. It's okay. " His voice was steady, too relaxed given the scare they just had.

"What do you mean *it's okay*?" she riled. "Jared, we are being followed! It is not *okay*!" She grabbed his cell phone from the console and jerked it open. "I'm calling your dad."

"No!" he snapped, accidentally grabbing her wrist instead of the phone. It was as if time froze. Neither moved, and the everyday sounds of life seemed to fall victim to the pressing silence. Jared released her hand, but it was too late. The red whelp around her wrist had already begun to flare. "T., I'm sorry. I..."

Tracy backed away. The sadness in her eyes told him she remembered. She remembered every home-run, every touchdown, every good grade, and every award that Jared raced home to tell his father about. She remembered shopping with Jared – Fathers' Day, Christmas, and birthdays – hoping that he could find that one special gift to show his dad how much he loved him. She remembered all the times Jared circled important dates on the calendar – ballgames, field trips, holidays from school, hoping his dad would just take the time to be with him. She remembered each missed opportunity Mr. Frazier had sacrificed when he chose work over spending time with Jared.

Tracy rubbed her wrist and thought back to the last week before Jared was hustled out of Newport. In that one week the football team had won the 5A state title and Jared had been nominated and selected for Oklahoma Boys' State. She had never seen him so proud. They waited and waited but his father never said a word about either accomplishment. That's the week she remembered that Jared had sworn he would never concern himself with his father again.

Moving closer, Tracy slipped the phone into his hand. She wrapped her arms around him and held him until the mounted tension left his body.

"I never meant to hurt you, T.," he whispered, "but we've got to keep moving." He kissed her cheek then stepped out of the car. He lifted his own cell phone from his pocket then dropped both phones to the ground, crushing each one with the heel of his boot. Scooping up the larger pieces, he launched them in varied directions around the parking lot then collapsed back into the driver's seat. "They tracked us." In a rush, he accelerated to the nearest exit, desperate to put quick miles between them and Newport.

Chapter 20

Keeping Tracy Sims and her uncle under surveillance had been FBI Agent Mike Richardson's priority for some time. But now that Jared Frazier had returned, that task would be even more of a challenge. So as he closed in on Jared Frazier's car traveling east on I-40, he detailed a new list of items his partner needed to arrange.

"Overheard his plans while he made reservations – they're heading to Memphis. Rent a car and get in touch with the FBI office there and tell them we're on our way. Have them get these kids a new car – outfitted for top security. And arrange to have one of the Memphis agents come on board with us for the next few days. Let's prepare for round-the-clock surveillance on these two." As the agent positioned his black sedan several car lengths behind Jared, he leaned back and popped in a CD-recording of witness interviews. The two-hour trip to Memphis would allow ample time to review his strategy for finally bringing the Sutherant investigation to an end.

***

Several miles to the west, Dennis Sims' temper softened as he closed in on the Oklahoma/Arkansas state line. After driving straight through the night and stashing her car at the repair shop, Selena Salgado had joined him and had helped to calm his shattered nerves in a way that only she could do.

"This thing works like a charm," he bragged, stroking the tracking device like a genie's lamp. "They're heading east – my bet is Memphis. I've waited too long for Frazier to turn up again, and I'm sure as hell not going to let that bitch stand in my way of getting him to sign that land over to me." He patted Selena's hand. "That's where you come in. You'll be her little distraction."

Chapter 21

Friday afternoon

Several car lengths ahead of Mike Richardson, Jared's rented silver Ultrex streamed along I-40 as soft rock eased the stress of their dash to safety. Tracy rested her head, closed her eyes, and tried to put some order to the questions ricocheting through her mind.

The steady rhythm of the tires matched her throbbing heartbeat - *pum, pum, pum, pum* – the steady cadence echoing a warning of what lie ahead. She rolled to her side and pressed her ear against the door trying to muffle the incessant noise. Two hours later her eyes popped open, bleary and disoriented.

"Hey," she breathed as she wiped the blur from her eyes.

He twined his fingers through hers. "I'm sorry about earlier. And I promise, if it comes to it, I'll get in touch with Dad."

Tracy squeezed his hand and nodded. "How long did I sleep?"

"You were out like a light as soon as we got out of Little Rock. It's been a couple of hours."

She rubbed her eyes and reached for her glucose meter.

"So who is Jim?" The serious look in his eyes surprised Tracy.

"Jim? From the *Tribune?*" She pricked her finger and slid the test strip against it.

"You were talking in your sleep."

"Nooo." Tracy rolled her eyes as she calibrated her insulin intake. "What did I say?"

"His name - - a lot."

"Must've been a nightmare," she quipped. "Don't worry. Probably just a little deep-set disdain seeping through. I really can't stand the guy," she added.

"At least I'll have some way to keep track of your thoughts." He laughed.

"Let's hope next time it's more interesting than Jim Crenshaw." Tracy shook her head then pulled her journal and notebook from her bag. "I was just thinking that since I'll have to lay low for a while, my publishing agent could help me finish this."

"What, a news story? Forget that, T. We'll be lucky to get out of this alive."

"We've got to expose them, Jared – my God, they are trying to kill you!"

Jared flinched with the ugly truth.

"Maybe I can't get inside, but we could find a reporter who could really make a difference," she pushed. "A national reporter so Sutherant and the Newport Police can't cover it up." Tracy grabbed a pen and blank paper.

"How would you get in touch with this reporter?" Jared watched her scratch some notes on her pad. "You know they'll be monitoring the press to see if you surface."

"I'll send it covertly. Dale Saunders, out of Nashville handles all my music submissions, but he works in all kinds of print publications. I'm sure he represents some freelancers who would love to have a crack at a story like this." She flipped to a new page.

"What are you writing?"

"A note to Dale. I have two new songs on my disc that I need to send and I'm explaining our situation. Don't worry –

only enough to see if he's interested. I touched on the airport incident and the deaths that have occurred in the past few years. And I think I'll mention those Congressional committees we talked about. There's something there. I can feel it."

"Just be careful."

"We'll send this over-night when we get to a hotel. Anything new we find can be sent with my next lyric submission. That way it is secured and only Dale will have access to it."

***

The interminable cotton and rice fields lining I-40 became a monotonous blur. Just as the afternoon sun began to ease, Tracy caught sight of the Hernando-Desoto Bridge spanning over the Mississippi River. The massive 'M' connecting Arkansas and Tennessee was a landmark of Memphis - a city that always made her feel welcome. As they came to the end of the bridge, Jared found his way onto Union Avenue. Tracy leaned forward in her seat, craned her neck to look ahead, and felt her heart pound when she saw Jared wheel into the parking lot of another Memphis landmark.

"Jared, are you kidding? The Promenade Hotel?" She wrapped her arms around his neck as he eased the car into valet parking. He winked at her and glanced at the console clock.

"Come on, it's almost time."

Grabbing the shopping bag from the backseat, he rushed her out of the car.

Waiting for the instant Tracy looked away Jared retrieved one small item from the shopping bag then pressed a wad of cash into the doorman's hand, asking him to have their bags delivered to their suite.

Chapter 22

Friday - late afternoon

As if in a romantic fairytale, Tracy floated on a cloud as Jared escorted her through the lobby of the South's Grand Hotel. Smiles and welcomes overflowed with true Southern hospitality. Like a passage back in time, their stroll transported them to a culture long-honored for its grace and grandeur – far, far away from the chaotic world racing right outside the door.

After checking in, they ambled along the storefronts lining the mezzanine until Jared made a stop at the concierge desk and arranged to have her lyric package sent express delivery. Hand-in-hand they mingled through the curious crowd which had gathered near the fountain as a loud Sousa march began to resonate. The crowd shifted for a closer look just as the Promenade Ducks departed the fountain, waddled along their special red carpet and made their way into the express elevator which shuttled them to and from the lobby each day.

"Come on. We get to follow them up," Jared beamed.

He guided her to the elevator, explaining that he had arranged for them to see the roof-top house where the ducks retired nightly. When the elevator doors opened, he led her out into the cool evening air. Instead of turning, Jared led her across the rooftop where a casual sundown reception was underway.

"I thought we were following the ducks," she whispered as she watched them waddle toward the pen.

He didn't answer so she followed him to a secluded area. A gentle breeze stirred as they approached the edge of the rooftop overlooking the beautiful Mississippi. Pink-blossomed crape myrtles and Southern magnolias lining Riverside Drive created a feeling of sheer seclusion – a welcome escape from the fears that haunted them. Soft music lifted on the air as a small combo band played some blues favorites, enticing couples to float away in dance beneath the sultry Southern sky.

In a dream, Tracy soaked in the scene, her mind swirling in the beautiful vision: the perfect God-touched Dixie sunset, Old Man River flowing lazily in the distance, lovers swaying to the musical serenade - all deliciously enhanced by the addictive aroma of Memphis barbeque and beer.

She propped her elbows on the ledge of the rooftop and watched a lone tugboat chug along behind a river barge. Jared embraced her from behind and as she leaned back into his chest, she felt his lips brush her ear.

"T, you've been the best part of my life for as long as I can remember," he whispered. Tracy smiled and lifted her cheek toward him. "I've loved you since we were kids and every day I know you I love you more." Somewhat surprised at how freely he was expressing his feelings, she turned to face him. "I know we've been apart for a long time, and I know you said you needed time to process all of this. But I can't imagine living without you another day because you are everything to me. You *are* my life. You always will be."

Tracy brushed his cheek and before she could reply, he kissed her – so gently she didn't feel him release. That's when she saw it…the love of her life slowly lower to one knee.

A hush fell over the small crowd as they turned to watch. Jared raised his hands and jittered as he opened the small velvet-lined cover. A flash of sunlight struck the diamond and Tracy's jaw dropped. She brushed her hair aside and heard a collective gasp move through the onlookers as they realized what momentous event was taking place.

"Oh, my God," she swayed. "Jared…" Her body began to tremble as he lifted the ring into view.

"Tracy, it's been four long years and I know you need time," he smiled and grasped her hand, "and I don't want you to make a decision until you're ready. But here's the thing, if none of this would have ever happened, if I had been able to stay home and take you to the prom and graduate with you and go off to college with you, then this would have been the next step anyway. I wanted to marry you then as much as I do right now. So waiting a little longer won't make any difference to me. I'll wait as long as you need. But just know this: I will never, ever leave you again and I will never stop loving you."

Tracy fell to her knees and locked her arms around his neck.

"I don't need more time. I love you!" She pulled his face close and kissed him. "Yes, Jared, yes, I'll marry you." Tears spilled onto her cheek and Jared kissed them away. Awakened by the cheers of the crowd, he pushed to his feet and eased the ring onto her quivering finger.

Raucous applause broke from behind as onlookers approached to celebrate their special moment. Tracy melted into Jared's arms and kissed him again, barely taking notice of the strangers graciously handing Jared glasses of champagne.

"A toast! To the happy couple," someone shouted.

Cheers and shouts of encouragement hailed from every direction as Tracy and Jared tipped their glasses and joined in the celebration. She lifted her left hand, unable to take her eyes off the beautiful diamond. In her next breath they were hustled to the dance floor by the enthusiastic guests as the band played an old Al Benson favorite. Jared wrapped her in his arms and whispered as they floated on a dream.

"Ever think we'd be dancing on a roof in Memphis?"

"I can see life will be full of surprises with you."

"Funny you should say that…"

Jared went on to explain his plans for the evening as he took her by the hand and led her to the dress shop on the first floor. "They've got a rack where you can rent formal clothes for dinner. Thought that would be fun since this is kind of a special night." He then suggested she make use of the Jacuzzi tub while he handled the details of sending the express package and then went on to explain the dinner reservations at *La Roux*, the after dinner dancing, and a horse-drawn carriage ride. "Thought we could try out a bar or two on Beale Street, you know, to get you in the mood for the room service couple's massage and the champagne dessert tray they bring up to your bedside."

"Ha! Pulling out all the stops, huh?"

"Did I mention the luxury king-sized bed?" he grinned. "But if you'd rather, we can go sleep in the Ultrex." He whispered.

"I'm not letting you go anywhere." Her kisses brushed the roughness of his cheek and settled into the curve of his neck. "I just have to stay awake tonight so I don't talk in my sleep," she added, smoothing her hands down his shoulders.

"I think we can handle that," he breathed, and all other thoughts fell away.

Your Touch

When you take me by the hand in my heart I understand
How loving you comes naturally - It's when I feel you
touching me

A gentle brush against your skin refreshing as a gentle wind
Loving you so easily anytime you're touching me

Late at night lost in a dream frightened by the things I've seen
I wake to find you holding me. I love to have you touching
me
It' s not hard for me to see your touch is everything to me

So take me by the hand 'cause in my heart I understand
That loving you comes naturally - when I feel you touching
me

It's where our love begins, a love that never ends
Loving you so easily anytime you're touching me

Chapter 23

Friday – early evening

Special Agent Mike Richardson took the first shift in monitoring the elevator bay and lobby area of the Promenade Hotel. He checked his watch - 6:20 P.M. He could not help but smile, reflecting on all he had observed since arriving at the hotel two hours before. From the moment he had shuffled unnoticed toward the roof top reception and witnessed Jared Frazier bend to his knee, a tender spot had worn in Mike's calloused heart. He had never considered himself the romantic type, but when he saw their closeness and the way they never released hands, he envied the pureness of their love. For a brief moment he regretted the path he had taken in life and wondered what it would be like to have someone to come home to at night. And while his gut told him the two lovers had nothing to do with the illegal affairs of Sutherant Petroleum, he knew he had a job to do.

Having never formally met Jared Frazier during the four years he had been assigned to the investigation, Mike could tell from his observation that Jared had character – a personality that did not seem tainted by the corruptive disease that had infiltrated his father's conglomerate. And as far as Tracy Sims - it didn't take his expertise as a seasoned criminal investigator to know an angel when he saw one. For that reason, and because they had unjustly been forced into separation during key years of their lives, he saw no problem in giving them a night of fun before leveling them with the truth of their connection to the case.

Sidestepping the expense of a private room, Mike opted for a double room to share with his partner, Agent Brody Craig, while they rotated shifts throughout the night. An extra agent would be coming from the Memphis office and could offer assistance in the morning. Once he arrived, Mike planned to approach Jared and Tracy to disclose all he knew of the investigation. Until then, he'd keep a sharp eye on the couple from a distance, confident that their night would be safe, peaceful and disturbance-free.

Chapter 24

Special Agent Brody Craig nibbled on a banana muffin as he eased through the second hour of his shift. His tired blue eyes squinted as he sipped his newly poured coffee and even in mid-swallow he had to stifle a yawn. Monitoring the lobby and elevator bays of the Promenade Hotel was not the most interesting assignment he had ever had. Accustomed to and often teased about his meticulous methods of detail, Agent Craig had taken thorough notes of every happening from the time he relieved Mike Richardson at 8:30 P.M. Three worn napkins bore evidence of all that had occurred throughout his watch. Aside from a mild scrapple he had observed between the security manager and an inebriated guest, his night had been uneventful – that is, until he saw Dennis Sims wander in from the rear entrance fifty minutes before at exactly 9:40 P.M. Knowing that Mike was not due to relieve him until well into the morning, Craig opted to maintain his distance and shuffled behind an overhanging palm to hold surveillance.

The well-hidden corner table gave Agent Craig the vantage point he needed to observe the full activity of the lobby area. Other than an occasional glance toward a young woman who sat against a far wall flipping through pages of a novel, Sims paid no special attention to anyone. Making note of every move Sims made, Craig sat in obscurity, keeping steady count of how many new drinks were delivered to his table. At three highballs in one hour, Craig chuckled to himself, wondering how a body could handle so much hard liquor in that short of time. Just as he noted number four, he received a text from Mike Richardson saying that he was going to get some sleep and that he would relieve him later in the night. Craig replied, informing him of Sims' presence. That's when things got interesting.

The businessman who approached Sims' table held an aloofness that brought immediate balance to Dennis Sims' down-home and bawdy persona. The man's tailored suit and "pop of color" scarlet tie put a new shine on Sims' worn jeans and snake skin boots. As the man slid the chair from the table, straddled its seat, and glowered at Sims, Craig sensed the two were old acquaintances. Few words were exchanged and the constant shift of eyes made the man seem nervous, or maybe preoccupied. Or perhaps he just didn't feel comfortable being seen in Sims' presence. Too noticeably different to be blood brothers, the bond read brothers in a different way. Craig recorded nondescript thoughts on a clean napkin: *College? Relatives? Inmates? Co-workers? Business Associates? Military?* He tapped his pen as he pondered clues as to their relationship.

The suited man stood and raised a forefinger to his eye with a mock salute to Sims. In response, Sims snapped upright and mirrored the simulated salute. Craig nodded and smiled. With a stroke of his pen, he underlined his last entry. *Military*.

The businessman exited through the crowd unnoticed, only to disappear into the shadows. Craig battled in indecision and considered following. Just when he pushed away from the table, he glanced up and saw that the businessman had doubled back to a corner of the front desk and was now staring directly at him. Craig froze, locked in a glare with cold, gray eyes. Craig pried his gaze and the businessman disappeared around the corner.

Turning back to the lobby, Craig realized the young woman had crossed the floor to Sims' table. She dropped a piece of paper beside Sims' hand then continued to the exit. Sims lifted it, read whatever message had been sketched in the border then looked in Craig's direction. Craig dropped his head and returned to his table, knowing his cover had just been blown.

Moments later Mike Richardson sidled to Craig's table and was given the rundown on what had taken place.

"Sounds like you may have shaken up their little plan," Mike reasoned. "Where are the kids right now?"

"Still in there dancing. Having a great time and don't have a clue I'm watching."

"Okay, stay here and keep an eye on Sims. I've got a few travel details to work out, then I'll go let them know they have company. I hate to cut their night short, but we need to get them back on the road. Wish I knew how Sims was tracking them," Mike added. "Agent Derrick Roberts of the Memphis office just phoned before I came down," he continued. "He's coming in now since things have changed. He's got the new car I requested for the kids so I think I'll have him drive Jared's rental back to Newport as a decoy. Maybe Sims won't notice the switch."

Chapter 25

Friday – 11:20

The room steward had just delivered the dessert and cheese tray to room 1200 on the Celebrity Suite floor. Inside, a feint light streamed through the Venetian blinds of the luxury suite. A disarray of evening attire and shoes paved the way to the bedroom where leftover remains of an empty bottle of champagne and two souvenir beer mugs from Beale Street lay scattered next to the bed. Upon the pillow-top comfort bed, Tracy and Jared collapsed, their chests rising and falling in laughter as they re-enacted one of many hilarious conversations they had shared with a local comedian. An air of pure contentment settled over them.

As she stretched and yawned in the lavishness of the king-sized bed, her bleary eyes fell on Jared and her heart jumped, amazed that he was real and safe and there. Catching her breath, she exhaled, relishing in the memory of the night's celebration, knowing that she was happy, genuinely happy for the first time in years. But just as suddenly, her smile fell away. One glance into Jared's peaceful face reminded her that one hotel room door was all that protected him from the threat that was bearing down.

Suddenly chilled, she pressed into Jared, gently resting her arm across his chest. He was everything to her and as she held him close, she felt so guilty – suddenly ashamed of the secrets she was keeping from him.

Jared smiled and slithered his arms around her back. His warmth smoothed across her skin as he brushed his lips to her ear.

"I want you..." Jared breathed

"Mmmmm," she moaned, sliding her finger to his mouth to trace his lips, his tongue, and the edge of his teeth. His hand joined hers, his own fingers sliding down to lift her engagement ring into view, rotating the stone in the light. In one smooth motion he rolled her to her back, kissing her lips, sliding his tongue across her teeth, and lowering his attention to her chin, her throat and her breast. As he sank lower into the sheets, she moaned with pleasure and snuggled closer, drawing the silky, satin around them. How could she fully surrender to him while withholding so many secrets? From deep within her mind she heard a tiny voice – *tell him, tell him, tell him.*

Without warning, she pushed away, knowing she could never enjoy the rest of this special night until she cleared her mind.

"We need to talk." Jared bolted upright, confused and frustrated, but she withdrew, grabbing her purse to retrieve the one thing standing in her way of honesty. "And please don't get mad – I don't think I could handle that."

She opened her hand to reveal her computer jump drive. Jared's face went pale. "While you've been gone, I've tried to find you, you know that. Working at the *Tribune* gave me extra access to private information, locked files, classified materials - things that will surprise you, information that may hurt you."

"Tell me what you know, T. To start with, what's on that flash drive?"

She surrendered the tiny memory stick. Jared snatched it from her hand and made for the desk, popping it in the laptop drive as Tracy moved in behind him. He scrolled through the material, scanning page after page of research confirming the fact that his father's company had fallen into corruption.

David Frazier's Sutherant Petroleum – suspected as central location in receiving and shipping of narcotics and illegal firearms through local airport and seaports...international operations... major U.S. political leaders and foreign investors implicated...prostitution, embezzlement... federal investigation underway in Newport, Oklahoma. "Unbelievable." Jared's eyes strained to read the small print.

"Believe it. And as of two weeks ago, the Newport Air Facility is surrounded by concertina wire. Looks more like a prison."

"This implies that government officials may be protecting the business. That explains the Congressmen I saw at his house."

"Yes, and read on. 'Washington insiders are suspected of manipulating Congressional votes to allow all of this to happen.' I'm telling you, Jared – this sounds to me like Sutherant Petroleum is operating an international crime ring right through Newport. By the way it looks they're connected to European and Middle Eastern underground. There's speculation they are importing and exporting contraband – possibly through those deep water ports Congressman Davidson oversees."

"All the drugs and weapons *we're* trying to keep out are being smuggled in by Sutherant Petroleum?" Jared asked.

"Or by whatever company or group Sutherant happens to be fronting."

Jared craned his neck to ease the strain. "Some members of Congress are allowing it to happen, huh?"

"That's what Lauren is trying to find out."

"And my good old dad is the ring-leader of it all!"

"We don't know that," Tracy countered. "It looks like there are a lot of players in this so let's keep digging until we get the facts." Tracy watched his shoulders sink as the burden of the truth set in. His body seemed to have aged ten years since he had been away.

"My, God, T., how long have you known this?"

"That's the thing – most of it has just come together this past week. I want to show you something else."

She scrolled to a different document. He perused a police report and two pages of notes as she explained her angle on the new information.

"Grant met me Thursday afternoon and let me download these files. Remember how I told you he is working on Clint Burris' murder case and he said the crime scene was similar to that one from four years ago when he first started the force?"

"Yes, a senator from Colorado, right?"

"Right. Senator Hastings was killed December 16th - right outside of Shiloh, the night you were hustled out of town."

That caught his attention.

"I've been researching reasons why he would have been targeted. When he started out, his voting record was consistently opposite the voting record of eighty-percent of the rest of Senate. He voted his conscience even when it wasn't popular. He ran on anti-drug, anti-firearm agendas all the way across the board."

Tracy scrolled to a different page of notes. "Now look at this report. After he got to Congress, he voted for bills that *supported* those same agendas he had been against. I'd be willing to bet he only thought he was voting his conscience."

"You mean someone was changing the text of the bill? Vote tampering?"

"Exactly," Tracy confirmed. "And I think Senator Hastings found out about it and was going to expose it." Tracy clicked on another excerpt. "This article ran about two months after his death. It includes the only interview his wife gave after his death. In that interview she confirmed he was being pressured and that she knew there was foul play involved in his death. She had plans to make allegations against some committee heads in Congress."

"Good for her!"

"Not really. The week after this article went to print she and her two sons were killed in a plane crash. As a matter of fact, they were heading to D.C. – subpoenaed for Congressional hearings. Perfect weather, veteran pilot, practically new corporate jet, yet they called it 'pilot error.' Flew right into the side of a mountain on take-off when leaving Colorado."

"Damn, is there any good news in all of this?"

"Maybe. Just before we left Newport, I called a contact at the Flight Training Facility in Oklahoma City. She's checking the flight records and the crash scene report for me. And I found an article dated four years ago, December 9th. This picture was taken at one of those high dollar fundraisers about a week before Senator Hastings' death. You'd assume only his real supporters would pay ten thousand dollars a plate for dinner, right? Well, notice his table guests. Your dad was there supporting Hastings. He was probably just as opposed to what was going on in Washington as Senator Hastings was."

"Maybe."

"Well, remember I said Hastings was murdered on December 16th in Shiloh, Oklahoma, right outside of

Newport? What if I told you a lawyer for Sutherant who was on his way to meet with Hastings was found dead that same night? Strangled in his garage. The police even tried to cover it up by calling it an attempted robbery. Two deaths in one night, five miles apart and carried out within minutes of each other."

"And both victims were affiliated with Sutherant?"

"Yes. And according to Grant Reynolds, both crime reports were falsified by the Newport police and kept out of the press. Within minutes of the murders, your dad rushed you and your mom out of town. My dad was killed two days later. I refuse to believe it's all a coincidence."

"Do you think my dad had something to do with their deaths?"

"No, I don't. Look again." Tracy scooted closer and traced her finger across the picture as she identified each person. "Senator Hastings, Leonard Osteen (the lawyer who was killed), your dad, and then two empty seats. I took the time to enlarge the photo. The names on the seating placards at the empty seats read Sheriff Lowell McClain and my dad, Mark Sims, VP of Finance. These are not the bad guys, Jared. I think this may be the group who alerted the FBI in the first place. But Lowell McClain made one mistake. He innocently informed the police force not knowing that his own deputy – now Chief Vincent - was a part of the corruption. Vincent leaked it to his group and before your dad and his partners could carry out their plan of exposing the corruption, two of his partners, Hastings and Osteen, were surprised by an assassin. So no, I don't think your dad had anything to do with the deaths. But I do think he found out about them and feared for your safety. That's why you were carted off into protective custody minutes later."

A noise from the outer hallway made her pause. They waited until the group of guests passed and then turned back to their research. "I think Daddy knew about the corruption too," Tracy explained. "I think that's why he spent so much time teaching you his computer system, just in case something happened to him."

"Jeez, Trace...just to keep all of this hidden?" As soon as he said it, he whipped around in panic. "Who else knows about this?"

"Nobody. I didn't get this material until yesterday."

"Is there anybody you trust at that paper?"

"Lauren. She helped me with some of the research."

"Can we really trust her?"

"Jared!" She popped him in the arm. "It's Lauren."

"Can you call her this late? Can you see if she can get some more information to you?" Tracy turned her new cell phone on and pressed Lauren's number while Jared explained the type of information he needed her to find.

"Hhh-hello?" Lauren mumbled, nearly knocking her bedside lamp to the floor.

"Hey, girl."

"Trace? Where the hell are you? I've been calling you all weekend." Lauren swung her legs to the side of the bed.

"I know. We need your help."

"Hold on," she said as she reached for her laptop. "It's like a madhouse around the office and by the way, your house? The police are calling it a bombing and they're trying to pin that guy's murder on Jared."

"What? That's ridiculous! That man was alive when we left there." Tracy turned and updated Jared.

"Not anymore. They found his body back behind your barn. His head was bashed in and they're even saying Jared *kidnapped* you. All kinds of rumors are flying. Stan's making us all go in to work tomorrow."

"I can't believe this! Well, whatever you do, never say that I called. I need you to send me as much as you can find on the dates around the time Jared left four years ago, particularly about his dad and the company. And while you're at it, everything you can find on my dad's accident."

"Okay. I brought all my current files home so I can get right on it. But Tracy you'll want to see something I found. Are you somewhere I can e-mail it to you?"

"Yeah, but anything you forward needs to be sent from your house. The office might be wired. To be safe, fax it to the Promenade Hotel in Memphis."

"Memphis? Are you guys okay?"

She glanced at Jared and smiled. "We're incredible." With a squeeze of his hand she added, "Tell you all about it when I see you."

"Can't wait to hear the details, but I have some things I need to talk to you about. Stan thinks there is someone in the office slanting the news. Somebody is deleting information from stories. There was even a palm pilot stolen. That's one of the things I'm sending. I want your take on it. Can I call you at this number? I can't get through on your old phone."

"I got rid of it. But Lauren if someone in the office is going to these measures to keep the news from getting out, it's too risky for you to stay involved."

"Don't worry. I don't talk to anybody around here. Even Jim – did you get that e-mail yet?"

"Jim? What about him?" Tracy reached around Jared and pulled up her e-mail.

"Remember that autopsy on Hank Tisdale, the airport manager? When Jim was meeting with the sports editor, I passed by his desk and happened to notice a folder sticking up in his file cabinet. 'FAA regulations' was written across the top and that made me curious. Anyway, I opened it. Not much there except one folded piece of paper near the back of the file, the autopsy report on Hank Tisdale."

"A copy of an autopsy? That's not unusual."

"No, it's the original, even signed by the coroner. It scared me so much I stuck the file under my arm and made a B-line to my car."

"No wonder it took so long for Grant to get the medical report. Jim had taken it."

"Right, probably to hide the real cause of death. They're still trying to say it was a heart attack. But scroll down the page. See the handwritten notes? Look in the margin and tell me what you think."

"WV- Mc.Sun…pot.chl….H.T. 381-2440 Okay, I give up. What's it mean?"

"That's what I was hoping you could tell me. These notes were written along the side of the autopsy report but I can't figure it out. The phone number there is to the airport."

"Airport phone number – then '*H. T.*' could be Hank Tisdale. *Pot.chl* - Potassium chloride. Grant said he had large traces in his blood. '*Sun*' – Sunday maybe. Wasn't he killed on a Sunday? '*WV, Mc*' I have no idea what that is."

"My first thought was Waylon Vincent. But why would his name be attached? Grant was the one who investigated the scene."

"Waylon Vincent. Wasn't he on the last execution detail? If so, there's your link. As far as I know, potassium chloride is one of the drugs used in Oklahoma executions."

"Oh, my God. You mean Vincent might have stolen the chloride and used it on Tisdale? Tracy, you're a genius! Now we just need Grant to find proof that Vincent stole it."

"Good luck with that. Just get the rest of that information to me as quickly as you can."

"Hey, wait. There's one more thing. It's about Eric."

"What about him?"

"Well, last night we got together to compare our research on Sutherant and uh, … he kind of asked me out."

Silence.

"Tracy?"

"Lauren, he works for Sutherant. His truck tag number was one of --"

"Yeah, I know. But he says your uncle had used his truck that day. Believe me, it'll just be as friends, but if you don't think it's a good id-- "

"No, no it's not that. Just please be careful."

"Always."

After talking a minute longer Tracy disconnected then turned to Jared. "Eric asked Lauren out."

"Good!" Jared sneered. "Hope she breaks his heart!"

"Jared!" Tracy shoved him. "She's on to something with Hank Tisdale's murder. And it's possible that Jim Crenshaw may be withholding evidence. He had the autopsy report hidden in his files."

"The same Jim you called out for in your sleep?" The sarcastic tone in his voice surprised her. She watched him look away and recognized the look. Being jealous of Eric was one thing. But of Jim?

She slid her arm around his waist. "Jim's close to sixty years old, as short as me and topping two-twenty, has a double chin, and reeks of cigarettes. Plus, he harasses women every chance he gets. Does that ease your mind?" Jared chuckled then looked on as she scrolled down the page of Lauren's e-mail.

"This is the actual autopsy report on Tisdale with the real cause of death. Jim must have been hiding it to protect..." Tracy stopped in mid-statement and read some notations on the second page.

"An airline ticket receipt?" Jared asked pointing to the screen. "From four years ago?"

"It's in my uncle's name. One-way to Pueblo Memorial Airport in Colorado. Oh, no."

Her face went pale. "That's where Hastings' plane had flown out of before it crashed," she added.

"You've got to get that crash scene report from the FAA," Jared warned. "If your uncle was involved in Hastings' crash, that may explain why he's kept you under lock and key all these years."

Jared's eyes shot open. "This is the kind of evidence they're trying to keep hidden, even by killing a whole family in a plane crash," he exclaimed, pointing to the computer. "The guy you saw at the fountain followed us four hundred miles! Who's to say he didn't follow us here?" The room began to swim as Tracy jumped to her feet. "Get packed! We've got to keep moving." He shut the laptop and tucked it under his arm.

In a daze Tracy wandered toward the bedroom then circled back to where Jared stood. "Jared, what do we do?"

"The same thing I've done for the past four years – stay one step ahead of them." Jared wrapped his arms around her and reached for a bottle of water. "Here, drink this. And you need to eat something."

She bolted the cool water and splashed a bit on her face. Jared opened a pack of cheese crackers and watched as she crammed one in her mouth. After a couple of crackers he handed her a piece of chocolate. Just as she started to regain some color, a loud knock rattled the door.

Jared threw his finger to his lips. He shoved her away from the door and waited as she recoiled against the wall. He approached the door and with an eye to the peephole, he slowly exhaled and his shoulders relaxed. Flashing a grin at Tracy, he swung open the door.

"Man, am I glad to see you! I never thought I'd be thankful to see your sorry ass!" Jared razzed.

A man shorter, heavier, and older than Jared paraded into the room. Sharply dressed in what appeared to be a high-dollar gray suit and red tie, Tracy wondered what kind of business relationship Jared had not disclosed. Jared slapped him on the back and they embraced as old friends.

"Hey, you finally get to meet her," Jared chimed. "Phil, this is Tracy. T., this is my good friend, Phil Murphy." Before Jared could finish the introduction, Phil pulled Tracy close into a warm hug. She smiled and endured his tighter than comfortable hold. But she liked him from the start and forgot her nervousness as she felt his presence fill the room.

"Tracy Sims – you *are* as pretty as he said! And he was right. Your eyes are like emeralds. But Honey, I've got to tell you, you could have done a helluva lot better than Jared Frazier," he chuckled.

Tracy smiled as Phil tightened his grip around her waist. Then her eyes narrowed.

"Have we ever met before? You look familiar." Phil released her and crossed the room.

"Darlin', I would have remembered meeting you," his words trailed behind him as he sauntered through the room. "And I apologize for interrupting you so late at night."

"That's alright, but what are you doing here?" Jared said. "I was planning to meet up with you in Atlanta later in the week."

"Aw, you know me, I break plans like I break hearts. I've just been a little concerned since I heard you turned up in Newport. And after your little pyrotechnics display, I thought you might need some help. Word on the street is that you're high on their priority list. You sure picked some heavy hitters to play ball with, Buddy Boy. Hope you know what you're doing."

Tracy led Phil to the couch and offered him a soda.

"Actually, I don't know what the hell I'm doing," Jared confessed. "All I did was go back for Tracy and now they're sticking me with murder, a bombing, and a kidnapping. You know it didn't go down like that, Murph."

"Yeah, I know." Phil stretched out and popped the drink top. "Well, if I'm going to be your hero looks like I better level with you about some things." Tracy looked up in time to notice Jared cut his eyes at Phil. On closer look she saw his jaw clench with tension.

"Hope you aren't about to tell me you're here to carry out some sinister deed on my dad's behalf. I'm not too trusting of folks tied to Sutherant right now."

Phil gulped down a hefty swig of his soda. "Hell, no. I'm here to help you put your old man away. And I plan to get you two to safety as soon as I finish this pop. But Jared, it's time you knew the truth. So answer me this," he leaned closer. "Do you trust me?"

Jared hesitated. "You're scaring me a little right now, but yeah."

"And you know I'm a friend, right?"

"The best, Phil. Now what are you getting at?"

"Just keep those two things in mind. When I met you years ago I wasn't totally honest about some things. I was actually working undercover as part of the investigation into Sutherant Petroleum."

A silence blanketed the room like a deadly plague. Over the years Tracy had witnessed most all of Jared's expressions. She could practically read his mind by the look on his face. But when she saw the life drain from his expression her heart began to break. She had seen that same painful air every time his dad had been too busy to notice him.

"I had to use some kind of ploy to stay close to your dad, so I fronted as his employee – Head of Security." Jared stared in stunned disbelief as Phil paved an explanation between them. "Truth is, I've been with the FBI for the past fifteen years and for the past five years I've been leading an investigation into international conspiracy and drug trafficking. That's where your dad and Sutherant come in."

Jared ran his hands through his hair. "But you helped relocate my family. You were part of our protection team and the U.S. Marshalls who moved us four years ago. I remember that."

"Jared, when things started getting hot, your dad had us move your family. We had to come up with a plan to get these guys off your trail."

Both men competed in a frozen stare. Long seconds passed.

"What the hell are you saying, Phil?" Jared hovered on the edge of his seat.

"I'm saying there never was a witness relocation for your family. Your dad made that up to get you and your mom out of the way."

Jared bolted to his feet and lunged at Phil.

"You son-of-a-bitch! How could you..." Tracy jumped into Jared's path just as he rared back to strike. Folding her arms around him, she held him, pushing against him until his anger cooled. His body began to tremble. "Jesus, Phil, I trusted you!"

Phil backed away with a tentative step. "I would have given my right arm to tell you sooner, Jared, but I couldn't blow my cover. We all felt it was best to just get you out of Newport. The kind of deals your old man had in the works put you and your mom right in the heat of things. It was best that you were out of the way."

"What the hell do you mean *it was best*? You're saying it was all a lie?" He motioned toward Tracy. "You kept us apart for nothing?"

Jared slammed a desk chair to the floor as he rounded the corner. He bolted to the window, thrusting his hands to his pounding head. Like a caged tiger he paced, darting to the windowsill to stare at the traffic twelve stories below.

"Four years of our life!" He fumed.

Tracy righted the chair and eased toward him, cradling him from behind as his body shook in rage. Turning to face her, he mouthed *I'm sorry* before resting his head to hers.

From across the room, Phil crept toward his friends. "If I could erase the past, I would. You guys got a raw deal and I'm here to do what I can to make it up to you. Now Jared, your dad is a powerful man, but he is about as corrupt as they get. And the guys above him are even worse."

Phil reached to squeeze Jared's shoulder but halted when he met his glare.

"Tracy, as pretty as you are, they'll kill you as quick as look at you if you cross them. And you need to understand they are down stairs waiting for you. They may try and take you back to Newport or they may kill you where you stand, I can't say."

"Then why the hell can't you just go and arrest them, Phil? Just get this over with!" Jared exploded.

"We've been gathering evidence on this company for so long I'm plain sick of it. But we need a little more time to get what we really need. We've got to get proof so we can indict the politicians who have been ram-rodding this whole mess. That's where you come in, Jared.

"Tracy's dad was working on his own little research project and whatever he stored in that computer probably wouldn't have mounted to a hill of beans if it had been buried with him. But he made one mistake. He shared some of his secrets with you, Jared. So their one goal is to stop you from exposing that data. My main goal is to see if you can access his files so we can get what we need to close this case before they can set up any roadblocks. I've had the top techies in the country try their luck but so far, nothing's worked."

"Access his computer? Will it get us out of this? Will it get my name cleared and..."

"Just don't worry about that. It'll all get straightened out. But your dad and those other cats from Sutherant – now those guys have me a little antsy. So far they've been pretty successful at following you."

"But we got rid of the phones. We haven't used any credit cards or made any contact...nobody even knows we're here."

"*I* did," Phil challenged. "*I* knew you were here." Jared rubbed the strain from his eyes. Defeat weighted his shoulders. "Truth is my guys followed you out of Newport. And Jared, if we could follow you, so could they. That's why we need to get you into that computer system as soon as possible so we can put a lid on this case. So if you don't mind my asking, what exactly was your plan before I showed up?"

Tracy pushed around Jared.

"Phil, I don't know if Jared told you, but I work - rather worked - at the newspaper in Newport," Tracy offered. "A co-worker of mine and I have been gathering research on Sutherant for some time now. We're even working with an investigative journalist from outside Newport. They're faxing some new material tonight and we had planned to visit my aunt in Jacksonville after we received it, but if you think we..."

"No, that's fine, Tracy. Go ahead with your plans. It will actually help me out to have a couple of extra days to get this thing prepared." Phil crushed the soda can and banked it off the back of the garbage can. Before it had time to settle into the trash, he spun back to Tracy. "This research material, you say it's regarding Sutherant?" Phil lifted his cell phone as his question trailed in the air.

"We've just been working on some leads and since --"

"I'm not that comfortable with you staying in contact with anyone in Newport. Who is this co-worker?" He pressed some numbers into the cell phone and suddenly became consumed in a text message. Whether or not he was actually listening for a response she could not tell. But as a journalist, the first rule she had ever learned was to never reveal a source. She whirled around to Jared and the alarm in her expression halted him.

Tracy shook her head in one short deliberate motion. "Do not expose Lauren," she mouthed.

The seriousness in her eyes set Jared on edge. He trusted Phil's advice, but he trusted Tracy's instincts more. As a distraction he kissed her, unleashing enough energy that Phil assumed they had been side-tracked by a sudden burst of passion. Before Phil could interrupt, a loud *TAP, TAP, TAP* pelted the door.

Phil's arm dropped to his side and in one breath his gun was steadied between two hands. He motioned to Jared. Tracy froze as Jared and Phil exchanged visual cues. After Jared directed Tracy to a far wall for safety, he nodded at Phil and approached the door in such synchronized rhythm to

Phil's side-stepping movement, Tracy wondered if the scene had been rehearsed. Jared leaned his body into the wall beside the door and palmed the knob, thrusting the door open into Phil's readied aim.

Phil's face went pale. He exhaled and cracked a smile as he focused on the heavy-set agent flashing his FBI credentials at chest-level, then slowly lowered his gun.

"Geez, Mike. How about some warning?" Phil sighed as his hands fell to his side. Agent Mike Richardson stood rigid as Phil holstered his gun and widened the door to allow him in. "Wasn't expecting you to make a house call."

"Murph?" Richardson stammered. "You're back?" The deliberate inflection in his voice seemed strained. Phil cowered under Mike's gaze. Tracy observed the reunion, noted their interaction: the tense facial expressions, the awkward exchange, the nervous glances. "Been what, two years? What the hell are you doing here?" Mike snapped.

"I've got a personal interest in this one. Weren't sure where you were on things so I flew in this afternoon." Turning to Jared, Phil made introductions while Mike entered and closed the door. "Jared, Tracy, meet FBI Special Agent Mike Richardson. Mike, this is Jared Frazier and Tracy Sims," Tracy brushed past Phil to shake Mike's hand. The warmth of his hand overcame the sudden chill that had settled in the room.

"The mall?" Jared pointed his finger remembering their strange encounter at the mall bench. Mike smiled, explaining his role in the case and disclosing how he and his partner had been following at a distance since leaving Newport.

"Okay, Mike, since we've got some undesirables downstairs," Phil began, "I was just about to explain that I'll be taking them down an old service elevator that the hotel doesn't use anymore. I'm going to have them drive their rental to Jacksonville to visit family and then meet up with me in Atlanta so we can plan our strategy."

Mike's jaw tensed. "Well, I'm going to trump you on that, Murphy," he interjected. "I've arranged for them to have a secure government vehicle and my partner, Agent Brody Craig and I had already planned to team up on protective detail." He threw a quick wink toward Jared and Tracy. "I've got a personal interest in this as well, Phil, since they *have* been in my charge for the past year." Turning to Jared he continued. "You two have some Sutherant boys on your tail and I'm not leaving your side until you're safely out of danger. That's a promise."

Phil rolled his eyes and trudged toward Mike.

"I assume this has all been approved?" Phil sniffed.

"Everything's by the book. You know how I work," Mike countered. "By the way, how did you know they were here?"

Phil stammered as if reaching for a response. "I *am* an investigator, you know."

Tracy's eyes volleyed between Mike and Phil as their verbal battle grew more intense. The more the pressure mounted, the more Jared's patience crumbled. He threw up his hands and retreated to the bedroom to pack their belongings.

Once Jared was out of earshot Tracy strode toward Mike and Phil, her stern hazel eyes ablaze. She cleared her throat and they took a step back, suddenly attentive.

"I don't know which of you is actually in charge here, but Jared and I aren't too trusting of anyone at this point – even FBI agents." Her voice was low and deathly cold. "It doesn't matter who is after us and I don't care why they are trying to keep Jared away from Sutherant. Finding evidence for your precious case means nothing to me. What *does* matter to me is Jared. And I will do anything to keep him safe. So while you two work out your petty little differences, you better figure that into your plan. Mike, we'll be ready in five minutes." Without waiting for a reply, Tracy stormed into the bedroom and slammed the door.

Mike glanced at Phil who was grinning from ear to ear.

"Hell hath no fury like a woman's scorn, eh Mike?" Phil snickered in Tracy's direction. "Hasn't changed a bit," he muttered to himself.

It was that same fiery spirit he had remembered from years before.

***

In a hurried daze, Phil led Tracy and Jared to a rarely-used service elevator on the eleventh floor. His voice blared, "Hold on!" just before he popped a lever that jolted the elevator into a free-fall to the lobby below. Tracy clenched her stomach. Between the recent lack of sleep and the gut-wrenching motion, she felt her body turn inside out. When the elevator jerked to a stop, she opened her eyes and the whoosh of the doors streamed a warm, pungent blast of night air into her face. Stepping onto the platform of the loading dock, the noxious odor of heat-decayed garbage slapped her hard. Blocking the stench from her mind, she deliberately blocked Phil's harsh voice as well when he muddled through an apology to Jared. While Jared accepted his handshake with an "I oughta kick your ass for not telling me sooner" warning, Tracy inwardly wished he would go ahead and do it.

"...my guys will be right with you and after you've taken some time to visit with Tracy's family, we'll meet up in Atlanta before we get you into that computer system." Tracy caught the last of Phil's instructions.

"Hey, one other thing," Jared remembered, grabbing a notepad from his bag. Ripping the top sheet from the pad, he held out the piece of yellow paper toward Phil.

"I paid a visit to the house where my dad's staying and overheard a private meeting going on outside. These are tag numbers of some of their vehicles. I recognized at least one Congressman who was discussing ports and shipping changes. Thought it might help."

Jared pressed the list into Phil's hand. Flipping the paper open, Phil stole a quick glance and just as quickly, crammed it into his pocket. "Never know...just keep me in the loop, brother."

Tracy stopped dead. Those words – *keep me in the loop, brother* - that familiar voice, that same inflection all triggered a distant memory. The exact time, the exact place, both long forgotten. Still, those words sparked a buried memory that convinced her more than ever this was not their first meeting.

Chapter 26

Saturday – 12:20 A.M.

Inside the lobby of the Promenade Hotel, guests mingled as the night began to unfold into another beautiful Southern memory. Just beside the lobby fountain, a pianist stroked the ivories, dazzling the late-night on-lookers with a long-forgotten blues melody. The tranquil tune competed with the crescendo of noise rising from the crowd who had lingered at the bar, struggling for position to view the mixing choreography of the bartender. From the camouflaged back corner of the lobby, Agent Brody Craig craned his neck to monitor one particular table whose lone occupant kept the waiter busy replenishing spirits and complimentary hors d'oeuvres.

Dennis Sims. His eyes remained fixed on the two bays of elevator doors that led to the upper mezzanine and higher floors. Several drinks into his extended wait, his alter ego took charge – angry, annoyed, and aggressively impatient knowing that somewhere above those lobby doors were his two reasons for tension. With every sounding bell of the approaching elevators, his eyes came alive scrutinizing each arriving guest, ensuring his targets had no chance to escape. Little did he know that several corridors away, his former army commanding officer, Phil Murphy, had altered the plan and devised his own scheme of escorting the two federal witnesses to a quick escape.

***

"Jared, Tracy, this is Agent Derrick Roberts. The Memphis office was gracious enough to loan us his services and this car until we get you two back to Newport," Mike explained as Jared shook Roberts' hand. "Let me show you what we have here," continued Mike as he led them to their new FBI-secured sedan. "Take this phone. It's synced with the car's GPS and phone aps so we can always track you. And there's a link between your phone and mine so I can pinpoint your location within seconds. If we happen to get separated, I'll know exactly where you are. That battery should last a week or more without a charge."

"Will we know where you are?" Jared asked as he searched through the phone applications.

"You bet. It will give you the nearest coordinates of my location. There's full wireless, a stocked fridge and some snacks. By the way, your local pharmacist isn't too private with your personal information," he admitted as he turned to Tracy.

Tracy searched through the bag and noticed new vials of insulin, antibiotics, and a new prescription of birth control pills, snickering as she read the labels. "He filled these?"

"Yeah, he didn't want you to run low," he blushed. "So about this car... the glass is mirrored and she's got a V-8 quad turbo to give you all the power you need." Mike pulled a business card from his shirt pocket. "I don't plan to lose you, but just in case, all my numbers are listed there." With a wink he pressed the card into Tracy's hand.

Tracy liked his smile. It was real - the kind of smile she'd get from the locals back home before Sutherant's poison seeped in. And when he grasped Jared by the shoulder and playfully rough-housed, Tracy looked on with a smile of her own, remembering how often her father had done the same before he died. Rather, before he *was killed.* The thought pounded in her mind. She stepped in and pulled Mike aside.

"These people killed my father, Mike. Maybe no one pulled a trigger and maybe they didn't intend for him to die in that truck, but Daddy died trying to expose their crimes. I want justice for that. And I want to see Dennis Sims pay for what he's done to my family."

Mike patted her arm. "That's my whole intention, Tracy. Now, you sure you two are up for this drive? It's already late and we have a long night ahead of us before we can stop for sleep."

"Between the fear and wanting to stop what's happening in Newport we have more adrenalin than we need to keep us awake," she smirked.

Beside her, Jared placed a call to the concierge alerting him of the in-coming facsimile from Newport. After confirming strict security measures to ensure privacy of the transmission, it was decided that upon receipt, the fax would be forwarded to the Opry Heritage Hotel in Nashville and held in Tracy's name.

"Here, don't forget her guitar," Phil approached when he saw it leaning against the car. "I'll keep an eye on Dennis Sims. My flight to Atlanta won't leave until in the morning and I want to make sure he doesn't try and follow you." Phil patted Jared's shoulder, threw a wave toward Mike then turned to walk away.

From behind, Tracy felt Jared graze her arm. He leaned in close and whispered just the right seductive sentiment to ease her mind. Her knees grew weak and she smiled, suddenly a world away from everything but Jared. Turning into his embrace, she caught a glimpse of Phil as he climbed the loading dock ramp. He reached into his pocket and crushed his fist together. Just as he passed the dumpster she saw a yellow wad of paper spiral from his hand – straight into the bin.

Her breath caught.

Stunned, her eyes roamed, counting three FBI agents and two security guards within a twenty-foot radius. Plus, Jared's arms secured her in a layer of protection. Still, she shivered in fear. Watching Phil disappear into the hotel, she was as terrified as those innocent cattle she once saw her dad prepare for slaughter.

***

The reverberating slam of the service entrance door echoed as Agent Phil Murphy hustled through the first floor hallway. He cracked a smile and casually rounded the corner, meandering through the lobby toward the front desk, gesturing a nod toward Dennis Sims before approaching the front desk personnel.

"Is that the fax from Oklahoma?" Phil inquired as he noticed the concierge retrieve pages from the fax machine.

"Yes, Sir. I'm just forwarding it as instructed," he answered as he stacked the multiple pages and typed in the number for the Opry Heritage Hotel.

"Wait! No need to send it on. I'm right here. Let me have those originals," Phil demanded. The concierge hesitated and then backed away from the counter.

"May I see some identification, Sir?"

Phil smirked and flashed his FBI credentials. "Special - Agent - in - Charge Philip Murphy," he enunciated. "Now give me the papers."

"I'm sorry, Sir. My instructions are to forward this according to precise detail, and I can only release the materials to the intended recipient of the facsimile. Hotel policy."

"But I need that information! It's vital to a case I'm working on."

The concierge shrugged and immediately loaded the stack of papers into the fax machine.

"Sorry, sir. As I said, hotel policy. And per my instructions, these originals are to be shredded as soon as the fax is forwarded." From his left an armed security guard stepped closer to the concierge.

Phil Murphy shook his head and then bolted from the desk. His eyes shifted aimlessly around the lobby in search of his next move.

***

In a back corner of the lobby, Agent Brody Craig lifted his phone to answer an incoming call. Before he could speak, Mike Richardson began relaying instructions.

"We're pulling out, Craig. Follow-up on that fax and make sure the hotel forwards it to Nashville. Agent Roberts is taking the Ultrex back to Newport as planned; grab his keys and you take his personal car to meet up with me in Nashville. We'll take shifts through the night so call when you're on the road." *Click.*

Craig wasted no time in following through with his new orders. He approached the concierge, but did not notice the young woman hovering at the far end of the front desk.

"Excuse me, I'm Special Agent Craig of the FBI, and I need to make sure a fax transmission arrived from Newport, Oklahoma." Agent Craig offered his credentials. "Could you tell me the status?"

The concierge studied Craig, adjusting his eyeglasses to the bridge of his nose.

"Just like I told the other agent." He jerked his head toward Phil Murphy who had edged near Dennis Sims' table.

Brody Craig followed the concierge's line of sight and recognized Dennis Sims. *Other agent?* Craig ducked behind the foliage to gather his thoughts. "The fax arrived and I sent it to the Opry Heritage Hotel as instructed," stated the concierge, "but I cannot release the information to anyone but the intended recipient of the transmission. I already explained this to your partner over there." Agent Craig glanced again toward Dennis Sims and the businessman he had seen earlier. *Partner?*

"Did you happen to get the agent's name?" Craig whispered.

"Yes, he made it pretty clear. Special Agent *in Charge* Philip Murphy," he mocked, mimicking the quotation marks for emphasis.

Agent Craig ducked his head and disappeared into the shadows off the front desk. Before he could fully analyze his next move, the young woman, having overheard Craig's entire exchange from the far end of the counter, bolted to Dennis Sims' side, holding her gaze on Craig as she twisted through the tables and chairs. After relaying what she had witnessed, Phil Murphy pivoted just in time to get a solid view of Brody Craig as he fled from the front desk.

Murphy grinned, holding his head high, so glad he had taken time years before to plant the surveillance camera in Mark Sims' home office. The time it had taken him to duplicate Sims' tracking device design was just starting to pay off.

Fumbling in his pocket, Murphy retrieved a business card and placed a call.

"Hello, Agent Roberts, this is Special Agent in Charge Phil Murphy from the Atlanta office. There's been a change of plans. I know Agent Richardson planned to have you drive the rental car back to Newport, but to expedite things we need you to fly to Oklahoma to assist with the investigation there. I'll be taking that rented Ultrex so meet me in the lobby in five minutes and I'll get the keys."

Disconnecting from Roberts, Murphy placed another call.

"Opry Heritage Hotel? I need to speak to the Manager on Duty, please." Once he finalized his instructions, he pulled out a chair and settled in to wait for Agent Roberts. He threw Sims a casual salute then popped the lock on his briefcase. Inside, the GPS tracking monitor sat motionless in its case. Phil Murphy flipped the switch. The familiar steady rhythm began to hum as the young FBI agent from Memphis made his way toward Phil to hand over his set of keys.

Chapter 27

Phil Murphy's disclosure of David Frazier's involvement in the corruption hit Jared harder than Tracy had expected. The icy silence during the first fifty miles to Nashville gave her more peace than she had wanted. To take her mind off the endless stretch of I-40, she moved from one distraction to another. A snack raid from the backseat stash, a curious inspection of the glove compartment, an ill-attempted manicure by flashlight, and a private game of billboard ABCs helped pass empty minutes. But after suffering through another forty miles, she realized her limit of silence.

"Jared, I'm really sorry about all that has happened. I wish we could somehow rewind to when we were seventeen and just relive it all. But we can't undo it. We're here. It's all really happening and we can't do anything but move forward."

Jared nodded and managed a half-hearted smile. She brushed her fingers through his hair.

"This material Lauren is sending…what is it you're hoping to find?" she asked.

"Some clues as to how wide-spread this corruption really is." He glanced at Tracy. "If all this is true, and if Congress is involved like we think they are, we may be in deeper than we realize. And if it's mob-related, they won't stop until they find us."

"So what do we do?"

"Fall off the edge of the earth."

Tracy waited for his words to sink in. But the words would not settle. They were too hopeless. *Fall off the edge of the earth.* No hope at all.

As every passing car sped by, each passing driver caught her eye. Had she seen them before? Were they with Sutherant? Were they part of some sinister mob? She peeked at Jared and saw the same anxious panic in his face.

Refusing to let the tension come between them, she unfolded the map to study the destinations around central Tennessee - seeking a place they could finish out the night, a place they could somehow escape the tension of the passed hours. She ruled out Nashville, knowing that if their pursuers were as lethal as everyone had said, they would most likely track the faxed package. Instead, her eyes fell on Foster Creek Falls State Park south of Cookeville, Tennessee. The very sound of it enticed Tracy. She circled the location, confident this was the hideaway they would find the peace and security they needed.

Chapter 28

In the subdued light of the security lamps in the parking area of the Opry Heritage Hotel, Mike Richardson wheeled his black sedan into a secluded space in view of the front entrance. Glancing at the console clock, he estimated that during the three hour drive from Memphis, Dennis Sims, or anyone else who may have followed their path, had been given ample time to arrange an ambush. For that reason, he had taken extra precautions to ensure Tracy's safe retrieval of the faxed material from the front desk.

"Tracy, the fax is in your name so you'll have to do the honors. I don't expect Dennis Sims to have followed, but just in case he alerted management in some way, I'm going to walk you through the pool area around back to avoid the main security cameras. I was able to get a layout of the property so we'll take an employees' corridor once we enter the building. Jared, just hang out by the front entrance in case we need you."

Tracy and Mike jogged toward the pool entrance while Jared mixed in with a band tour bus that was unloading near the entrance. Moments later he overheard the guest services agent greeting Tracy while Mike strolled close behind. Jared watched the young employee retrieve a package from the rear credenza and set it on the counter. But when Tracy reached for it, the clerk slid the package away, gripped it in her hands, and grabbed a phone mounted on the back wall.

Jared stiffened. He searched for Mike and found him surrounded by three men in dark suits. A glance to Tracy confirmed she was unaware of danger. Rushing through the band members, Jared repositioned, straining to hear the hotel clerk's voice. The words *"fax transmission from Memphis"* rolled off her lips. In a panic, Tracy spun around, searching for Jared in the distance.

A diversion – Jared reached for anything, hoping to God he could someway distract the clerk. Just then, in walked his answer to prayer - a gorgeous, silky-haired stunner with the shape of a goddess drifting through the tour group.

Jared mindlessly grabbed her by the arm and whispered, "Please, I'm in a real jam here. Could you just play along and help me out?"

The fear in his eyes must have convinced her. She glanced around the room, nodded, and flashed a skeptical smile.

Jared looked toward the front desk and saw that the clerk was on the phone, still clenching the package in her hand. In a panic Jared pulled his partner to his side and raised his voice above the crowd.

He glanced to Mike, to the men, to the front desk clerk, and to Tracy - all eyes were on him. He dropped to one knee and looked into the girl's eyes. "Babe, I know it's late at night, but in front of all these people, I'm asking you to be my wife," he bellowed. The girl hesitated then replied with a quick nod. Applause from sleepy band members broke the silence and Jared jumped to his feet. Before he steadied his stance, the girl grabbed him by the collar and kissed him – deeply. She pressed herself against him and wound her arms around his neck, grinding to the synthesized Muzak piping through the speakers. Every eye in the room zeroed in on their embrace.

Tracy had the best view of all.

Her hazel eyes ignited. Blood heated her cheeks and her hands began to tremble. Like an angry child, she lunged across the credenza, snatched the package from the hotel clerk's hands and stormed toward the door. Her laser beam-eyes pinned Jared to the wall as *Jezebel* worked her hands through the maze of his body. Tracy never noticed the two dark suits bounding down the spiral stairway to block her exit. She never noticed the onlookers clearing a path to avoid her rage. Instead, her steely, cold eyes fixed on Jared. And no one dared stand in her way as she stampeded through the exit.

Mike shoved his way through the circle of men and yelled for Jared to follow. With an awkward wave to his co-star, Jared turned to flee, adrenaline pumping with every pounding stride until he caught up to Tracy.

"Whew! That was close!" he gasped as he slung his arm around Tracy's waist in mid-stride.

"Don't touch me!" She snapped.

"Tracy?"

Her dagger-eyes flashed another warning. Jared held back as she rushed to the car, flung open the passenger door and plowed in. Slammed doors and thrown facsimiles gave no satisfaction so she slid to her right, pressing as tightly against her door as possible. Her face rumbled like a Titan ready for launch.

Jared scrambled into the driver's seat and took refuge in the silence. He started the car, dropped it into gear and spun out of his space just ahead of Mike. A small group of hotel employees were spilling through the door of the front entrance, so he gunned it and drove the opposite way. Above the whine of the engine, he heard Tracy struggling not to cry.

Several miles lapsed before Jared finally gathered the nerve to approach her. He brushed his fingers along her elbow, but with a violent twist she jerked away. A few moments later, he tried again. This time her arm relaxed to her side. He caressed her skin and slowly, the tension in her face subsided. With nervous fingers he massaged her shoulder. Long, slow rotations loosened her stressed muscle. Her head lolled from side to side, glancing slightly his way. He feathered the back of his hand along her clenched jaw. Soft, soothing motions. He slid his finger just beneath her mouth, tracing her lips, brushing his thumb along her velvety cheek. Unexpectedly, she clenched his fingers and pressed them to her cool lips. A tear rolled from her eye and she swiped it with the back of his hand, burying her face into his rough, calloused fist.

"T, it was just an act. It didn't mean a thing."

He could hear her soft gasps as she began to cry. With his warmest touch he wiped her cheek. Sliding his arm around her shoulder, he pulled her close, tucking her head beneath his chin.

"Don't ever do that--"

"Shh…never again. I promise."

***

Knowing that they still had a another hour's drive to the state park and sensing that Tracy was still upset about the girl at the hotel, Jared pulled into an all-night Cup-a-Joe so they could take a needed break. He was tired and they both could use a kick of caffeine.

"Let's get some coffee and read through these papers."

Tracy turned and saw Mike follow their exit. Jared wheeled the car into the near-empty lot and parked in front as Mike pulled to the side of the building. Before Tracy could open her door, Jared grasped her hand. She turned his way and he kissed her cheek, whispering close to her ear.

"Sorry."

She laid her head on his shoulder and hugged him as he smoothed his hand along her back. She found his lips, releasing all her built up tension into a warm, lingering kiss, knowing that nothing and no one could ever diminish the love she had for this man. In the darkness of the car, she ran her hands underneath his shirt and as she tightened her hold around his waist, she kissed him again, this time so sensuously and with so much love that the girl at the hotel became a blur, a buried insignificance.

The sultry motion of Tracy's lips immobilized Jared, altering his mind like a euphoric drug. As her touch ran hot across his skin, his mind and body reacted. He craved her. The public area, the confinement of the car, Mike waiting in the distance – none of it mattered. In one easy move he could lift her over the seat to finally find their private Heaven. But just when he slid his hand beneath her thigh to make his move, Tracy pushed away and bolted from the car into the cool night air leaving Jared dazed, confused, and wanting. She stifled a laugh as she closed her door, watching from the corner of her eye to see him crawl from the driver's side.

Jared sent a quick text to Mike who declined coffee and opted to wait in his car. Then as he entered the bistro, warm, delicious aromas attacked his senses; as his eyes locked on the curves of Tracy's hips, he nestled into her back and wrapped his arms around her. She held her focus on the menu overhead.

"Where did that come from?" He pressed his mouth to her ear, hoping she would forget the coffee and follow him back to the car.

"Just wanted to make sure you knew what you would be missing if you ever pulled a stunt like that again."

"Never again," he promised.

"Good. Because I'd hate for you to pass up what I had planned for later today," she jibed. "Coffee?"

Jared managed a nod and swallowed hard.

Tracy greeted the employee and placed her order while Jared hovered alongside, rubbing the small of her back as his eyes wandered across her body. When the barista turned away, Tracy looped her arm through Jared's and brushed her lips against his ear.

"The sooner we get through this fax material, the sooner we can get to our cabin," she whispered.

Jared grinned then rushed to a table. By the time Tracy arrived with their coffee, he had already plunged eye-deep into the fax that Lauren had sent and had phoned to check on Mike who was keeping watch from his car. Tracy settled to the table and took a sip of chai tea. Jared's face went pale as he pushed a page of the fax her way.

Bold font stretched across the top of the wreckage scene of Jared's F150 pickup lying mangled in a barbed-wire fence at the base of a cottonwood tree. Tracy skimmed the lines of copy: *Local Cattleman/Oil Industry Specialist Loses Control on County Road.*

"I guess I was in the hospital when this went to print," she managed as she let it fall to the table. "Or else Lauren kept it from me all these years."

Jared scooted a separate handwritten page toward Tracy. It was a note from Lauren confirming that Sheriff McClain and Everett Hadley were the officers at the scene. "She must have been skeptical enough to dig a little deeper. According to the police report she was given, Police Chief Vincent said your dad lost control on an icy road and lists the cause of death as severe head trauma. No autopsy, no seatbelt."

"No seatbelt? That doesn't sound like Daddy."

"No, it doesn't. And read on. Lauren checked with the National Weather Bureau in Norman; the temperatures were unseasonably warm on the day of the crash. The weather was clear and the high that day reached fifty-two degrees. The accident happened at 5:15 P.M. The roads couldn't have been icy. But T., this is what I really think you need to see."

Jared pointed to the picture again, this time to the rear cab window.

"It was a head-on crash and that back window was not damaged before the accident."

Tracy did not say a word. She didn't have to. It was obvious that the small hole and spider-web of cracks had been made by a bullet.

He handed her another page of notes from Lauren. "She and Grant are on to something. Officer Everett Hadley died in a car crash that same week– two days after your dad. Oddly, he lost control, too."

Tracy flipped the page around. "Where did she find this? Is she sure?"

"Police interrogations. Her notes say Officer Vincent sent Hadley out on what Grant says was a bogus emergency call. Grant was told to stay at the station which evidently was against protocol since his duty was to ride along on every call."

"They were making sure there were no witnesses." Tracy re- read Lauren's note. "There was no autopsy and the squad car was sent straight to impound to be destroyed."

"Wonder if his car had a shattered back window, too," added Jared.

They both huddled more closely together and read the information Lauren had forwarded regarding the car tags Jared had seen Thursday afternoon.

"Eric's truck, which supposedly had been driven by your uncle," Jared quipped.

Tracy popped him on the arm. "There's no reason not to believe him." Jared shrugged and continued his list. "A car registered to S. Bradley, a U.S. Senator from Arkansas, two rentals registered to Kyle Monroe of Arkansas, and the last to Leanne Sebastian of Texas. Do those names mean anything to you?"

"Not yet. I'll have to research it. But look at this..."

Behind the printed copy of Lauren's e-mail message Tracy spotted several photos and articles about David Frazier. The first photo showed Frazier at a company gala he had hosted in Newport the second week of January, just two weeks after his family had supposedly entered the witness protection program.

"He certainly wasn't keeping any secrets – an announcement about his New Year Gala and four press releases introducing Sutherant's new managers and board members for the upcoming year. He even held a second reception in Washington for his national and foreign financiers." Tracy tapped her pen on the table. "He got you and your mom out of town then came right back to Newport," she surmised.

"Just like Phil said, he got us out of the way – probably to hide his crimes from us."

"I don't think so," she shot back, tossing her pen aside. "Look at these pictures. This is not a man who is hiding anything. He's *promoting* himself."

"Yeah, trying to show how *innocent* he is. What an asshole!" Jared sneered.

"Actually, I think your dad is trying to make himself look guilty. It looks to me like he wants to be identified with Sutherant Petroleum. Think about it. Two of his partners were killed in one night. He got you and your mom to safety. Then my dad...well," she stammered. "Anyway, your dad's life had been turned upside down losing his best friends and seeing his family split apart. So he returned to Newport – publicly and in the limelight, making sure the press reported that he was still in charge, still a viable part of Sutherant."

"Proving he *is* part of the corruption." Jared rolled his eyes.

"One thing I've learned from reporting - things may not always be as they seem. To be certain, we need to get his side of the story. Personally, I think it was all an act to make it look like he supported what was going on – maybe in order to protect your family."

Tracy sat back and sipped her tea. Jared propped his elbows on the table and thumbed through the photos. He shook his head then lifted one particular picture from the pile.

Tracy slipped the photo from his fingers, studied it then swiped it down his nose with a smile. "See what I mean?" It was an old candid of her father and David Frazier standing side by side cheering from the stands at one of Jared's home football games. "He probably made it to more of your games than you realize," she grinned.

But Jared wasn't smiling. He was too busy concentrating on the unusual scenes playing out around the coffee shop. He pressed his finger to his lips and grasped Tracy's hand to get her attention. But she was way ahead of Jared. She nodded as he motioned toward a young woman who had just entered the coffee shop. Tracy had noticed her seconds before, crossing behind what looked like a silver diesel pickup. Strangely, the girl had entered alone while the driver had pulled to a back corner of the parking lot. Pretty enough – too heavy on the eye liner and mascara and a bit too Gothic in the black fatigue-style pants, but she seemed innocent enough. Still, something about her...

A second look saw her lift a small compact from her purse. Was she checking her make-up or was she actually slanting the mirror toward Jared? Either way, Tracy noticed the shift of her eyes and the way she scrutinized each person behind the counter. One regular coffee – size medium. Nothing unusual about that. Still, it seemed odd that she came inside while her companions waited in the darkness of a vacant lot. Why not use the drive-thru window?

Jared clenched Tracy's knee. He slid his phone toward her and pointed to the text he had just typed: *Too many eyes and ears in here.* But Tracy did not need a cue from Jared to recognize danger. Blame her sixth sense, that innate acumen she had trusted time and again when that tingle coursed her spine.

Monitoring two other customers who had just entered, she realized how suspect they seemed. Her eyes grew wary of the older woman in the flowery blouse as she nursed her Frappuccino. Was she as engrossed in the romance novel she held at eye level or was that just a prop to keep her hands occupied? One thing Tracy made note of: the lady had not turned a page since she had sat down five minutes before.

The young intellect waiting in the corner sported a tan blazer and jeans. Was he actually surfing the web on his smartphone or was he just pretending to look engaged in his search? The casual manner in which he had stepped outside to his car to place a call cast a bit of doubt. While Tracy could not guarantee it, she thought she recognized a sticker on the man's front bumper. "David Priest's, Okie's Way Bar & Grill" - a favorite watering hole in Oklahoma City. Could it be that he was far from home on an errand for Sutherant Petroleum?

It was then that Tracy's eyes returned to the young girl she had noticed before. As the girl adjusted the lay of her jacket, she absently fidgeted with her hair. With a tug, the lighter blonde curls shifted, exposing velvety black hair at her neckline. Was this ill-fitted wig some attempted disguise?

Tracy's eyes diverted to Jared's as she watched him study the same customers. When he opened his phone pretending to search directions, she took another sip of tea, nervously attempting to appear unaware of their surroundings. She watched as Jared scratched down a couple of hotel chain names on the napkin in front of him, purposely situating the napkin in the center of the table.

"Okay, I found a hotel. It's just down the road," Jared announced to everyone in earshot.

Tracy flinched at his change in volume but then read his lead, gathering their materials and sliding from her chair as Jared tossed their cups in the nearest bin. Like an obedient child, she followed, not daring to speak until they reached the privacy of their car.

"Jared, don't ask me how I know, but Denny is behind this. It's almost like I can feel him watching me."

"All the more reason I'm glad Mike is with us. Maybe that hotel info I left will throw them off our trail for a while."

Tracy cowered into the seat, unnerved by the sudden drama. Peeking over the dash, she felt the sinister eyes of the customers inside shift directly to her. That small voice she had befriended long ago whispered a warning. *Trust no one...trust no one.*

Hot anxiety rushed through her. She pressed hard against her ears, squeezing violently to stop the spinning. Collapsing her head against the headrest, she wrenched her arms to her stomach and shivered, closing her heavy eyes to drown the echo of Eric's words that had yet to escape her mind – *Jared is interfering with their plan. Jared is interfering with their plan.*

"Everything will be alright, T."

In a panic, she thrust her arms around him as her body began to tremble. Jared cradled her to his chest as she fought hard not to cry.

"I've got you, T."

It was barely a whisper, yet like magic, his words took her to a different time, a different place when he had breathed them once before. They were eleven and it was late spring. They had ditched the bus after school and had walked home, intent on hiking to the creek that cut a path through her back pasture. In spite of Jared's warning that the recent rains had made it too swift to cross, Tracy rolled up her jeans and stepped in. She was pulled under before he could stop her. Jared jumped in to grab her, struggling to keep her head above water. Several yards down-stream, he was able to latch on to a tree branch and pull them to safety. "I've got you, T. I've got you." he repeated between gasps for air. She had never forgotten the look of terror in his eyes, and as he held her now, she saw it again.

Jared rocked her gently as he studied the scene from inside the coffee shop. He watched the young girl make her way to the back parking lot. The young man slipped his phone into his pocket and cleared his trash from the table, glancing over his glasses toward the window. The older woman continued to read her novel.

Jared grabbed his phone and sent a quick text to alert Mike Richardson of what they had witnessed in the coffee shop. Once done, he reached to help Tracy with her seatbelt, reassuring her again that this would all be over soon. Just as he was about to whip the car from the parking space, his phone vibrated with a message from Mike: *Already on it.*

Head out. I'll catch up. Jared wrenched the steering wheel and maneuvered to the parking lot exit. He glanced in his rearview mirror before merging into traffic. The last thing he saw was the chaos of flashing blue lights as two squad cars sped into the coffee shop parking lot.

***

Random headlights and center lines melded into a blur of solitude as the passing miles led them farther and farther from their home. Tracy's eyes glazed over with memories of family.

She thought of her mom, remembering how close they had once been, before *cancer* became a household word, before childhood came to an abrupt end, before all the sadness set in. Those early years were filled with good memories: the 'take your child to work' days when her mom wrote television ads in Oklahoma City, or rolling out pie crusts and weeding the garden, playing dress-up and taking walks, piano lessons and Laura Ingalls Wilder books on the porch swing. Tracy could still hear her voice – *Love is what matters the most.* That sweet Southern drawl, so gentle, so loving – passing on more in twelve short years than most mothers do in a lifetime.

And when not trailing her mother, Tracy was shadowing her father. Riding to the feed store or herding cattle, plowing the fields or *fixin'* anything that needed *fixin'* or stealing a taste of his coffee as they enjoyed their weekly dinner date in town. He was stability and all things honorable and good. And no matter how many times she tried to imagine what God might look like, images of her own father always came to mind.

But as Tracy thought of her parents, she knew the best memories came from simply being together. Sharing breakfast every morning, lazy horseback rides through the pasture, or their nightly routine of bedtime prayers. These were the kind of memories she had so dreamed of making with Jared and their own children. But with such an uncertain future on their horizon, she wondered if they would ever even have a place to call home.

Saddened by that somber thought, she grabbed the flashlight from the backseat and pulled out her notebook and pen, hoping that a little writing would ease her mind.

"It's been a long time since I actually wrote on paper," she sighed as Jared changed lanes to pass a semi.

"I remember how much you used to write when we were kids. What's that your dad always called it?"

Tracy thought back to the little girl in pig tails sitting at her Daddy's feet as he read the sports page, her own paper in hand, filled with misspelled words and silly rhymes. She smiled at Jared, fascinated that he remembered so many small moments of her past.

"Paper dolls," she nodded.

"That's it. You hardly ever played with real dolls but you always had your writing. Your *paper dolls*."

"Still playing with them," Tracy agreed, waving her hand across the materials in her lap. "As much as I love using pen and paper I do miss my computer." Somewhere in the conversation, an interesting theory came to Jared.

"Computers. Your dad taught me everything he knew about the Sutherant systems. Yet, according to Eric, he left the password with you. Does this make sense to you?"

"Not at all. You're the hacker."

"Exactly. He knew you were a writer. He knew you didn't like computers. Why would he have left the password with you?"

She shrugged. "Two are better than one," she snickered as her voice fell away.

"What?"

"From the Bible. 'Two are better than one, for they have a good reward for their labor.' Daddy would always quote that to guilt me into helping him. He probably just figured I'd be helping you find..." she continued. But she stopped short. Her thoughts had trailed to frequent afternoons and weekends in the past when her dad had rambled through one computer program after another, quizzing Jared on data entry, programming processes, and security access. *He taught Jared everything he knew.*

Tracy turned in her seat. "Reward... " she finished. As each shared moment at her dad's computer surfaced in her memory, a smile stretched tighter across her face. "He wasn't just teaching you the system, Jared. He was telling you his secrets. He was giving you clues!"

Jared narrowed his eyes and focused on the traffic. Suddenly, his face brightened as he grabbed her hand. "His computer – the one he used to bring home. Where is it now?"

"I guess at Sutherant. But you remember what Eric said. Sutherant will never let you near Daddy's computer."

"We've got to try. And we've got to figure out his password."

"Tonight?"

Jared laughed – his deep, hearty laugh that she had not heard in years. The fatigue and worry had left his face. He looked younger, happier, and confident.

"It can wait. Besides, I owe you a trip to Jacksonville and we still need to meet Phil in Atlanta. We'll need his help getting into Sutherant."

Tracy cringed inwardly on hearing his name. Still, for some reason she could not bring herself to share her feelings about the man.

"By tomorrow we should hear from Dale. We sent it same day express so he will have had time to review my notes by then."

"And you're sure that Sutherant information won't fall into the wrong hands, right?"

"That's why I sent it with my lyrics. It will look like a regular submission packet. Dale's the best. We've got a really good relationship."

His brows creased with worry. "So how close are you two anyway?"

"Oh, I don't know. I mean we don't share kisses in hotel lobbies or anything." She shot a cool eye his way.

***

Shortly after, they arrived to Foster Creek Falls State Park nestled along the Cumberland Plateau. Driving through the rustic entryway they were welcomed into another world. After checking in with late registration and winding along the secluded road, they were drawn into peaceful isolation as breath-taking waterfalls roared in the distance, plunging into deep gorges below. Through the open window of their car, nature whispered a secret - a gentle lullaby of welcome. Tracy leaned her head into the breeze and breathed in the fresh mountain air.

Kudzu-coated tree monsters lurked along their path as they followed the gravel road to their cabin, rustic and private. Ascending the cedar steps to the deck of their mountain hideaway, Jared paused to listen, relaxing against the banister to take in the view. A blanket of cool pre-dawn air wrapped around them as they fell under the spell of the whippoorwills' serenade. From the distance the bullfrogs' chorus rolled in with the damp fog, carrying every sound deeper and deeper into the woods.

Tracy made room in the porch swing as Jared collapsed and opened the paper bag of sandwiches they had picked up at an all-night drive-thru. An owl hooted from above and as the serenity settled around them, the gentle creak of the swing chimed in rhythm to the forest sounds. Moments later, a flash of headlights and the crunch of gravel put them back on alert. Mike Richardson stepped from the car and labored up the steps.

"Just wanted to let you two know I'll be out here watching things so you can rest easy. Brody Craig will be here in an hour to relieve me. I'll be back on duty at noon and then later this afternoon I'd like to get with you to compare notes on some of this." He kicked a pinecone from the step. "I'll stop by the office when they open and tell them we'll be staying tomorrow night as well, then we'll plan on meeting Phil Murphy in Atlanta first thing Monday morning."

"Take the extra room, Mike," offered Jared as he stood to hand him a sandwich. "Might get chilly out here in your car."

"This is when my real work begins and I can do that much better from my car. Not expecting any trouble since we swapped out cars. By the way, that man at the coffee shop checked out to be a tourist visiting family. And the lady was a regular – came first thing every morning and brought a different book each time. As far as the scare at the hotel, all I can figure is that Sims got word to them. Anyway, you got your package."

"What about the girl?" Tracy asked.

"Girl?" Mike questioned.

Jared glanced at Tracy.

"The one at the coffee shop. You didn't see her?" Jared tensed as he remembered how quickly the girl had taken off once he and Tracy exited.

Mike shook his head. "Sorry. Must've missed her. But you two rest easy. That's the whole reason I'm out here."

Mike trudged back to his car. The car door slammed and all was quiet again.

Jared shook his head. "Can't believe he didn't notice her…"

Tracy shook her head and dropped her sandwich into the wrapper, suddenly no longer hungry. She loosened the scrunchie from her hair and shook it free.

"I'm way too tired to think about it."

"Come on," he reached for her hand to help her from the swing. "We better get some sleep while we can. It'll be time to meet with Mike before we know it."

***

An hour later, just below the deck on the winding gravel road that led to their cabin, a government-issued white midsized inched slowly up the drive, casting an eerie spray of dust across the hood of Mike's parked black sedan. Brody Craig lowered his window.

"I've had enough coffee to stay awake for three days. Best take advantage of it and get to bed. Later on I need to fill you in on an encounter I had after you left."

"Hmm. What happened?"

"It's about Phil Murphy but it can wait. I know you're beat."

Mike didn't argue.

Brody waved as he watched as his partner's car pull away, then reached for his side arm and released the safety.

His eyes and ears went on alert, scanning the wooded terrain for any signs of movement.

Chapter 29

Saturday - early afternoon

The light, mountain drizzle had just begun to subside as Jared and Tracy slowed to a cool-down pace. A post-nap jog had taken them along the highway in full view of the granite-cliffs and waterfalls, and as they wound down from the three-mile run, Jared stripped his shirt off to wipe the sweat from his forehead. Side by side they followed the narrow foot path and when they ducked underneath an overhanging pine branch blocking their way, Jared slapped it, unleashing a cool spray of water down Tracy's back.

"Aahhhh! Jay!" Tracy cringed from the shocking chill then turned to see a covey of dove shoot from a nearby brush pile. She swiped the cold, wet beads from her arms and neck as a smile spread across her face. Just as Jared reached to hug her, she plunged into him, tackling him to the underbrush of pine needles beneath the trees. As they fell onto the soft earth, their laughter filled the air. He flung his arms around her and tickled her, rolling her defenselessly to her back.

"I win," he gloated.

Standing, he stifled a laugh then snatched her up into his arms to heave her to his shoulder. He paraded her in a slow-motion victory jog, every step bouncing her higher into the air. Unable to catch her breath from laughter, he eased her to the ground then pressed his sweaty chest against her and mockingly shook his soaked hair in her face.

She rocked him in her arms and felt his hot breath race across her skin. "I get a rematch when we get back to the cabin," she crooned.

"Rematch it is." He grinned as he ran his finger down her cleavage. "Now that we've had a nap maybe we can make better use of that bed. Unless you'd rather call Phil's office and fill him in on the fax," he snickered.

"You know what I want." She slid her own finger from chest to abdomen and tugged lightly at the waistband of his shorts. "And you can save your call. I think I saw Phil drive by where we crossed the highway. It sure looked like our Ultrex anyway."

***

Before returning to the cabin, Jared and Tracy made a short detour to the guest lodge to access the internet, hoping to have a reply from Dale regarding her lyric submission. Delicious aromas of bacon and coffee greeted them as they opened the main door. A faux fire blazed behind the hearth in the corner of the room and a family who had taken over the couch and loveseat were discussing their day's plans.

Tracy rounded a corner toward a separate, glass-enclosed computer/library. With a punch of an electronic code, wireless internet business equipment was at their use. While the glass walls lacked visual privacy, the business center did offer a relatively sound-proof area to work. As they entered the room, Tracy settled in to open her e-mail and without taking time to read the entries, printed off the notes Lauren had sent.

"Here's a message from Dale. He's already lined up a publishing agent and they're taking the story. They've wired an advance of three-thousand dollars to my Nashville account. They must be serious. Goes on to say 'anonymity of all involved parties is guaranteed' and they want exclusive rights to the story." She hesitated then faced Jared who was searching the headlines. "I think I'll forward the money to Lauren if it's okay with you. We don't need it and she's doing all the work."

"Fine with me. And let her take all the credit for it. I don't want our names linked to it."

"Good. Then you should like this. Dale says there is 'a very interested International Press reporter waiting in the wings' until we send word on how to pursue the project. He says submitting the material with my lyrics will be the most secure method and that they'll handle everything from there. Dale will oversee all the editing so that will keep us out of the loop. Goes on to say he loved the new lyrics, he's glad you are back so I will get my head out of the clouds, *yada, yada, yada*, he's looking forward to meeting you and he'll be in touch."

Jared stretched back in his chair and latched his hands behind his head, stealing a glance at the curves underneath her compression running shorts. Without saying a word, she knew what was on his mind. It was the same thing on her mind. She tousled his hair and leaned in to kiss him, patting him on the rear as she pushed away.

"Let's get some lunch. Then I'll race you to the shower."

Jared cleared the computer history and gathered the printed copies before starting for the door. But Tracy had frozen in mid-turn. He rushed to catch her, thinking her blood sugar was low. But her transfixed eyes told him something else was wrong. He mirrored her line of sight, searching the main room for whatever had caused alarm. He saw nothing out of the ordinary - a handful of guests strolling through the guest services area, some history show on the television, a mother and child carrying a lunch tray. Still, Tracy's face was flushed, expressionless.

"T., what is it?"

"He's here." Her eyes shifted through each corner of the room, passing judgment on every person within range. Defensively, Jared bolted forward, erecting his protective frame to shield her.

"Who's here? Where?" His hands clenched into fists.

"Denny."

One word and Jared was in motion. He grasped her forearm and before she could focus, he propelled them forward.

"Get to the cabin!" Bulldozing the door, Jared seized Tracy's wrist, charging them both to safety. "Stay off the road! Take the path."

Hand-in-hand they fled into the cover of the trees. Sweeping the area with every pounding step, Jared dodged tree limbs, all the while wrenching Tracy to his side. Gasping for air, he shouted, "We'll get to Jodie's."

Breathless, they reached the clearing. Jared stepped onto the footpath that led to their cabin but stretched his arm to block Tracy's progress. She scanned the area from behind him. In that one quick look she saw their black sedan parked at the foot of the steps, rain puddles and muddy footprints trailing from the porch (theirs from that afternoon). Small leaves and tiny redbud blossoms sprinkled the ground and as she craned her neck, she spotted a second fresh set of footprints leading from the tree line and down the drive. Thoughts of cut brake lines, her father, and Everett Hadley churned in her mind. She inhaled. Something was not right.

"That car down the way – was it there when we left earlier?" she questioned.

"I think that's Brody Craig, Mike's partner. He came sometime while we were sleeping. Mike said he'd be standing watch today."

Tracy stepped to his side then noticed another car parked at the end of the drive behind Brody. Mike stumbled from the car and when she saw the anxious look on his face, she froze. Jared pushed around her.

"Mike, what's the mat…"

"Get inside! Go!" Mike ordered as he rushed toward them. Jared clutched Tracy under his arm and half carried her up the stairs to the cabin. He bolted through the door and before he could steady himself, Mike pushed him from behind shoving them deeper into the safety of the room. He slammed the door then crouched to the window to look outside. "Get your things, hurry!" he thundered.

"What is it?"

"Jared, they're here. We've got to go!"

Mike lifted the curtain as Jared rushed Tracy toward the bedroom. Two minutes later, Jared plowed by Mike and dropped three duffle bags at the door. Tracy stumbled into the hallway fighting to pull jeans over her running shorts. Mike was wringing his hands. His bleary, bloodshot eyes wandered aimlessly around the room and when Tracy touched his shoulder, tears trickled onto his cheek. He grabbed for a chair a moment too late before collapsing to his knee.

"Mike?" Tracy breathed as she flung her arm around him.

"They got Brody," he stammered.

"Oh, God…"

Jared bolted to the window to see Brody's car, but Mike held him back.

"No! Stay down!" Mike peeked through the side of the curtain then let it slip free. His head fell into his hands.

"Found him in his car. They were probably waiting for you here. Must've taken off when I pulled up."

"Dammit!" Jared mumbled.

"The Bureau is sending a unit to secure the scene, but I need to get you two out of here. Phil wants you in Atlanta this afternoon and then I think he plans for you to lay low in Jacksonville for a few days. "

Mike's face turned an ashen gray. He seemed to have aged ten years overnight.

"Phil isn't here? I thought I saw him in the park this morning," Tracy questioned.

Mike stood, studying her while an uncomfortable silence pulsed between them.

"...in the Ultrex we had rented," Tracy added.

With a turn he walked to the window, glanced through the curtain then settled his gaze on Tracy. His teary eyes scanned her like she was a specimen, as if he were weighing her thoughts. Finally, he shook his head and raised his hands in question.

"He said he was in Atlanta waiting for us," he exhaled. "I just talked to him."

Like a dampened fire, the spirit of the room grew cold. Even the warm glow of the sun peeking through the clouds faded into the floorboards. Tracy tried to brush her speculations away, but one thought pelted her mind like a droning echo - Eric's final warning: *Jared is interfering with their plan.* Her stomach knotted as she realized the *'their'* could be the very ones who killed Brody and *they* might be just beyond the door waiting for Jared.

"Jared, I need you to drive," Mike sighed. "Between this and not getting a wink of sleep I better not try."

Before Tracy could prepare, Jared clutched her hand and bolted through the door on Mike's heels. In a panic, she lunged toward Jared, throwing her arms around him to shield him from harm.

"JARED!" Fear spewed from her eyes. He pulled her close and rushed in Mike's shadow, descending the stairs two at a time with Tracy under the cover of his body. Just as they cornered the trees at the base of the stairs, Mike flung open the car door, gun aimed toward the tree line guarding the area for the unseen enemy. Jared shoved Tracy into the passenger's side, and then skidded across the hood of the car to the driver's side. Mike leapt into the backseat, knocking Tracy's guitar to the floorboard.

"Floor it! GO! GO!" Mike roared from the backseat.

Gravel flew. Jared accelerated, spraying dust and debris into a rising cloud. Gunning the engine, he careened onto the main road of the state park and sped toward the exit.

"Follow the signs for the highway!" Mike pulled himself upright in the backseat and searched the area.

"There's the lodge! We're almost to the exit." Jared checked for oncoming cars. But when he caught the death-like stare in Tracy's eyes, everything else fell away.

"What's wrong?" His foot eased up on the gas and the car began to slow. Mike's booming command to hurry fell on deaf ears as Jared's full attention went to Tracy.

"It's Denny!" Tracy managed as she cowered into the seat. That single name cut like a knife. Dennis Sims equaled four years of her life. The taste of bile lodged in the back of her throat as she thought of how Sims had caused so much horror in her life. She lived for the day they could slam his ass in a federal prison. But right now, to see him stepping from his truck within a hundred feet made her want to slink away and hide.

"That son-of-a-bitch!" Mike snarled. "Just look straight ahead Jared. Nice and easy." Mike's voice was quiet and

muted, as if he knew Sims was listening. He peered toward
the lodge and watched Sims and a female companion traipse
toward the entrance, unaware they were being watched. Jared
coasted forward and exited onto the main road.

When they reached the highway, Tracy found her voice
and spun in her seat. One look into Mike's eyes and he fell
powerless, pinned to the back seat by her lethal glare.

"Get this straight! Jared and I have nothing to do with
this. I don't care about this investigation and I don't care
about FBI procedure or whatever the hell you call it. Before
we go any further, you're going to do something for us. Pull
up all the information you can find on Sutherant's computer
system – the network and programs they use in Newport and
Savannah. I want to know about security clearance,
passwords, badges, whatever regular employees use to access
the system. I want printed layouts of the two branches. And a
gun. With ammunition. And once and for all, find out how
my psycho uncle is stalking us. He found us in Memphis and
he found us here. You are FBI, for God's sake! Do your job!"

Tracy sank into the seat just as her tears began to flow.
With half her focus turned to the passing scenery of the
Tennessee hills, she leaned against the passenger door and
listened as Mike placed a call to Phil Murphy. She overheard
bits and pieces of his conversation and quickly realized Phil
and Mike had no solid plan for gaining access to Sutherant's
computer information. The more she listened, the more she
sensed the FBI's main motivation: not to blow their cover
until the last possible moment. Nowhere in the conversation
did she hear any intention of returning to Newport.

Mike's exchange with Phil came to a quick close. To
avoid another angry outburst, Tracy tuned him out and
pretended to sleep. Her hand fell listlessly to her lap and as
she heard Jared whisper to Mike, she knew she had

succeeded. In the following moments, she clung to every whispered word passed between them – *get guns and ammunition...change identities... leave the country...surface when it's safe...have no contact.* His plan had merit. But the longer she eavesdropped on the muted discussion taking place beside her, the more she knew she had to find her own way to protect Jared. So she began to construct a plan of her own.

Chapter 30

The sparsely populated parking lot of the federal building in Atlanta slowly emptied as the few security guards and groundskeepers who were scheduled to pull Saturday duty began to depart. One lone west corner office on the fourth floor of the local FBI headquarters remained illuminated. Marcia Treadway, Phil Murphy's administrative assistant, had been called in on "urgent business" to gather materials needed for a classified case. Adhering to the instructions given in the morning phone call, she assembled the requested items then locked the files and office doors as directed. Knowing that Phil Murphy had plans to arrive the following day to meet with federal witnesses, she never questioned her task. But as she closed down the office and scanned her security badge at the exit, she considered again how unusual it was for her boss to be working on a case he had been removed from two years before.

Hours later when Murphy walked into his office after the long drive to Atlanta, his desk was organized, and stacked in the middle were detailed building plans, fabricated Sutherant security badges, blueprint diagrams of the inner workings of various computer systems, a mock entry keypad and electronic key, a selection of handgun pamphlets and the address and phone number to a local gun shop that Marcia Treadway confirmed was open on Saturday night and was capable of expediting the background check for a gun permit. Phil palmed the small business card and his secretary's note and slid them into his pocket. Before diving into the task of reviewing the gathered collection, he took a quick look around his office. He quickly moved around the room removing personal photos, wall hangings, and military commendations from their places and stashing them in a lower desk drawer. Minutes later, after taking another sweep of the room, he placed a call to Washington, D.C.

Senator Baird Mackenzick's thick northeastern accent was undaunted and smooth – as smooth as the thirty-dollar shave he had just received in Concourse B at Washington Dulles International. He shifted his carry-on to his left shoulder as he made his way to the shuttle bound for a small on-site general aviation hanger.

"Got a name on that reporter she's working with, but right now there's more pressing business. David Frazier is getting a little too cozy with some of those boys from Arkansas and there's a secretary in public relations who's making waves. Seems her friend, some young hotshot named Kyle Monroe, is running for state senate in Arkansas and she's raising a stink to get him elected. Anyway, I'm heading there now."

"I'm right behind you," explained Murphy. "But I know Jared Frazier. He's been out of pocket for two years and I'm not about to scare him away now. I'll have him there within the week and once he locates that shipment, he's all yours."

"Just remember, one slip could make Soon bolt back to North Korea."

"Yeah, and one gutsy senator or even a smart-ass reporter from the Newport *Tribune* could shut this whole operation down – our whole economy right along with it," Murphy quipped.

"Relax. Half of Congress is keeping this afloat. And I don't have to remind you how much you and I stand to profit when we finally get access to those Sutherant bank accounts. And yes, I left Sims out of the equation. He should have been cut from the loop a long time ago."

Murphy pursed his lips. Being micromanaged by a former sniper did little for his anger management. "Dennis Sims is our link to Soon and if Soon stops printing money, we're all out of luck."

Phil Murphy glanced at his watch and headed toward the elevator, eager to meet the rental car representative who was due to retrieve a car.

***

Across the street at the Book-Buyer's Emporium, Marcia Treadway stretched from her seat and looked through the window. After leaving the office, she had stayed in town to do a little shopping and just as she was taking a bite of her blueberry scone, to her surprise she noticed Phil Murphy lingering outside the federal building. She sipped the foam from her latte and watched as a rental car company van drove toward him.

"Hmm, that's odd. Thought he wasn't due back until tomorrow," she mumbled to herself.

A passenger got out, accepted keys from Phil, and drove off in a silver Ultrex GS. "Mr. Cheapskate splurged on an Ultrex?" Treadway chuckled. And then it occurred to her. Why did he not return the rental at the airport when he arrived back in town? Curious, she watched Murphy walk back inside the building. Remembering the travel itinerary, she recalled it said nothing about a rental car for his trip. And why had he returned to Atlanta a day earlier than he had planned?

Treadway gulped the rest of her latte, picked up her bag, and headed for the door. As she stepped outside, she looked up in time to see the car tag numbers of the Ultrex as it passed by. With a suspicious nod, she went home to do a little more checking on her own.

***

A few minutes later, Jared pulled the sedan into the Federal Building parking lot. Phil rose from the lobby chair and crossed the room to unlock the door. His slow, painstaking lumber was in sharp contrast to the energetic step he had flaunted at The Promenade. A dark, heavy shadow shrouded his face and he had lost his youthful and easygoing demeanor.

"Hey, kids. Come on in," Phil sighed as he held the door.

Phil gripped Jared's shoulder and as Tracy entered, she accepted Phil's outstretched hand, taking notice of the dark circles under his eyes. Mike Richardson ducked behind Tracy and excused himself to find a vacant office to tie-up some loose ends on a lead he had received. With plans to meet back in an hour, Phil waved Mike toward the conference room then guided Jared and Tracy to the elevator. Three floors later Jared wandered to Phil's desk and picked up a small paperweight, moving it casually from hand to hand.

"Phil, I'm sorry I was so short with Mike, it's just..." Tracy's voice broke.

"No, I'm sorry. We tend to get bogged down in the case sometimes, and we need to stay out in front on this one. But I've got everything you need to avoid a situation like that again." Phil moved toward his desk, but Tracy caught him by the sleeve.

"I also wanted to say how sorry we are about Brody Craig."

They locked eyes for an instant, but Phil looked away and brushed past.

"Thanks, he was a good kid."

Waving them toward the materials, Phil paused at each item as he explained.

"Building layout, computer room schematics, electronic entry mock-up, fake IDs, and while I can't legally provide you with guns, I have the specs on the one I recommend." Phil handed Jared a brochure. "Course it's not my 23, but it's a beaut, same one you trained on in Arkansas so it shouldn't take much to get the hang of it again. There are several local dealers, but they're all closed. Besides, you're looking at a week or more for the background check." Phil's poker face was unreadable.

"Nobody sells guns on Saturday?" Jared clarified.

Phil hesitated, shoving Marcia Treadway's note deeper into his pocket.

"All of 'em closed earlier today, sorry."

Tracy blanched as she studied the gun information. Granted, she had handled guns while confronting snakes around the pond banks, but realizing she may need to use one on another human being was disconcerting.

"You okay, Sweetheart?" Phil scooted beside her and placed his hand to her shoulder. Sweeping away his concern and moving to a small table, she grabbed a bottle of water and gulped a long drink.

"Hon, I wish I could say something to make you feel better. We knew they'd be following you, but they still managed to surprise us," Phil explained. "So we need to prepare you in case it happens again." He winked at Jared. "And don't forget, Jared is pretty capable when it comes to handguns."

Her mouth fell open. "You are?" she asked.

Jared scanned the spec sheet then dropped it to the desk. "I can usually hit where I aim."

"Tracy, Jared and I spent a lot of time together in the past few years. I was technically undercover as Sutherant's security, but I kind of had a hidden agenda in teaching him all that I know. I knew one day he'd probably have to take on the company, so while we were together, I used my time to get him up to speed on some things - firearms for one."

"What were the other things?" Tracy grinned as she twined her fingers through Jared's.

"Let's see – taught him how to boost cars, how to break into safes and security systems, defensive driving, got his pilot's license in a twin engine plane (although I wouldn't trust him on that one). He can get around a kitchen. He's a helluva good mechanic, and as I remember, I got him to jump out of a plane a few times. But he's got some other fine talents that I guess you'll just have to discover on your own."

Phil tossed a paper wad at Jared's head and chuckled.

"I think you about covered it, Phil," Jared hedged.

"I can't wait to discover some of those talents," she whispered beside Jared's ear. He rolled his eyes, restrained another laugh then pressed his hands to her cheeks.

"You'll have that chance tonight because we *will not* let anything keep us apart any longer," Jared whispered. "And if Jodie starts to talk too much we'll go to a hotel." He tightened his hold and Tracy swayed in his arms. But Phil pushed between them as he made his way back to his desk.

"Okay, you love puppies - settle down so we can take a look at these floor plans. It looks like the Newport and Savannah offices are pretty similar, so I'm thinking we should access the computer system in Savannah since Newport is so hot. We'd never get past Frazier's guys. Access one computer and you have access to the whole shebang."

Phil led them over to his computer and retrieved information about the Savannah, Georgia branch of Sutherant

Petroleum. As he whisked through page after page of data, he explained his relationship with the Savannah office and divulged his personal eagerness to bring their corruption to light. Besides having invested more than five years of his life infiltrating and monitoring the operations of the company, his family business had taken a major hit three years before when Sutherant Petroleum opened a plant in Southern Georgia.

"My brother and I started a small water craft and tour business. It wasn't much but it took all my brother had to get it started. He was all set to offer water tours throughout Georgia – white-water rafting, air boat charters, house-boat rentals and sales, deep sea charters...the whole bit. We were eventually forced to file Chapter Eleven bankruptcy when Sutherant opened the Savannah branch."

Tracy followed Phil's explanation but in the back of her mind, she recalled the Congressional names linked to the subcommittee overseeing deep water ports such as Savannah. She made a mental note to have Lauren see if there was a connection.

Phil strained from his chair and made his way around the desk toward a credenza on the far wall of his office. Tracy and Jared watched as he slid a drawer open to retrieve a half-empty bottle of top shelf whiskey. He tilted the bottle and a clean glass toward Jared and Tracy, and as both declined, Phil grabbed his coffee cup and allowed a generous jigger to mix into his freshly poured java.

"Sutherant Petroleum has that much leverage in Georgia?" Jared asked, going on to question how such a large operation could have grown from small-town roots in Newport, Oklahoma.

"They used their deep pockets to persuade the state to give them priority over the waterways. One bill after another passed through the State Legislature and before we knew it, they were overtaxing every business that needed to use the shipping routes. Georgia officials more or less put everyone other than Sutherant out of business. Nobody else could afford the damned levies."

Tracy remembered one piece of research she had read that linked Sutherant Petroleum to a smuggling operation in and around the ports of Savannah. Looking at the map of the area, she speculated that the intersecting major interstates and the intra-coastal waterways that ran along the eastern seaboard would be a prime location for international shipping – and smuggling.

"I'd give my right arm to shut that company down." Phil ran his finger around the rim of his coffee cup. His ruddy face stiffened and the more the conversation revolved around Sutherant, the more the blood vessel near his temple throbbed.

Tracy followed the conversation, but the thought of Phil driving through the park in the Ultrex that morning blurred her mind. Could his anger over Sutherant have gnawed so deeply that he would resort to brutal murder? Then again, her own anger surged each time he slammed the company her father had devoted so much of his life to building. She watched Jared's reaction and wondered if Phil's denigration of Frazier, Sr. affected him in the same way.

"So what should be our first move, Phil?" she prodded, eager to end the meeting. "How much more information do we need to prove their guilt?"

"My father heads up internal investigations in the Washington Bureau, and he has been following this case for the past couple of years since so many Washington elites have been linked to it. It's become a major focus in both the FBI and the DEA. We have evidence of their actions, but we still need proof of all the players...documented proof of everyone involved, both stateside and abroad so we can expose the whole operation, most importantly our friends in the U.S. Congress."

"And you think all that information will be in my dad's computer system?" Tracy leaned over to take a closer look at the computer data on Phil's computer.

"Securely hidden, but yes, I think it's all there. Records of all their supporters and contributions, inventory lists of the products they're shipping, and most importantly, proof that our own government officials are the ones initiating these transactions."

Phil pointed to a world map that highlighted the branches and company-owned properties of Sutherant Petroleum.

"You two need to realize this is a very large, very powerful operation. It's part of a conglomerate which has multi-billion dollar interests in foreign oil. There's a network of small branches scattered throughout the States which outwardly appear to be functioning as independent businesses. In reality, each branch location is a front, disguised in such a way that the operations inside go unnoticed by the local townspeople in the area. And unfortunately, Jared, your dad runs the Newport branch which is the center of it all."

"So behind the front, Phil, what exactly is going on at Sutherant Petroleum?" Tracy studied the chart of suspected criminal activity and had to buffer the sharp pain that flared as she realized the kind of company her father had been a part of. Still, she remembered the last picture of her dad surrounded by friends. If David Frazier was the 'center' of the corruption as Phil said, why was he at a table with those who were trying to uncover it?

"I don't think we'll fully know until we get on the inside, Tracy. There're all kinds of rumors: oil, drugs, military arms, mercenaries..."

Phil glanced at Jared. Tracy noticed Phil's sudden discomfort and sensed his anxious rush to gather the materials. "I know this is a bit much for you to hear. I'll do my best to keep you both from getting too involved in this."

Jared slammed his hands down on the desk. "Dammit, Phil! We're already involved. As soon as I went back to Newport they had a shoot to kill order on my head. They want Tracy back. They want me dead. We're as involved in this as we can be. We *can't* stop until we get to the bottom of it." Jared's voice cracked. When he turned, his clenched fists were bloodlessly white and his veins were bulging under his skin.

"He's right, Phil. Don't you dare question our judgment on this!" Tracy shouted, leaving little room for Phil to reply. "My God, look at us. Do you honestly think we want to be here planning a break-in? We've been separated more than four years and now that we're back together, these psychos are trying to kill us. We want to be alone, making up for lost time and planning our wedding. But we're here, looking at gun brochures and planning... our survival! So don't question if we're up for this."

Tracy spun around and withdrew into a corner of the office. Then with one anxious turn she bolted to the credenza and snatched the Gold Mark whiskey. Twisting the top from the bottle, she tilted it, filling a shot glass to the brim. As her onlookers gawked in awe, Tracy closed her eyes and slammed back the whiskey in one smooth motion. She pressed the empty glass to her lips and allowed the liquid fire to trickle down, then exhaled a long, slow breath as her head started to swim.

Straining to focus, she noticed the inscription along the side of the small glass. *The Black Tulip, Boston*. With little thought she lowered the glass back to the shelf. But with a second more curious glance, a recent memory triggered her mind. She whirled toward Jared and saw that he had fallen back into conversation, pouring over schematics with Phil. Palming the glass, she studied it again – the long stemmed black rose, the heavy block letters, the Irish inscription – an identical replica of a glass from Jim Crenshaw's collection at the *Tribune* office. She replaced the empty glass, and with a cautious glance toward Phil, slid the credenza door open a little further. Phil's entire personal collection came into full view, each small glass a mirror-image of those she had seen in Jim's desk on so many occasions as he had bragged about the places he and his unnamed friend had visited. *Mr. O'Malley's Boston Pub; O'Rooney's Times Square Tavern; Celtic Green Pub, Chicago; Paddy's, Washington,D.C.; Bracken Head Pub, Dublin; Three Queens – London* – each glass an apparent souvenir of places Phil and Jim had visited – together. Jim Crenshaw…Sutherant's "good ol' boy. The very one who was burying key information about Sutherant was a close friend of Phil Murphy.

Tracy peered over her shoulder toward Phil, peeled away the layers of lies and deceit that disguised him, and saw he was unaware of her discovery. She eased the cabinet door closed and felt her hand tighten around the small glass, clinging to the proof of her suspicions.

Her eyes wandered aimlessly through the upper shelves of more memorabilia – dust-covered awards and plaques of recognition melded into a dizzying blur as her stomach churned in disbelief of the man Jared had so revered. Books of law and federal guidelines loomed on high daring her to accuse their owner. As she swore in her mind that she would

Lyrics and Lies

take that dare, her eyes settled on the one personal effect Phil must have overlooked while hiding evidence of his involvement. The framed photo of the golf three-some had undoubtedly slipped his mind as he had prepared his office for their visit. Tracy internalized each subject in the frame: her co-worker, Jim Crenshaw, her own uncle, Dennis Sims, and in the center with his arms stretched wide across their shoulders, Phil Murphy. A heart-halting chill raked her spine as she realized Phil Murphy was linked to the people she most distrusted. And the way he had degraded both Mark Sims and David Frazier made her question Phil Murphy's credibility even more. Plus, his determination to "get into the computer system" told her not to trust him one bit. He had suddenly become her biggest enemy. She shut her eyes and pushed the truth to the back of her mind, searching the length of the room for her one safety net - *Jared*.

The look in her eye shouted a warning to Jared. It was a glare he knew by heart, that twinge of urgent warning that had protected him time and time again. The same look from years ago that kept him from crawling into the car with Steve Wynkowski who Tracy knew had been drinking and who minutes later flipped his Camaro into Banyan Creek, winding up in critical condition for the next two weeks. The same look that cut Jared down one day in tenth grade and kept him from following their chemistry lab partner who tried to get him to join in the bottle rocket prank that caused a fire in the teacher's lounge. He remembered the same worried look had convinced him to defy his coach's mandate during the spring of his junior year. Because of the glare in her hazel eyes, he had waited out a rising storm instead of walking to spring football practice, narrowly avoiding the tornado that touched down along the very path he would have taken. And if he had

261

only taken notice, he would have seen that same look in her eyes years before on the night he was whisked out of Newport. Even now her pleas from that night rang clear, begging him not to leave. If only he had listened. Tracy had sensed danger then and by the look in her eyes, she sensed it now.

Tracy's hands began to tremble. Jared cautiously steered Phil's attention to the map, giving her the chance she needed to collect herself. In her next breath she grabbed the slender photo frame and slipped it underneath her shirt, securing it in the waistband of her jeans. She eased toward the chair where she had placed her purse and while Phil continued to drone about Sutherant operations, she gripped the frame and stuffed it deep into the corner of her bag.

She exhaled then suddenly felt the room sway. *The alcohol*, she reasoned. A surge of warmth rose inside her. Floating over to Jared, she reached out and ran her fingers through his thick, wavy hair.

"You okay?" Jared chuckled.

She nodded and pulled him close, focusing steadily on an obscure painting on the far wall of Phil's office - a seascape with a flock of gulls breezing over the saw grass as a young family looked on.

Family.

Suddenly, her strategy for what had to be done became clear. She tightened her arms around Jared's neck and initiated the first step of her plan.

"Let's go see Jodie." The gravity in her eyes bore through him. Before he could respond she whirled toward Phil and in her best effort, kept her accusing eye at bay. "Phil, I don't guess you could hook us up with a shower could you? We're still in our jogging clothes and it'd be nice to get this sweat off us."

"Yeah, sure." Phil gathered the schematics and the gun pamphlets and slid them toward Jared. "Mike mentioned you were out for a jog this morning."

You know damned well we were out for a jog you sonofabitch! You were there. With Brody Craig! As Tracy thought it, her eyes glued to his and she wondered if the expression "if looks could kill" might hold a little truth. She laughed to herself and thought how much she was going to love bringing this man down. But she had to be patient. So she collected her purse, held it tight against her chest, and smiled, unwilling to hide the spite in her voice. "Yes, we were. Best time of day to take in the scenery." Her face heated when she stared into Phil's eyes. "Only saw two cars along the highway," she sneered.

The room closed in and suddenly Phil was under her microscope. He loosened his tie and she could only hope it was out of nervousness. But Phil was good. He covered his every emotion with the experience of an FBI expert. She knew his innocent façade would be hard to break.

"Over there at the firing range, there's a full gym, showers, even a spa." He glanced at his watch. "It's three-thirty. I'll get you checked in then we can grab some dinner before you head to Jacksonville," Phil stammered as he stacked the papers stretched across his desk.

"And what about Sutherant? What's your timeframe for getting us in their office?" Tracy pressed.

"End of the week."

Tracy halted in mid-motion. Phil's monosyllabic reply floored her with a right hook. *End of the week.* She thrust a hand to her mouth and tackled the hangnail that had been worrying her – anything to fight the urge to scream.

She moved to assist Jared with the materials, but inside, her nerves ignited. Her head pounded as she calculated the time that would be wasted in waiting days to get into the company's computer system. She thought of Jared, his safety in jeopardy until they secured and returned the money Sutherant demanded.

Feeling the rising blood color her face, she swallowed hard to slow her heavy breathing. *End of the week.* Not soon enough! It hit her that it was only Saturday. Jared had returned on Thursday morning – just two days before. In that short time they had lost their home, been framed for murder and had been chased across three states, ambushed at the hotel, and had lost an agent in the line of duty. Now she realized the one person Jared had put his trust in was Satan incarnate. Her eyes ricocheted across the room searching for an escape, wanting nothing more than to drive straight to Newport and bolt into the computer room to see what she could find. Then reason caught up to her. Phil was a wild card. She had to be sure when to play him.

Still lost in conversation, Jared and Phil rambled through various security measures that Sutherant had added in recent years. For a brief moment, they turned away from the desk. Before taking time to think, she snatched one of the security badges and a printed diagram of the Sutherant offices. Slipping them into her purse, she moved to Jared's side.

"Ready to go?" she brightened.

***

Hot, steamy water streamed across Tracy's face, allowing the soothing shower to cleanse her mind. Lathering her hair for the second time, her fingers massaged deeply while an alternative plan of action slowly came together. She watched the suds trickle through her toes and down the drain. Hot tears pressed the back of her eyes. Her muscles tightened and as she thought of the danger that threatened Jared, she sank to her knees and began to cry.

Unable to combat the mounting strain, she wrapped her arms around her stomach and began to tremble. She lifted her head and allowed the warm water to run free wondering how she would ever have the strength to carry out her plan. She wiped her eyes with the back of her hands, turned off the water, and then followed the escaping steam through the shower door.

As she tightened the towel around her, she looked around, feeling oddly out of place in the governmental training facility – the hunted amidst the hunters – a desperate victim on the run surrounded by federal agents she no longer trusted. An antique cherry-wood grandfather's clock chimed in the next room and as the melody ended, four reverberating *BONGs* echoed through the room.

"Four o'clock," she sighed.

After a quick bite they could be on the road and make Jacksonville by ten. She glanced at the clock again and just under the face was an engraved quotation. She squinted to read it from a distance and the more the words came into view, the more they drew her in.

Most of the important things in the world have been accomplished by people who have kept on trying when there seemed to be no hope at all. ~ Dale Carnegie

She moved closer and read the imprinted words again, thinking of Sutherant, the brutal killings, and the families who had been destroyed. She thought of Jared, how four years of their lives had been stolen and how Sutherant was keeping them from living even now. At the same time, Eric's last words echoed – a simple warning meant to save their lives. *Jared is a threat... Jared is a threat.* As the engraved words settled in her mind, she knew what she had to do. There was only one way to keep Jared safe.

In the privacy of the empty dressing room, Tracy took the first steps toward enacting her plan. She pulled her phone from her purse and as soon as she heard her friend's voice, she fell into relaxed, easy conversation, putting the chaos of her life on hold.

"So how was your date?"

Lauren snickered. "It was...informative," she evaded. "We just met for dinner. Ended up comparing notes on Sutherant and Company. Where are you anyway?"

"Atlanta." Tracy hesitated and then went on to say what she had considered keeping to herself. "We're being followed, Lauren. An agent who was with us was killed this morning. And now I just found out that the one person we were counting on can't be trusted. I'm really scared." A chilling silence invaded the air.

"Can you handle a little more?" Lauren sighed.

"Tell me."

"You know that lawyer named Osteen - the guy who was killed in his garage the day

Jared disappeared?"

"Yes, along with Senator Hastings – same time, same place."

"Right. I think I may have found a connection between the two of them," Lauren began.

"How?"

"Phone records. Stan Dothan's niece works in billing down at the phone company. Plus, her boyfriend happens to work in wireless sales. Never knew how much you can find out about a person through their phone bill."

"So what's the connection?"

"Osteen, Hastings, David Frazier and your dad talked quite a bit. Sheriff McClain told me they were all friends and he confirmed that the week of the murders they were actually planning to turn over state's evidence, so the frequent conversations made sense. But one thing bothered me. Most of Hastings' in-coming calls were local with the exception of one from Maryland and that one number kept popping up."

"He's a U.S. Senator, Lauren. A call from Maryland wouldn't be unusual."

"I know. But why did this caller not use Hastings' government cell phone like his other associates? His personal Oklahoma cell was hardly used – just local calls and that one Maryland number. And here's the clincher: Osteen's cell phone record showed the same Maryland number ten minutes before he was killed. Oddly, the call lasted two seconds, as if Osteen answered then disconnected right away."

"Maybe it was the caller who disconnected. Did you trace the number?"

"Came up as unlisted. Grant ran a more intensive search for me and when Senator Baird Mackenzick's name came up, he got very interested, especially when he remembered Mackenzick being in town the night of the murders four years ago. Pulled him over in a traffic stop."

"A traffic stop?"

"Yeah, speeding of all things. It all fits, Tracy. This Senator Mackenzick flies his own plane into town using the name of John Smith (according to some old records that Hank Tisdale's widow kept around), he makes the fifteen-minute drive to Shiloh, then flies out of the Newport Air Facility just past ten that night and is back in D.C. by eight o'clock the next morning to oversee the passage of a bill on school funding. His cell number appears on the phone records of two victims of execution-style murders. Baird Mackenzick's only mistake was that there was a witness."

"And Grant is sure that it was him?"

"Absolutely. Grant was majoring in Political History at the time and probably could have named every cabinet member and most of the members of Congress. He said he can testify to the whole conversation Mackenzick had with his ride along partner, Everett Hadley."

"Baird Mackenzick...it does sound familiar," added Tracy.

"It should. He was Majority Leader three years ago. He heads up the Armed Services Committee that deals with emerging threats and military capabilities. You see his picture all over the news when terrorism or military technology stories air."

Tracy sat up and the photo of the golf-threesome crossed her mind. *Military capabilities.*

She jumped to her feet and grabbed her duffle bag, digging into the sides to find the golf photo of Phil. She ran her fingers across the frame.

"Lauren, write this down. Check military records for Jim Crenshaw, Phil Murphy, Dennis Sims, and this Senator Baird Mackenzick. If you can, get me a history of each military career – where they were stationed, what places they may have served together..."

"You got it."

Tracy had played golf twice in her life – once during college with some friends and once when Eric took her on one of their first dates. Those two times were enough to learn that golf was usually played in groups of four. She tilted the frame in search of a clue. That one thing – a piece of clothing, an extra golf bag, a score card – anything that could identify a fourth player. And as she moved to lay the frame down, one odd detail caught her eye. The visor of the golf cart was lowered and angled in such a way that a distorted image had been captured in the mirror. She brought the photo closer, turning it left and right to see if she could make out the image. And then she saw it. The image in the mirror was a reflection of the photographer, the fourth player.

"Also, I need you to check with Lane Kirkland to see if his editing equipment can enlarge and enhance an existing photo image." Tracy flipped through her notes and another idea crossed her mind. "One other thing – I need you to do one of your cross-reference checks you're so good at. See if you can find anything suspicious about Congressman Davidson who heads the sub-committee on deep water ports. Specifically Savannah, Georgia."

"Okay, anything else?"

"Yes, I think it's time to pull Jim Crenshaw's prize-winning story. Run a very thorough credibility check on the story and the sources he cited."

"Now you're talking. Let's hang his ass!"

"Who else knows about all this, Lauren?"

"Just Levi Daniels, the investigative journalist your music agent found. He called from New York last night and I had to get him up to speed."

"Nobody else can know. From here on out, just you, me, and Levi."

"No problem. Where do you want me to send this information you need?"

Tracy hesitated.

"I'll let you know." Tracy glanced at the clock to see that time was slipping much more quickly than she had wanted. There was more she wanted to say but knew the more she told Lauren, the more she was pulling her into danger. With that fear, she changed the subject. "So, you and Eric, huh?"

"Oh, who knows? Sure you're okay with it?"

"Just don't get hurt, Lauren. I couldn't handle that."

"Ha! I think he knows you'll kick his ass if that happens. Don't worry. I know what I'm doing."

After another five minute rundown to update Tracy on all the Newport gossip, they disconnected. With greater urgency, Tracy devised a personal strategy to mount her own defense against Sutherant. She pulled up a different contact on her phone pad and typed a detailed text message to set her plan in motion.

"Don't let me down," she whispered, praying her message would get through in time.

She finished dressing in a casual top and jeans, dabbed on some make-up, and gathered her damp hair into a ponytail. Collecting her toiletries and luggage, she made her way toward the door, stopping briefly at the clock to draw strength from the prophetic words one final time.

"...people who have kept on trying when there seemed to be no hope at all."

Tightening the grip of her duffle bag, she strode toward the elevator. Reaching the lobby she spotted their car through the front glass doorway and saw Jared climbing from the driver's seat. As she passed the reception desk, Mike Richardson came from behind and eased the duffle bag from her hand.

"Have a nice visit with Phil Murphy?"

Tracy spun around in surprise, exhaling her nervousness as he draped a protective arm across her shoulder. His warmth was a comfort, as was the release of the heavy duffle bag. She caressed the blood flow back into her fingers and considered sharing what she had discovered. The trust was there...somewhat. But as she brushed her thumb across the diamond engagement ring her heart began to race. *Jared.* His safety was in the balance. Confiding in *anyone* would be too great a risk. So a simple nod was her only response.

Jared held the door open for them as they exited the building. "Phil called to say he had an unexpected meeting so won't be able to join us for dinner."

"Hmm. Not surprised," Mike mumbled.

"Let's grab something on the way to save time," Tracy suggested as she climbed into the car.

"Stop anywhere you like," Mike offered. "It's on me since you're driving. A bit more sleep is just what I need. I feel a long night coming on."

Chapter 31

Saturday – late evening

The lingering glow of dusk melted into a swirl of color – soothing warmth dancing on the horizon. A fresh coastal breeze streamed in through the open windows as Jared wound his way through the light traffic on I-10 west of Jacksonville. Tracy, having spent the last hour of their trip updating him on all that Lauren had discovered, powered down her laptop. Battling with indecision, she kept her suspicions of Phil at bay. The less Jared had to worry about the better, she reasoned. Turning in her seat, she stole a quick glimpse to ensure Mike Richardson was still sleeping soundly. Satisfied, she scooted closer toward Jared and enjoyed the landscape changes as the miles vanished behind them.

"Everything okay?"

"I just hate that you have to face all of this. Your dad, learning of my father's death, the investigation – it's all so much. Not to mention that if I had just stayed in Newport they may not be after you now."

"T, I spent four years away from you. I've got to know why they were so determined to keep us apart."

He released her hand and turned off the radio.

"But if all this scares you too much, we'll stop right here and find a safe place to ride it out. Tell me what to do."

Tracy pulled her feet into the seat.

"I want answers. Why were you taken away? Why was my dad killed? And I need to know what Daddy stored in his computer program. But Jared, the important thing is that you stay away from Sutherant. Promise me you'll stay safe."

"I'll keep us both safe, T.," he snapped. Then his tone softened. "So how long has it been since you last saw Jodie?"

"Four years. It was a few months after Daddy died when she took me to New York for a week of shopping."

"Bet that burned your uncle's hide," Jared grinned.

"Wasn't much he could say. Jodie insisted that I see some of the world outside of Oklahoma."

"Then why the hell didn't you get out of there, T.? You didn't have to stay in Newport."

"Sure, I did."

"It wasn't like your uncle was holding you prisoner. There was no reason for you to stay there." His words cut her like a knife. Her throat tightened and it was all she could do to speak.

"I had to…"

"You should've just left Newport and…"

"Jared…" she stammered. She shifted in her seat and turned away. Her soft whisper trailed behind. "I was waiting for you."

Silence.

Jared's face drained. A sharp pain stabbed his chest. He tried to swallow, but the impact of her words got in the way. He exhaled a long, regretful sigh as he saw, really saw the sacrifice she had made because of him. *Waiting for you.* The words slapped him like a gust of that harsh Oklahoma wind. She *had* to stay - hoping he'd come back for her.

Tracy curled her legs beneath her and felt the cold distance grow between them. The same thought kept flashing through her mind. *Do I matter to him at all?* She adjusted her engagement ring and considered all the sacrifices she had made to be with him and wondered if she had made the right decision. She fought back the tears as truths became clear. The truth of how she declined the music scholarship from UCLA and settled for the local state college – *for him*. Taking the part-time job at the *Tribune* just so she could stay in Newport – *for him*. Putting her social life aside – *for him*. Remaining faithful and spending most every breathing moment thinking of one thing - *him*.

The frenzy of emotions made her withdraw and for a moment, she was a child again, swathed in the memories of family. "Girls only" sleepovers with her mom. Her father's laughter as he fielded her pop flies. Baking cookies on Saturday nights. Walking with her dad through the fields as they longed to rekindle the joy that had died with her mother.

An easy smile lifted as Tracy recalled when that joy eventually returned – with Jared. Passing through months of grief together until carefree talks opened the long-closed door of laughter. Jared became her escape. Her strength. And as those dark months slowly evolved into the happiest years of her life, their love took root.

She looked Jared's way and wondered how she could ever question his love or doubt God's perfect plan. A sweet forgiveness rose within her. She slipped her hand into his and felt the awkward tension crumbled.

"I'm so sorry I haven't been there for you, T. And I promise I'll never leave you again."

She wiped her eyes and leaned closer.

"And I'll never leave you," she sighed. The words were a mere whisper and nearly caught in her throat. Guilt made her look away. She realized that was the first time in her life she had ever lied to Jared.

***

Chapter 32

The orange and purple strains of fading daylight streaked across the Jacksonville sky and as Jared exited the interstate, Tracy glimpsed the position lights of an eastbound jetliner. She followed its course, imagining a madcap escape with Jared. But she knew it was not that easy. Not without getting some answers first.

As they turned into her aunt's neighborhood, Mike began to rouse in the back seat. Jared wheeled into the circular drive and before the car came to a full stop, Tracy bolted from the car and dashed across the yard to meet Jodie, who had just stepped from the porch.

Aunt Jodie was forty-six and aside from her auburn hair and hazel eyes, shared nothing in common with her sister, Shannon. While Shannon was content to stick around the farm in Small-town, USA where they had both been raised, Jodie had set out in search of adventure the day after her high school graduation. Destination: Pensacola Beach, Florida - The Miracle Mile. The first day there, while looking for seashells on the beach, she met Kevin. He was twenty-one at the time and had just taken out a loan for a used 35' commercial fishing boat. The story shared at Thanksgiving dinner for the next decade was that it was love at first sight, and within three weeks of meeting, they had begun to plan their wedding. Surprisingly, it had lasted. Two children and twenty-nine years later, they still held hands as they stepped from the porch to greet their only niece.

Kevin Mason's laid-back charisma put everyone he met at ease. Soft gray streaks framed his tanned face and his anytime-u-see-him attire (khaki shorts, linen shirt, and deck shoes) made him look years younger than his forty-nine years. Having purchased that first fishing boat nearly thirty years before, Kevin had used pure sweat and his country-boy drive to turn his dream into one of the premier deep-sea fishing expeditions along the east coast. While he was not the type to ever disclose his wealth, Tracy knew that she and every other member of the family would be well taken care of in the future.

Kevin's greatest reward had come in co-sponsoring a foundation with their daughter, Whitney, who had recently graduated from the University of North Florida with a degree in marketing. Together, they had founded Sweet Escape, a non-profit camp for children with special needs. While his daughter handled the managerial side of the organization, Kevin blocked twenty units of a time-share resort he co-owned and donated the use of his fleet of recreational boats, tour guides, and services sixteen weeks out of the year. Their generosity afforded an average of twenty-two hundred children per year an all-expense paid week of fun and mental escape from physical and emotional challenges as a full staff of doctors, nurses, dieticians, and volunteer staff provided them with recreational and medical care.

"My girl – my sweet little girl," Jodie sighed. The reunion was just as Tracy had imagined – warm, full of laughter, and as comforting as a mother's lullaby. As soon as Jodie loosened her hold, Tracy flashed her left hand in the air. That was all it took for her to be swept into Jodie's arms again. From that point on, the wedding was the topic no matter how many times Tracy insisted it would be some time before they could actually have a wedding. Still, unpacking was put on hold, bedtimes were postponed, and everyone else was left to wait as Jodie suggested one idea after another for a ceremony.

An hour later, Jared pushed away from the table and stretched out his legs. "Jodie, that rum cake was killer. I can't hold another bite," he groaned. After helping to clear the table, he and Tracy spent the next half-hour sharing every detail of their ordeal, ensuring that Jodie and Kevin fully understood the magnitude of their struggle.

"Tracy, your dad knew what was going on. I see that now," Jodie offered. "He wasn't happy at Sutherant with all he had witnessed those last years. I assumed he was stressed about the farm income, but now I see it was more than that. Last thing he told me was that he was going to make things better for you."

Tracy shrugged, "Never got the chance."

Jodie went to the kitchen and returned carrying the last of an opened bottle of cabernet. She refilled Jared's glass, stroked his hair then leaned down to hug his neck.

"You'll never know how much we've missed you," she whispered. Jared smiled and squeezed her hand. Turning to Mike she added, "We were thinking about giving them a tour of downtown tomorrow. Can you join us?"

"I go where they go as part of their protection," Mike smiled. "But right now, I think I'll head out to my car to read a little. It's eleven o'clock and a back-up unit is scheduled at dawn. We'll be on duty 'round the clock so you guys rest easy."

Rest easy? Tracy questioned his casual tone. She watched as Mike shook hands with Kevin and while she tried to push her suspicions away, she could not escape the hint of distrust invading her mind. How could he not have noticed the girl at the coffee shop? And why had he arrived almost two hours early to relieve Brody Craig? He had planned to change shifts at noon yet he arrived before ten. Was it a coincidence?

Mike stood from the couch and offered a final wave as he walked toward the door. Tracy followed him onto the porch and caught his arm.

"Mike?" She hesitated. "We trust you to get us through this," she warned.

Mike smiled and squeezed her hand. "I'll see you in the morning."

Returning to the living room, Tracy saw Jared move toward the front window.

"Must be tough losing a partner." He lifted the curtain to look outside.

In his distraction Tracy pulled her phone from her pocket and saw a new text message. She quickly responded then put her phone away.

"Guess it'll be a long night for him," Jared continued as he turned around. "Eating on the run and reading by flashlight – not much of a life. But it sure is good to know he's keeping an eye out for us."

Jodie smiled, standing to clear the empty wine glasses. "Well, I know you two must be exhausted. Tracy, you know the layout upstairs. The balcony room was always your favorite but, well, I'm sure you two can figure out your own sleeping arrangements," she laughed and reached to hug Jared. "I'm so glad you're here Jared. It just feels right to see you and Tracy together again."

They said goodnight and headed upstairs. Tracy hesitated at the foot of the stairs, returning to where Jodie was standing. She clenched her arms around Jodie and together, they swayed in a warm embrace.

"Thank you for everything." Tracy began to pull away but Jodie stopped her.

"We're family, Tracy. You know we'd do anything for you two. Anything," she stressed.

With a gentle nod, Tracy turned back to Jared and climbed the stairs that led to the room she had always loved.

It was a comfortable house that sat on five acres on the east bank of the St. John's River. Their room had a private veranda and when you listened closely, you could hear the light bump of the pontoon boat as the current pushed it against the dock. Then a sudden quietness fell across the room. Their eyes met and the same thought occurred to them at once: there was a reason interruptions and fatigue has kept them apart the past two nights. Because here they were now – the most beautiful room in the most beautiful setting either could have imagined. This moment had been carved in time for them alone. The perfect time, the perfect place. No moment had ever felt so right.

Together they fumbled through clothing, taunting each other's own eagerness as they collapsed onto the bed. Jared lowered his head and paused at her neck, absorbing her scent, craving everything about her. His lips brushed softly across her skin, cuddling her and whispering softly how much he loved her. His breath blanketed her with warmth – sultry, moist heat like the steam that rose from the pasture after a summer rain. He kissed her skin with a new unhindered passion, feeling her curl beneath him as he brushed his lips against her breasts. He smiled as she closed her eyes and fell in love with her all over again as he watched her enjoy all the sensual pleasures he could give.

Tracy's own apprehensions melted away as his arms entwined her. Passion swept through her like a wildfire, searing the core of her body. With a sudden urge, she grasped his hand, mindlessly clinging to the one she most trusted to lead her into this new unknown experience. Sliding their gripped hands to her side, she arched herself into him, running her fingers through his hair as her body found rhythm with his. For the briefest moment she opened her eyes and saw him smiling at her. This was truly her Jared – back in her arms again. He had not changed a bit. Still her best friend, her protector, her soul mate, her lover. Her very world.

She pressed her lips to his ear. "I always knew you'd come back for me."

He raised his head and found her eyes. "I love you so much, T."

Swallowing back the tears that kept struggling to break free, Tracy pressed against him and whispered, "No matter what happens, you are the most important thing to me. You are my life, J." She shuddered slightly, trying desperately to ignore the danger they faced. But, as in so many times in the past four days, her senses lost all control as she floated away with Jared to that paradise where lovers go to shut out the world and be totally alone. When Jared's arms tightened around her, his gentle touch lifted them into romantic flight and all other thoughts faded away. She welcomed the precious night she had so anticipated and surrendered herself completely to him. She had never felt so free.

Watch Over Me Tonight

Angel in the window whispering my name

Spread your wings and fly to me, lead me home again

Winds of change and storms of life have carried me far from home

So sing a prayer to God above so I won't be alone

I wandered 'round and lost my way without you by my side

Out here I walk a lonely road with no place left to hide

Lead me through my darkest hour by Heaven's Holy light

My angel in the window watchin' over me tonight

Sing your song and carry me home so I won't be alone

Wrap your arms around my soul 'cause there's no place left to go

Angel in the window watch over me tonight.

Just sing your song and lead me home, watch over me tonight

I know my angel in the window is watching over me tonight.

Sing a prayer to guide me home; watch over me tonight.

Chapter 33

Sunday Pre-dawn

Peaceful sounds drifted through the darkened room: a warm breeze stirred just outside the open window, the light whirr of the ceiling fan, and the sweetest tune of all - the steady hum of Jared's soft snoring. Even the rustle of cotton sheets as he rolled to his side moved her like a love song in the night.

Tracy stood at the foot of the bed soaking in the beautiful harmony, cherishing the fullness of the moment. With one small duffle bag in hand, she gazed at Jared, fighting back the burn of tears. She could not breathe. She could not move. Her heart broke more with every shallow pulse, but her mind was clear on what she had to do.

A sudden vibration from her cell phone startled her. She glanced at the message and her muscles fell limp. It was time. She slid the phone back into her pocket. One last look around to ensure she had all she needed – clothes, medicine, research materials, passport, the Sutherant security badge and schematics she had taken from Phil's briefcase the day before, and part of the cash she and Jared had combined. As an afterthought she grabbed the wig and crammed it into the side pocket of her duffle bag. Then, with a heavy sigh, she slipped the strap over her shoulder.

She swallowed hard, trying to ease the horrific throbbing in her throat – a searing heaviness that ached deep in her chest. She feathered her fingers along Jared's bare leg. A smile came to light as her thoughts whisked to two hours before when they had made love. *Unbelievable* – was that the word he had used? All she knew was that she had never felt such passion and total surrender. Perhaps knowing it might be their first and last time had made all the difference.

"God, please keep him safe," she whispered. With a turn, she crept to the door and made flight. Just as she reached the foot of the stairs, a movement caught her eye.

Jodie rounded the kitchen door.

Tracy's breath caught and her body went rigid, unable to move from the sudden fright. She waited, expecting the reprimand. Instead, Jodie's face softened. She took Tracy's hand and smiled.

"I can't let you leave without saying goodbye." She brushed Tracy's cheek.

"Jodie, I…"

"Shhh, I know. I figured you were making plans when I saw you texting earlier. Just promise me. Don't let anything you find out change the way you remember your dad. He was a good man."

Tracy nodded. "Jodie…Jared can't know…" Hot tears began to spill. "He can't follow me. As long as we're together he will be in danger."

Jodie hugged her tight. "Just finish what you have to do and come back to us."

Tracy forced a smile and turned toward the door. She hesitated then pointed toward her guitar propped against the closet door.

"Keep it safe for me?"

"It'll be right here."

Unable to speak, Tracy fled through the back door to avoid Mike's watchful eye. Jodie stepped out behind her, mindlessly trying to protect her from unseen harm. Sprinting through the side lot and the easement to the north of Jodie's property, Tracy rounded a grove of trees well out of sight of Mike's view. As she approached an intersection several hundred feet beyond Jodie's driveway, a sudden flash of headlights at the end of the road broke the darkness and Tracy darted in their direction, thankful her planned getaway was on schedule. But just as she slowed to a jog, a lone truck turned from a side road and blocked her escape. The headlights were not on. Fear paralyzed her as she recognized the all-familiar sound of the diesel. With her last burst of strength, she dove from view behind a hibiscus hedge.

Crouching near the ground for cover, she watched as the silver quad-cab edged closer – a vision she had come to detest when her uncle pulled onto her property every day. Even from ground level and in the black of night she could make out his face - that seedy glower that would forever sicken her.

She held her breath trying to avert her eyes, but one look to the passenger seat immobilized her. That was all it took to recognize the girl. The dark clothes, the turquoise earrings - even without the wig Tracy knew it was the girl from the coffee shop. And as she thought about it, the full truth dawned on her – *his girlfriend from Colorado*. Her muscles tightened as she wondered how long the two had planned this snare.

The truck inched forward. Then it dawned on Tracy why they had come. *Jared!* Horrific fear unleashed and beyond anything else at hand, she knew she had to warn Mike. She jerked the phone from her pocket and pressed Mike's speed dial.

"Mike, here." His voice was alert, anxious.

"Dennis Sims is in a silver pick-up three blocks away. He's heading your way."

Before Mike could respond, Tracy disconnected. She bolted into the street into the path of the diesel with one thought driving her forward – *Jared's safety.*

Brakes screeched. Tires swerved on pavement. Tracy stood erect, daring him to cross the line she had drawn. Anger shot from her eyes like lasers and as Sims' confused gaze found hers, she slammed her hands against the hood of his truck.

"You sick son-of-a-bitch!"

An evil grin lifted from his mouth and before Tracy could break away, he revved the engine and lifted an open bottle to his lips. He said something to the girl and Tracy saw her head fall back with laughter.

"You want me?" Tracy raised her fist and hammered it against the hood with a force she never knew she had. "Then come and get me! I'll be in Newport!"

His smile crumbled and those beady eyes became deadly as he passed the bottle to the side. He shifted the gear and the truck lunged forward, throwing Tracy off balance shoulder-first into the curb. The driver's door flung open. She struggled to her feet, praying that the further she got from Jared the safer he would be. With each frantic stride that burden grew heavier. She heard the diesel roar to life and what little hope she had of escaping faded. But she strained to keep moving, fighting with all her strength to lure her uncle from the only thing she cared about. And from the depth of the heaviness of her heart, an inspiration lighter than air breezed by.

"Most of the important things in the world have been accomplished by people who have kept on trying when there seemed to be no hope at all."

Air filled her lungs. Every pounding crush of pavement moved her forward, giving her strength, building her confidence. She reached the intersection and felt the drone of the diesel close in. Then, from up ahead a flash of headlights cut the darkness. A sports car shot from the curb – whirring through gears as the tires held on for dear life. Her accomplice had come through.

"Thank...God," she wheezed, fighting for air as her uncle accelerated. The turbo 360ed to a screeching stop. The passenger door flew open. Tracy dove into the seat and the car thrust back to life. Zero to sixty in four seconds flat.

Dennis Sims hammered the dashboard. His anger echoed through the cab as he hurled threats. The diesel slowed to a crawl; he took a draw from his cigarette and watched the blur of red taillights disappear into the distance.

Tracy collapsed against the headrest and fought to catch her breath. Flipping the visor, she trembled as the image of the diesel quad-cab grew smaller in the vanity mirror. Her blood-tight grip of the duffle bag strap relaxed and she saw a red whelp where it had cut off her circulation. She rubbed her shoulder and saw that it was bleeding. Exhausted, she exhaled and only then acknowledged the driver.

"Thanks, Eric."

Her fingers shuddered as she tugged her seatbelt into place. With her arms wrenched across her chest, she recoiled into the door. She swiped a tear from her eye and tried to settle her mind on what was ahead. But as the whining roar of the turbo softened to a purr, all she could think of was Jared.

***

Tracy had sworn that Eric would never get her into the air in his family-owned Cresta twin-engine. During their early afternoon text volley she had tried to hold her ground. But his argument of being able to get into Jacksonville and back to Newport faster and more discretely than a commercial airline won her over. The added benefit of being able to take off in the middle of the night undetected convinced her further.

Having dozed off on their way to the airport, Tracy opened her eyes to see they had made the thirty-mile trek without incident.

"Nice rock," Eric noted as he whirled the rental into the hanger lot.

Tracy smiled, brushing her fingers across the marquis solitaire. Then she felt the awkwardness. "Eric, I hope you understand. And I can't thank you enough for doing this and…"

"Don't even say it. My dad hardly uses this plane. Besides, Lauren misses you. She wouldn't have let me back out if I tried," he winked.

Chapter 34

Sunday morning

Newport

By mid- morning, the Cresta 414 had made it into the Oklahoma City airspace and as planned, Eric landed at the Wylie Jones Airport west of the city to avoid being seen in Newport. Once he secured the plane in the hanger, he grabbed Tracy's bags and hustled her across the tarmac.

"I hope you know you're harboring a wanted fugitive here. Just drop me at the rental car place and I'll go to a hotel," Tracy warned.

Eric rolled his eyes. "You're not renting a car and you're not staying at a hotel. Lauren has her spare room ready. Besides, she told me to bring you straight home."

Home. The word hung in the air like a dissonant minor chord. This would never be home again without Jared. All those years she had prayed for him to return, and now she was praying that he would stay as far away from Newport as he could. *Home?* Not here. Not without him. She closed her eyes and felt that lonely isolation of the past four years set up residence. Like a bolt of lightning, the thought of enduring another separation jolted her senses.

"No!" She shouted. "There's no time. I need to get to Sutherant. And I've got to see the computer system my dad was using."

Eric looked at his watch. "It won't be safe until after hours. Even though this is Sunday some people are..."

"Eric, Denny knows I'm here! He probably has half the town out looking for me. I can't waste time."

Eric ran his fingers through his hair - his tell-tell sign of worry.

"I can't guarantee you won't be seen," he stressed.

Tracy shrugged. "It's the only chance I've got."

"No, there's one more," he suggested. "Let's stop by Lauren's for a disguise."

***

One quarter of a mile. That was the distance between Lauren's house and downtown Newport. And as many times as Tracy had casually walked, jogged, biked, or driven that short span in her life, the drive toward the Sutherant Petroleum office now seemed like a never-ending road to Hell. A town that had at one time been a welcome mat of comfort and warmth was now confining and cold. Tracy scanned the storefronts and houses stretched along Main Street and felt the walls slowly close in. Her throat tightened and once again she pictured those cattle head gates from the farm. Phil Murphy crossed her mind and with that vision she felt as trapped as those cattle, aimlessly stumbling toward slaughter.

Eric circled the perimeter of the Sutherant complex before choosing a parking spot. Instead of the reserved employee lot where he normally parked, he opted for a space in an empty lot across the street where he knew security cameras would not be in use. As the engine died, so did Tracy's confidence. Her nerves were so tangled she could barely breathe. She turned in her seat and scanned the old familiar buildings. Only new addition was the deafening pulse of the neon sign flashing in her mind: *danger, danger, danger!* But her need to keep Jared safe pounded louder. She closed her eyes and inhaled, trusting that the key to Jared's safety lie hidden within those walls.

"We'll go straight to the back and use the employee door. Keep your head down and just act like you belong here," Eric cautioned.

Tracy adjusted her wig and reading glasses and pulled the belt of Lauren's gray business suit a bit tighter. Eric straightened his own tie and grabbed his briefcase before casting one final glance Tracy's way.

"Once we're inside, my office is just a couple of doors down," Eric explained.

"I know where the computer offices are," Tracy smirked. The sweet memory of visiting her dad at work so often sparked in her eyes, but the bitter pain of returning to his workplace for the first time since his death was tough.

"Well, nobody's expecting me to be in today so once we get to my office we shouldn't have any interruptions," he encouraged. He patted her hand. "It'll be okay."

Tracy exhaled and forced a smile, reflexively reaching over to hug him.

"I'm so sorry about all of this, Eric. You've already risked your job and..."

"I want to help." He jerked his head toward Sutherant. "I've spent four years trying to figure out your dad's research. The FBI and some of the best computer techs I know have gotten nowhere. I'm counting on you to work a miracle in there."

Still holding her in a loose embrace, he leaned in and kissed her forehead and for a moment, the familiarity of her touch drew him closer. Tracy hesitated then loosened her hold. Suddenly aware of her unease, Eric pulled away. A smile broke at the corner of Tracy's mouth and on impulse she unlatched her seatbelt, turned in her seat, and shook her head.

"If you had told me a week ago I would ever feel uncomfortable in your arms, I would have said you were crazy," she chuckled.

"Lauren seems to like 'em," he teased, playfully pushing her away.

Tracy looked more closely into his eyes. "And if you ever hurt her you will deal with me. Got it?"

"Message received. Ready to do this?"

"Yes," she lied.

They stepped from the truck and crossed the street to the rear entrance, out of view of the front security gate. Eric swiped his security badge through the slot and with a slight click that seemed oddly subtle for such a high security facility, the lock popped.

When the door swung open Tracy went on alert. At the far end of the hallway a janitor leaned against his cart. Tracy stiffened, not knowing why the sight gave her such a start. But the more she studied the man – his light blue jumpsuit, the embroidered Sutherant Petroleum logo emblazoned on the sleeve – the more she was certain where she had first seen Phil Murphy.

"That's where I know him from," she whispered. "Right after Daddy died. Phil Murphy came to the house with Denny. He was wearing that same blue uniform."

"A janitor?" Eric questioned.

Tracy nodded. "In disguise."

She went on to explain Phil's constant appeal for her father's password, the incessant attempts to access her father's computer system, the agitated search of her home, and his choice of words to her uncle when he turned to leave – "Just keep me in the loop, Brother." It all had become suddenly clear. Phil Murphy had been a part of her uncle's corruptive ploy all along. But one other memory of that night weighed on her mind more than Phil Murphy. He had not come to her house alone. Sheriff Lowell McClain had accompanied him.

Once they made it to the main computer offices her father had managed years before, Eric paused to scan his security card. Tracy noticed the updated placard on the door.

Integrated Technology and Finances – Eric Williams, Manager. "Looks good," she nodded. She floated her fingers along the inscription, inwardly remembering her father's name in its place.

The heavy steel door swung open exposing a darkened unfriendly room. Eric flicked on the lights and Tracy's attention came alive at the sight of the spotless, white-tiled floor and bare walls – white walls, screaming for a personal touch. Rectangular six-foot, white granite-topped slabs stretched across the floor, meticulously arranged in formation like a military barracks. Perched atop each 'bed' sat pristine bays of cold, state-of-the-art computers, all symmetrically white to match the sparse furnishings: swivel chairs, copiers, waste baskets, telephones, and fluorescent light fixtures. Each neighboring bay identical - starkly white, obsessively clean, rigidly organized. Sweeping the computer room from corner to corner confirmed the mirror image of some kind of hospital ward – a sanitized, secure unit for the mentally unstable.

"Love what you've done to the place," Tracy sneered.

"Thank the new board of directors for that. They made some changes a couple of years ago – about the time I really started to hate my job," he grimaced.

Easing further into the coldness of the room, Tracy swept her hand along the equipment, impressed by the advanced technology. Remembering the exterior façade, she saw the place for what she had discerned it to be – an international business that was covert, corrupt, and crooked in every way. She had one chance to uncover the truth. Knowing Jared's safety was in the balance, she strode to the mainframe and powered up the system, praying for a miracle.

Chapter 35

Sunday morning

Jacksonville

"Dammit, Mike! It's not my safety I'm worried about. Tracy's gone!" Jared leaned against the kitchen counter and yanked yesterday's jeans over his boxers. He had just rolled out of bed to find his life turned upside down. "If she's in Savannah I've got to go and help her. I've seen her dad's program. She'll never break those computer codes without me."

Jodie set a cup of coffee on the counter and rubbed Jared's shoulders. Mike lifted a manila file from his briefcase and spread the contents across the kitchen table.

"We have no proof that's where she is. Now, I was going to wait on this, but I'll go ahead and get you up to speed on some things." He fanned handwritten notes, surveillance photos, and various case files in front of Jared.

Jared sat in silence as Mike referenced each piece of undercover intelligence – information depicting the latest evidence of Phil Murphy's suspected involvement in the criminal activities surrounding Sutherant Petroleum. Admitting that Tracy's own assertion of Phil's presence in the state park had been a key turning point in the investigation, Mike explained that it had become apparent that Phil had been secretly collaborating with Dennis Sims to destroy evidence in order to protect members of Congress.

"He's not alone, Jared. Five years ago your dad was working with Lowell McClain to gather his own evidence against some of Sutherant's political investors. When Tracy's dad stepped forward and produced records of their financial crimes, the FBI went undercover to monitor foreign suppliers and international trade negotiations. Senator Hastings of Colorado came on board to testify against several members of Congress. That's when Phil was assigned to the case."

"To protect my dad. That was a few months before we left town," confirmed Jared.

"Right, but what you may not know is that's about the time everything started to fall apart. Hastings and the company lawyer were killed so your dad was forced into hiding. That left the business wide open for a take-over." Mike sipped his coffee.

"Eric Williams said Tracy's dad stored the bulk of the incriminating evidence in his private files," added Jared.

"And shuffled so many financial accounts around it practically pushed the company into bankruptcy."

"Intentionally?"

"Actually, yes, it was part of your dad's plan. He had Mark hide the liquid money until the investigation was over. So Mark locked the company assets and most of the laundered money they planned to use as evidence into untraceable accounts. That was right before he died. Your dad gradually built their holdings back up, but the majority of Sutherant's money has been inaccessible."

"That's why Phil is so eager to get me into the system."

"I'm sure he's after the money, but he also has to keep you from discovering their counterfeit ring."

"Counterfeit ring? Phil was like family. How'd I not see it?" Jared snapped. Jodie topped off Jared's coffee.

"He posed as a U.S. Marshall in front of you and your mom. For others he was just another member of security for Sutherant. In reality, he's been an agent for the FBI, but obviously he's gone bad. He can't be trusted."

"And my dad lied about the witness relocation and purposely kept me away from Tracy!" Jared shouted.

"Not away from Tracy - away from Newport. And it's a damn good thing he did. It probably saved both of your lives. What's more, if he hadn't covertly hid your family in Wyoming, Phil would have found you sooner." Mike explained. "When Murphy found out you had surfaced, he reappeared. He's been waiting for you to figure out that computer."

Jared thrust his chair back and bolted to his feet. He pressed his hands to his head and paced the floor, his shoulders shuddering from the anger.

"I'm going to Savannah!" Jared snapped.

"You can't, Jared. You could end up getting killed. Give me a chance to figure this out. Besides, Phil concerns me. Nobody's heard from him since your meeting yesterday."

Jared shuffled to the couch and collapsed into the cushions. He unfolded Tracy's note, straining to hear her voice in the cold words.

You'll be in danger as long as we're together. Find a safe place and wait for me. You know how much I love you, and you know I'm only doing this for us.

Always ~ T.

Word by word his heart chipped away. He let the note float to the floor then raised his hands to unleash his fingers through his hair. His face reflected who he really was – a man whose whole world had come crashing down. Mike placed his big burly paw across his shoulder.

"I know you don't want to hear it, but the best thing you can do is let me help protect you until this is over."

Jared snatched up the note and crushed it in his fist. Taking two steps at a time, he raced up the stairs to pack his things. With or without Mike, he had to follow his heart.

Chapter 36

Sunday – late morning

Newport

Eric sat patiently as Tracy scribbled one combination of password possibilities after another in her attempt to access the program. Having learned the mechanics and operations of the system, she still could not break through the security wall that her father had designed. It would take the one unique password and electronic security code sequence to gain access.

It was almost noon and Tracy was tired, discouraged, and hungry. Between the lack of sleep and the knot of worry wrenching her gut, her focus was sporadic at best.

"I need a break," she moaned. "Take me back to Lauren's and I'll try again after lunch."

***

Once alone in Lauren's guest room, Tracy stretched out on the bed, mentally re-living her morning. Just hours before, she was nestled beside Jared, post-euphoria, listening to the soft hum of his breathing. Now the closest thing she had was the series of text messages he had sent begging her to return his call. She took another look at his most recent message and weakened, almost giving in. Almost. Once she heard his voice, she knew she would be past hope and would agree to anything he said. But she could not risk Jared knowing she was in Newport.

After a long, steamy shower she tightened the towel around her and scrunched her fingers through her wet hair, processing her jumbled thoughts. She plopped down on the bed and noticed her phone screen saver was fully illuminated. She smiled - *Jared again*. But at the moment, her mind was focused on another Frazier.

She slipped into some jeans and a Henley tee then entered the living room where Lauren and Eric were talking.

"Lauren, I need a favor. Drive me to Frazier's house?" Lauren glanced at Eric, unsure of how to answer. "I have to talk to him," Tracy added.

Eric scooted to the edge of the couch. "Tracy, Frazier is not the kind of man you just pop in on and if you…"

"I need to talk with him," Tracy snapped. "Or do you think I should just invite him over here?"

Eric's eyes widened.

"I didn't think so," she scoffed.

Chapter 37

Sunday - late morning

Newport

An unexpected cold front rode in on a northwest breeze. The perfect sky faded behind a veil of gray clouds. Distant thunder rumbled as Lauren searched the horizon. Stepping onto the front porch, she threw a quick wave to Tracy who was waiting in the car. Eric bumped her with his shoulder.

"Weather's turning," he warned.

"We won't be long."

"I know it wouldn't do a bit of good to try and talk her out of this."

Lauren pointed to the sky. "You could sooner change the direction of that storm than Tracy's mind. And I'm not about to let her go to Frazier's alone." She started down the steps then glanced back. "Will you be here when we get back?"

Without answering, he stepped down beside her. His kiss was light and tender.

"I'm not going anywhere."

"Good," she smiled. "Make yourself at home."

Lauren darted to her small sports car. As she climbed in, Tracy closed her notepad and fastened her seatbelt.

"He's worried," Lauren admitted. "So much has happened this past week he's afraid Frazier may have some company who may not want to be surprised."

"It's not Frazier's company I plan to see," Tracy quipped. But seeing the concern on Lauren's face, she softened. "So what happened this past week?"

"A secretary from Sutherant came to the *Tribune* to see Jim Crenshaw." Lauren waved to Eric as she backed out the drive. "According to Gavin who's been working the front desk, it was the third time in two days she had been in asking to see him. Naturally, I was curious."

"Someone from Sutherant actually came to the paper? I thought they usually faxed or emailed their stories to us."

"She wasn't bringing in a story," Lauren corrected. "She was there to *dispute* a story that was already in the works. Evidently Jim had run a couple of commentaries about a friend of hers who was running for State Senate."

"Commentaries?"

"More like allegations – you know Jim. He was hammering the guy for cheating on his wife, so Sutherant pulled their political support from him because it was about to go public. But the girl swore that Jim had fabricated the whole scandal."

Lauren stopped for on-coming traffic.

"Surely he checked his sources," Tracy wondered.

"Well, she sounded pretty sure he didn't. She accused Jim of using the press to destroy her friend's chances of being elected. Started yelling..."

"Yelling?"

Lauren nodded. "Evidently her friend discovered evidence of kickbacks and unethical favors between some political big wigs and Sutherant investors."

Tracy shook her head and adjusted her seat belt.

"You know the strange part?" Lauren continued. "Jim never denied it. He just closed down his computer and walked out the door."

"So what's your take on it?" asked Tracy.

"I did some background checks on Kyle Monroe this morning," Lauren confided.

"Who is that?"

"That's the girl's friend, the one running for State Senate. He owned one of those cars whose tag you had me check from Frazier's little meeting. According to Grant this guy is squeaky clean. Very respected over in northwest Arkansas. Has a lot of big business support around Fayetteville and until this information from Jim came out, had a spotless reputation. Real choir boy."

Tracy opened her pad and scribbled some notes. "And Jim still plans to run the article?"

"Unless I can prove he's lying."

"Have you told Dothan any of this?"

"Not a word. He was out of the office all weekend and I didn't go in today so he doesn't know. The reason I told you is because you're about to see Frazier and I want you to know what you're walking into."

Tracy leaned back into her seat. Suspicions and speculations were swimming in her mind and coming back to Newport suddenly felt like a huge mistake. Jim Crenshaw, Waylon Vincent, and her uncle were working together to keep Sutherant's crimes hidden. Jared's confidant, Phil Murphy, was being investigated by Internal Affairs as a possible accomplice in the murder of Brody Craig. And in four more miles Lauren's car would pull into the drive of the man who was controlling them all. How would she approach him? What's more, once she did, how would he react? And what would he do knowing she was back in Newport trying to access the evidence that would destroy his company?

Lauren slowed as she approached the business district. She passed the post office and waved when she saw Connie

Wright, her science teacher from eighth grade. Tracy cowered into the seat, fearful of being seen in Newport. That's when the truth backhanded her in the face: she was as much a fugitive as Jared and hiding was now an inescapable part of her life.

***

The long, foreboding driveway seemed to cast a spell over unsuspecting visitors. Lauren edged through the gate and proceeded up the winding incline toward the mansion. Tracy felt herself being drawn into danger. She likened it to a beautiful spider web – an enticing trap luring prey until the spider could pounce, expose its sharp fangs, and inject its debilitating poison. And here she was - the powerless prey.

Lauren slowed to a stop in the shadow of the massive doorway. As Tracy opened the passenger door, every sound carried, as if the entire estate were a vacuum in and of itself. Even the groan of the car door vibrated through the air. With every step toward the doorway, she felt her pulse rush. Her only calming diversion was to think of Jared. With that thought, her heart slowed, saddened by the fact that he had once lived this terror day to day.

When Tracy reached the front door, it opened from inside. A brawny man dressed in gray slacks and a tight navy pullover held the door as she waited. She tossed a futile wave toward Lauren who remained in the idling car, then followed the man into the foyer.

In a dizzying spin of the room she felt suddenly small and inferior in the shadow of the high, cathedral ceiling. The cryptic, dark paneled walls swallowed her and she weakened in the vastness of the room. She thought of Jared and for the briefest moment, felt his presence. Maybe it was wishful thinking. Or maybe it was that she was scared out of her mind and needed him. Then again, maybe she finally understood what it had been like for him to have grown up in this kind of cold, overbearing environment.

"Wait here." Tracy whirled toward the command. The door shut with a *check-mate* finality and moments later she heard footsteps coming from the other direction. And suddenly, there he was -- David Frazier: aloof, domineering, and untouchable - everything Jared would never be.

He was taller and heavier than she had remembered and the thick wavy, brown hair she had always admired had thinned and dulled to a salt and pepper gray. Still, she could easily see the resemblance and had to hide her smile as she sensed how truly handsome Jared was destined to be as he aged. She calculated the numbers and guessed Frazier to be fifty-five, recalling that he was five years older than her dad who had died four years ago at forty-six. His faded boot cuts and Green Bay Packers sweatshirt took her by surprise. But the look suited him, and again she had to hide a smile. The Packers. At least there was one thing he and Jared had in common.

"Tracy Sims." His baritone voice was melodic, almost friendly. But the expensive furnishings and the Gatsby-like display screamed crime and deceit. Tracy was reminded of the spider's lure and she instantly went on guard.

"For now anyway. Jared and I are engaged." A twinge of pain shot through her as the spiteful words spilled out. Her announcement took him off-guard, she sensed. As if reading her mind, his face contorted, and as the wrinkles spread across his brow, she saw how much he had aged.

"I see. Well…then… welcome to the family."

Tracy heard the struggle in his voice. But as she looked on the man who had caused such pain and heartache for Jared, she felt nothing but resentment. This was not how it should be. For so long she had dreamed of being beside Jared as they announced their engagement. But in all the times she had envisioned this very moment, she had never imagined it feeling so empty, so deflating.

"I'm sure he would have rather told you himself, but in light of the fact that your *security* has been instructed to shoot him on sight..."

"Things aren't always what they seem." His face softened. "But it's not safe for either of you here," he added in a near-whisper.

"I'm only here because I need to know if we can trust --" He shot his finger to his lips. He extended his hand and led her toward a door at the rear of the long hallway.

He unlatched the deadbolt and waved her into a small tree-lined courtyard, then deeper into the yard.

"Some fresh air will do us good," he whispered as they shuffled along the gravel pathway. He didn't say another word until they reached a hedge lining the back fence.

"Now, you were saying something about trust?" The stress-lines had disappeared from his face, and as Tracy studied his actions, she saw some of the familiar qualities she used to admire begin to surface: the way he held the door and helped her through the gate, the whimsical twinkle in his eyes when he smiled, his soft voice and gentle touch she remembered from years ago when she first became friends with Jared. And as she replayed their mad rush to exit the house, it hit her that he had not been rude at all. He just could not speak freely in the confines of the house.

"Yes. So why have your employees been threatening us?"

"As I said, things aren't always as they seem."

"No, they're not. Like the fact that Jared and I have obviously been confused with someone else. We don't know anything about a code or computer password or whatever else your company needs. We have no part in any of this!"

"You and Jared have much more to do with this than you realize."

"And I guess once we tell you our *great big secret* there will be no reason to keep us alive. I get it."

"No, Tracy, you don't get it," he lowered his voice and continued. "Do you really think I would harm you?"

She looked down at her hands, up to the trees – anywhere to avoid his eyes. Her answer was clear.

"Years ago when the company really started taking off, your dad and I discovered some of the investors were using Sutherant as a front for their own business ventures. By the time we realized it, small minor indiscretions had spread to blatant illegal trade between Congressional leaders and some of our overseas investors. Your dad started keeping records, accounting for every dime that was spent and every action that was done under the name of Sutherant Petroleum - backing everything up on his personal computer. That's when we got the FBI involved."

Personal computer – the words caught Tracy by surprise. Her dad had no personal computer. The only computer she ever saw him use was the company laptop he brought home from time to time.

"Some of these investors served together in the military and had enough skills to infiltrate the business without ever being noticed. They had so much influence in foreign markets that before we could stop it, they had taken control of every part of the company and had secured foreign investors to protect their interests. Sutherant became an international network of kickbacks and conspiracy almost overnight."

"Using U.S. seaports to import and export their goods, right? Savannah? Galveston? Tacoma?"

Frazier turned in surprise. "You've done your research." Just to the right of the pathway was a small granite bench in the shade of a magnolia tree. Frazier slipped his hand beneath her elbow and with his free hand, brushed the stray petals and twigs away. The gesture, she noticed, was as considerate as what his son would have done. She smiled and scooted to one side to make room for him.

"Once they heard there was an investigation underway, they took every measure they could to keep it all hidden. Your dad worked night and day to gather evidence while I kept the investors close and maintained this façade of running the company." He waved his hand around the property and as Tracy followed the sweeping motion, her stomach churned at the overwhelming size of the property. "To some I am Sutherant Petroleum – the most lucrative oil manufacturer in the Midwest. To others, I am the driving force behind the most covert organized crime ring in the United States. And still, there is a handful of trusted friends who know the real me – a man who has been betrayed and swindled out of everything I own, trying to find justice, and maybe regain a little peace I lost along the way. But right now, my only concern is to protect you and Jared. So I'll say it again. Things are not always as they seem."

Tracy felt her throat tighten and had to look away. But knowing that she and Jared had been used as innocent pawns fired new anger through her.

"My father was killed. And you alienated Jared for most of his childhood. You even sent him away from me and now we are running for our lives. I hardly call that protecting us."

Frazier looked over his shoulder. A commercial jet streamed a trail far in the distant eastern sky and even that triggered a cautious glance. Frazier leaned closer and whispered. "Believe me, Tracy, every decision Mark and I ever made was to protect you and Jared. That night, your dad --"

Tracy whirled around. "I know, I know...you were already safely out of town the night my father was killed!"

Frazier shook his head and exhaled a long breath. "What I was going to say is that Mark called me to let me know he was on his way to a meeting. He wanted to meet with Sheriff McClain before we turned over the evidence to the FBI."

"Wait – you mean Daddy knew how to reach you?

He nodded. "And he could not risk telling you. Jared was already in hiding and contacting him would have been too dangerous."

"Daddy knew all along and didn't tell me? Do you know what that separation did to us? Do you even care how much Jared and I needed each other?" she gasped.

"We never planned on a separation. Your dad was actually arranging to send you with Jared but it all happened too fast. But not telling you probably saved both of your lives. In fact, Mark had agreed to a deal with your uncle and his partners to plea bargain your and Jared's protection."

Tracy glanced up. "Those papers," she thought aloud. "The night your family left, my uncle had Daddy sign some papers. That power of attorney was to help Jared?"

"Your dad was willing to give anything – even control of his farm if it meant keeping you and Jared safe."

The idea of her father protecting Jared in his last hours made years of doubt crumble away. A part of her had always resented her father's motives and now she saw just how much he had tried to help them.

"Unfortunately," Frazier continued, "he didn't find out your uncle was double-crossing him until after he had signed."

"But his will negated the power of attorney," Tracy mumbled to herself. She saw Frazier's confusion. "Jared met with a lawyer who explained that legally Daddy had signed the farm over to him in a will."

"Well, if your uncle knows this that explains why they are hunting Jared."

Tracy's heart skipped. Her uncle, she knew, would do anything to keep Jared from gaining control of the farm. In that instant she wanted to trust Frazier with all that she knew. She locked eyes with him and like a cool breeze, Dale Carnegie's words whisked across her mind - *keep on trying when there seems no hope at all.* Her only hope was to trust him with everything. Suddenly, a huge weight lifted from her soul. "I need to tell you what Jared and I know."

In her next few breaths she confided all she had learned about Sutherant Petroleum: the military connection, Phil Murphy's involvement, her suspicions of her uncle, Jim Crenshaw, and the Newport Police Department, the Congressional Committees and the suspected murders of Senator Hastings and family, Hank Tisdale, Officer Hadley, and her father.

"I regret so much in my life, Tracy. I never meant for you and Jared to get mixed up in this," he sighed, rising from the bench. "When we lost Alli, all I could do was pour myself into this company. I couldn't bear to be in that house. In a lot of ways, I couldn't bear to be around Linda or Jared. It just never felt right. I just never stopped to see how much Alli's death had affected them."

He leaned closer. His face was worn and full of regret. Still, she saw so many traces of Jared in him – the same shallow cleft in his chin; his full, broad shoulders that carried so much more burden than they ever should; the strong, calloused hands that felt so tender when they slipped around hers. And like Jared, the emotional pain of the past had left lasting scars.

"I sacrificed too much time with my family trying to make this company successful – your dad tried to tell me that so many times. Now I 've had to spend years trying to keep others from destroying it." Tracy nodded and felt his arm stretch across her shoulder. It felt so much like her own father's touch from years before she let her head fall against his chest. "Which brings me to now. I called Linda last night and told her I've fought this corruption too long – played by the rules and did everything the FBI said, waiting and hoping they could finally bring me some justice. I'm to the point I'm beginning to think they are dragging this investigation on intentionally," he chuckled. "But to Hell with it! You and Jared are too important. We won't sacrifice your safety any longer."

For a moment his choice of pronouns made her pause, but she brushed it away to get more answers. "Why are we such a threat? Are they still afraid of something Dad found in his research over four years ago?"

A squirrel shimmied down a nearby tree and rustled the leaves. Frazier flinched at the noise then explained. "Have you heard of a black market cartel called Green Dragon?"

His low whisper put Tracy on edge. She nodded and the mood became suddenly grim.

"North Korean underworld," she acknowledged. "Terrorist group back during the nineties – like our present-day Taliban, or so I've heard."

Frazier ran his hands through his hair and Tracy could feel the nervous heat emitting from his body. She watched as his arms collapsed to his side and just before she glanced away, saw his hands tremble.

"They're still active, Tracy. Stronger than ever. There's a masochist named Te Lei Soon who operates out of Chicago. Gets his kicks marketing hallucinogens – opium, ecstasy and the like. Most of the meth imported into the U.S. is tied to him in some way. Along with drugs he targets teenage girls as his playmates. From what I hear, yanks 'em right off the street."

"I've seen the name in an article about sex-slave trade and child prostitution."

"Right family, wrong generation. That's his father's claim to fame. And not a damned thing our government can do about it. But my concern is in Te Lei, the son. The FBI has evidence that he helped orchestrate a counterfeiting operation for some Congressional leaders and a group of investors from Eastern Europe. Your dad stumbled across a fraudulent trade deal they were hatching and because it stemmed from Sutherant, he started asking questions. He threaded together such a tight paper trail he could have indicted half of Congress. It's all right there in his computer files."

"And they think Jared and I have access?"

Frazier nodded.

"That's one of the reasons for the security." He waved his hand around the grounds. "I don't have to tell you the measures they will take to keep anyone from finding that information. Can you imagine the ramifications of exposing Congress as a counterfeit operation? We'd be signing our death warrant. So far I've been pretty convincing at playing my role – the unaware owner who shuts his eyes to every illegal action. But I have a very select group in place, who along with the FBI, are continuing what your dad started."

"Adding to the paper trail?"

"And watching my back," Frazier added. "Politically, we have support and they can arrange a safe house and a new identity for you."

"Safe house? No! There is no way I can leave this undone."

"Tracy, one of the most powerful operations in our history is at work here, and if news of this gets out that the billions they have been using are counterfeit, the outcome would be catastrophic for our economy. Your dad never thought…none of us knew how big this was until it was too late. And I kind of half laughed a minute ago, but I truly believe the FBI is not here to put a stop to it; they're here to make sure that evidence stays hidden. From what I hear, your research in the past weeks has made them nervous. Not to mention Jared is no longer under their protection. Can you understand how critical it is for you both to disappear?"

He reached into his pocket and pulled out his wallet. "Here, I want to show you something." He slipped a dollar bill from an inner compartment of his leather tri-fold and handed it to her. "Did your dad ever tell you he was the one who gave me the loan to get the company started?" Tracy examined the bill. "He may have carried the title VP of Finance, but he was also Co-owner. This happens to be the first dollar Sutherant Petroleum ever made. Your dad and I signed it and I have carried it for twenty-five years." He pointed to a penned message as Tracy looked on.

Faith, Family, Friendship, Fortune: May we always know their strength.

Tracy ran her finger across the inscription and smiled as she traced her dad's signature. How many times had she heard her father recite that very sentiment? She handed it back and watched Frazier slide the bill back into his wallet. "Your dad knew what was important in life. His only thought was to protect you. That's why he shared the codes with Jared – thinking that would somehow give you leverage if anything ever happened to him."

"Until my uncle found out."

Frazier nodded. "Stay away from him. Now that his little enterprise is unraveling he'll be like a shedding snake – panicking and striking at everything within reach. Your dad never realized how dangerous it would be for you. Believe me, Tracy. He wouldn't want you to get in any deeper."

Tracy looked back toward the house, aware that Lauren was waiting. "I need to go. But could I ask a favor?"

"Anything."

"Talk to Jared. He's so broken. He's carried so much anger over the years and if he could know how you feel…"

He hesitated then cleared his throat.

"I will. And I hope after this…well, just try and understand that everything was done with the best intentions. It's time for all of us to be a family again."

Tracy listened to his words and found she was doing just that – trying to understand. He had a way of mixing words that made it hard to follow. But oddly, in just the few minutes they had been together, she trusted him. After exchanging personal cell phone numbers, they shuffled along the path toward the courtyard gate. Frazier released her hand to lift the latch then offered a final warning.

"Remember – eyes and ears." He pointed around the perimeter and pressed his finger to his lips.

Once inside the courtyard, the abrasive Frazier returned. Tracy cowered in his shadow. When they approached the front foyer, Frazier waved the *sentinel* away and once their path to the door was clear, he took her by the arm and whispered.

"Leave Newport. Stay as far from here as you can until we can find a safe house. And Tracy, do not trust anyone."

He squeezed her hand and she saw a subtle wink.

"Miss Johnson," his voice boomed. "We have no further business and as I said, the *Tribune* will just have to find another source for your story on Oklahoma oil production. Now, good day."

Tracy backed out of the door unable to look away. The layers of doubt and fear had been scraped away and as she looked on him now, she could see so much of his son in him. The stature, the softness around his eyes, his playful grin, the compassion, the honesty – all melding to form the man Jared now mirrored.

From inside she heard the telephone ring and shivered as she thought of the articles she had read about the Soon family connections. She turned and hurried to Lauren's car, straining to hear the doorman's voice – eager to know if the call had anything to do with her. But his low, gravelly voice was overshadowed by Frazier's ominous warning still sounding clearly in her mind. *Leave Newport...find a safe house.* With more urgency than ever, she rushed to the car and finalized her plan to break into the Sutherant offices.

Chapter 38

Sunday – early afternoon

Jacksonville

A thousand miles away Dennis Sims hunkered deeper into the seat of the compact rental and eased his cell phone from his left pocket, somewhat comforted by the familiar sound of his girlfriend's voice. The driveway of a vacated neighbor's house provided an ideal view of both the front and rear entrance to Jodie and Kevin Mason's house. At Sims' right side, the tracking monitor emitted an array of green and red trails of light. The incessant humming had not stopped since the early morning hours when he had first pulled into the riverfront community – about the same time Tracy had shot out into the street and scared the Hell out of him.

"How much longer do you plan to wait?" Salgado asked as she negotiated Sims' diesel through freeway traffic just east of New Orleans.

"It was the middle of the night when that little bitch slipped away. That tells me Jared Frazier didn't know she was leaving." Sims glanced at his watch. "It's going on twelve-thirty. That agent has kept everyone inside all morning. He's either trying to figure out where she is or he's holding up in there until she comes back. Either way, I don't move until Frazier does."

Sims popped a handful of sunflower seeds into his mouth and recited instructions for Salgado. "Find her as soon as you get to Newport and don't let her out of your sight. When I finish with Frazier, I'll be on my way."

***

Several hundred miles northeast in a small rural town in northern Virginia, covert government activity was a normal way of life. Various business owners, school administrators, and local homeowners in the surrounding area had come to regard classified government operations as commonplace, routine. For that reason, the procedures around the obscure airstrip and aircraft maintenance hangers went unnoticed. Few suspected that the FBI was conducting undercover operations behind the ordinary aviation front.

The aviation hanger came alive toward mid-morning when word came down that Robert Murphy, Director of Internal Affairs for the FBI, and Carol Mayhew, Assistant Director of the FBI, would be accompanying a special investigative team to Savannah, Georgia, to examine shipping operations of Sutherant Petroleum. Two Longsteane jets, a Drug Enforcement unit, and two teams from the Office of Firearms and Explosives were assembled for the on-going internal investigation of two sub-committees of Congress.

***

In Jacksonville, Mike Richardson shifted the phone to hear the final details of Operation Southport, the FBI infiltration of the Savannah branch of Sutherant Petroleum. Jared paced beside him, nervously twisting a kitchen towel between his hands. Mike glanced at Kevin who was helping Jodie clear dishes from the kitchen table. His conversation came to a close and as soon as he disconnected, Jared peppered him with questions.

"So it's a go? They approved the flight? We're heading to Georgia?"

Mike held his hands at chest level. "Hold on, Jared. Yes, they want to fly us out. They want us in D.C. for a debriefing then on to Savannah where they can," Mike emphasized the quotations visually, "'tighten' your security." Mike scanned the faces that were staring back at him. "But I don't like it. We're not going to Savannah. I'm getting you back to Newport."

Jared chunked the towel to the floor. "Are you insane? We just barely made it out of there alive! Why the Hell would I go back to Newport?"

Mike stared him down. "Because Director Robert Murphy, who happens to be Phil's father, just told me in confidence that Tracy is there. He's sending his entire unit to Savannah as a decoy, but he's going with us to Newport."

The room closed in. Jared collapsed into a chair and cradled his head. "Oh, my God."

Mike rolled up his sleeves and swept the scattered papers back into the file. He lowered his voice then ushered them all into the living room.

"We've got company outside. Everybody stay away from the windows and do what I say. I'm going to put a little diversion in the works to help us vacate the premises. Kevin, Jodie, sorry to say that includes you as well. I need you to pack a bag and get to a hotel for the next few days, just until I know it's safe. Register in a name other than your own. No credit cards, cash only. And Kevin, if you can take a few days off work to just lay low, that'd be best."

"Whatever we need to do, Mike," Kevin confirmed, draping his arm around Jodie's shoulder.

"Jared, you and I are going to catch a private charter to D.C.," Mike continued. "Director Murphy has been following this case as long as me. He needs you to take a look at some of the evidence he's compiled and I'm sure he will want to conduct a formal deposition. Then we'll head to Newport. Knowing the danger involved, that'll be the last place anybody looks for you."

Kevin ducked away to gather a couple of duffle bags and his personal automatic handgun that he would loan to Jared. Like Tracy, he too had a sixth sense when it came to measuring trust. The protective nature inside him wanted to get to Newport as fast as he could to find Tracy. But the business-side of him knew to stay calm – read all the players' faces and be certain of the next move. That's what had him on edge. Mike Richardson had one helluva poker face. Truth was, Kevin didn't know who to trust.

Chapter 39

Monday – early evening

Newport

With the blinds drawn to conceal her presence, Tracy reclined on the couch passing the first real alone time with Lauren since the whirlwind of her ordeal began. Sharing pretzels, iced tea, and gossip, they lazily tossed a small stuffed toy into each other's lap as Snickers, Lauren's cocker spaniel, licked and pawed her way between them. Tracy relaxed into the carefree frolic, realizing that whatever had stressed Lauren since their run-in with Frazier's guards had disappeared.

While much of the conversation gravitated toward their research and latest discoveries, the freedom to share in intimate girl talk quickly returned. Tracy hugged her knees into her chest and smiled as the topic turned to Jared.

"Sounds like you two just picked up where you left off back in high school," Lauren ruffled Snicker's fur and stretched her legs toward Tracy.

"It really never ended," Tracy mused, "even while we were apart I guess we were both still committed to each other. And God, he was so worth the wait," she blushed.

"You're glowing, girlfriend."

"Most perfect night of my life…until I had to sneak back here to Newport." Tracy felt her eyes moisten and quickly changed direction. "How are things with Eric? Tell me about that."

Lauren fluffed her pillow and chuckled. "Aw, you know me. Just having a little fun." She tossed a stuffed toy toward Snickers. "I mean he's great, don't get me wrong. Helluva kisser, as you well know."

"You don't sound very serious," Tracy urged. "By the looks of things, you two…"

"Don't read anything into it, Sherlock," Lauren interrupted, attaching the endearment as she often did when Tracy was close to uncovering something big. She snatched another pretzel from the bag. "Not really sure if he's my type. Besides, I'm not ready to be…exclusive."

Tracy's memory flipped through the years and landed in their early teens – a late-night game of Mystery Date as she watched Lauren swoon over the various "studs" the board game had to offer. With every opened door Lauren found something good about the man who appeared – even the "dud" who, Lauren insisted, had irresistibly sexy eyes behind those broken glasses. Tracy shook her head and smiled. "Just like high school - me and Jared, you and -- "

"Please don't say, 'all the rest,'" Lauren giggled.

Tracy rolled her eyes. "I wouldn't dare. I was going to say whoever was lucky enough to have you." Tracy shook the fuzzy from Snickers and tossed it to Lauren. "Have you told him how you feel?"

"He knows where we stand." A twinge of unease made her look away. "Don't say anything to him, but I kind of have a feeling there's more to his role in this. Something just tells me to keep my dis…"

Before Lauren could finish, Snickers unleashed a warning and Eric bolted through the door weighted down with a keyboard, monitor, and bulky desktop computer balanced between his arms. Tracy scrambled to help with the load while Lauren cleared the coffee table and held Snickers out of the way.

"Just figured it would be safer to bring the work to you," he explained to Tracy. "You seemed to know what you were doing this morning so you may as well work from here. I can tap into the Sutherant network and nobody will ever know."

Once he had the computer situated, he leaned into Lauren to whisper in her ear. Lauren grinned then tossed the stuffed play toy back into Tracy's lap. Grabbing Eric's hand, she ran with him to the door. Tracy listened as they giggled and chased each other out to the car, returning seconds later with two pizzas and a chocolate cake.

"I ran into Stan Dothan in town," Eric explained as he held the door for Lauren. "He stuffed two twenties in my hand and told me to buy this. I'm to remind you both that you owe him an exclusive when you finish your research." Eric set the food on the table then turned to Tracy. "He also said that if I happen to run into you to tell you he'd better be invited to the wedding."

Tracy grinned and grabbed a slice of pizza. "What makes you think we didn't already get married?" she winked.

Lauren popped her on the leg. "Because I made you swear I could be your Maid of Honor!"

"True," Tracy admitted as she chomped into the pizza. "Umm...the old Deadline Demon came through!"

Eric looked confused.

"Anytime one of the reporters lands a big story," Lauren explained, "Stan always brings in pizza for the staff. Says it's our reward for hard work."

"And if a reporter has a big lead and lands the story before it hits the media, we celebrate with chocolate cake. He says that's his secret weapon to make us better journalists."

Tracy wiped her mouth and glanced at Lauren. They both paused as the sudden realization hit them.

"Guess he's figured out what we've been researching," Lauren thought aloud.

Tracy stopped chewing. "And if he's figured it out, so has everybody else in the office." They locked eyes as worry swelled around them. Tracy flung her pizza in the box.

"I'll call Dale," she mumbled as she grabbed her phone and hurried toward the kitchen.

"Right. We need to get a rush on this." Lauren closed the pizza boxes and scrambled to gather research notes. She strained to listen as Tracy made delivery arrangements with her Nashville publisher.

"The sooner I get this new material out of my hands, the better, Dale. I'll send it now - inside my lyric submission." Tracy paced the floor, nervously biting her nail as she confirmed details. "Have Levi call Lauren as soon as he gets it."

She shoved her phone into her pocket and popped an encrypted disc and some notes into a mailing envelope.

"I need you to take this to the airport." She rushed past Eric toward Lauren. "It needs to go 'counter-to-counter' so Dale gets it tonight."

"Will you be okay here? Eric can stay, or maybe I should get Grant to come over."

Tracy peaked through the window blinds toward the street. "I'll be fine. It'll give me some time to concentrate on finding this password."

Lauren nodded then went to the bedroom to change clothes. Two minutes later she reappeared, pulling one arm through her blouse while zipping her jeans with her free hand. Shouldering a phone to her ear, she stammered from the bedroom, her expression so frantic that Eric hurried to her side. Tracy braced herself, certain it was tragic news about Jared.

"Cynthia Latham..." she sighed, gripping Eric's outstretched hand. She faced Tracy. "That secretary from Sutherant, the one who came to see Jim Crenshaw this week... her body was just found in the Canadian River."

Tracy dropped to the edge of the couch.

"Oh, Jesus!" Eric mumbled. "She worked down the hall from me. What happened?"

"Somebody bashed her head in," Lauren exhaled. "I told Grant about her confrontation with Jim. He wants me to meet him at the *Tribune* so I can be there while he questions Jim. And Tracy, another agent named Derrick Roberts just arrived from Memphis. Grant is sending him over to watch the place. Don't worry. Nobody else knows you're here."

Eric offered to take the envelope to the airport. Tracy hesitated and gripped the package against her chest. Her own warning echoed in her mind. From here on out, it had to be just her, Levi and Lauren who knew the truth of what had been uncovered.

"Lauren, take it before you meet Grant. And here," Tracy pulled the golf photograph from her bag and handed it to Lauren. "Lane Kirkland was going to see if he could enlarge this so I can see who is in that reflection." Tracy pointed to the oversized mirror inside the golf cart.

As the photo passed before him, Eric's eyes widened and his face went pale. He snatched it from Tracy's hand.

"What is this? Who the hell is this?"

Tracy hesitated, and then traced her finger across each subject. "That's Jim Crenshaw...my uncle...and Phil Murphy, the FBI agent I just met with in Atlanta." She waited for the tension to settle. "I took it from Phil's office."

Tracy glanced at Lauren and saw the same confusion in her eyes.

Eric's voice was barely audible. "I've waited over three years to see that face again. That's the bastard that killed my sister."

"Eric?"

Lauren touched his arm but his attention shot toward Tracy. "Dana was the one who got me the job with your dad. It was right after she was hired by Leonard Osteen."

"The attorney?" Tracy asked.

Eric nodded.

"Osteen..." Tracy reminded Lauren, "the lawyer found dead in his garage the night Jared was taken."

Eric slid his wallet from his back pocket and opened it, shoving a picture their way. As Tracy looked at the photo, it crossed her mind how frequently Eric had opened his wallet in her presence. Never once had she ever seen the picture. Never once did he mention his sister. But there she was – shoulder to shoulder with the brother she so favored. The same short dark hair, the same clear blue eyes, and that smile - so genuine, engaging.

"Eric, she's gorgeous," Tracy sighed. "You never even told me..."

"When I was on my last year at Baylor, I came to visit her. Dana introduced me to your dad when he was at the law firm one day. We hit it off and one thing led to another. Anyway, he arranged an internship during my last semester. I lived with Dana for a while and between helping your dad research and hearing what she worked on with Osteen, I found myself in the center of the Sutherant scandal before I was even officially hired."

Eric's smile crumbled. He shoved his wallet back into his pocket and drew a deep breath. "She called me one night a couple of months after Osteen was killed. She could barely talk she was so scared - crying and talking crazy about this federal agent who had been calling her, threatening her about interfering with the investigation. He was on his way to meet with her to supposedly record what she knew about Osteen's killer."

"She found something she shouldn't have," Tracy determined.

"Proof that the police had lied about Osteen's murder," he nodded. "His wife had found his cell phone between the front seat and the console. Somehow Osteen managed to record the whole attack on his phone."

"It must have fallen out of sight during the struggle," Tracy assumed.

"The police report called it a robbery," he snorted. "It even stated Osteen got tangled in his seatbelt and choked to death. Osteen's wife let Dana hear the recorded footage. The killer had pulled Osteen's necktie so tight it snapped his neck. It was an obvious cover-up, but I guess his wife was too scared to take legal action."

The room grew cold. Tracy shivered and hugged her arms to her chest, suddenly uneasy about staying alone.

"I knew Dana was in trouble when she called that night. I hung up and called the police and then raced over there. She was fifteen minutes away and I..." Eric caught his breath. "This guy..." he glared at the golf photo trembling in his hand, "was leaving her apartment." Lauren stroked his arm. "She was – God, he just left her there choking in her own blood. All I could do was hold her."

He pointed an accusing finger at Phil's image.

"I will never forget that son-of-a-bitch's sneer when he brushed past me."

Eric walked toward the window and pinched the bridge of his nose. He relayed the scene of finding her: stumbling through overturned furniture, stepping over smashed computer equipment, and collapsing to his knees as he found her gasping for air with her own kitchen knife lodged into her throat.

"It took close to half an hour for the cops to show – that's when I realized our own police were part of the corruption. When they finally submitted a report saying she must have *surprised a robber*, I just went along with it 'because I was too damned afraid to question it. That was almost four years ago. This is the first time I've told anyone what really happened."

***

The apartment had lost its welcome. From the moment she had watched Lauren's sports car back out the drive, Tracy had regretted staying behind. Truth be told, she was scared to death. She jumped at every noise, holding her breath each time Snickers growled at some unseen noise. Passing a wall mirror in the hallway she looked at her reflection, half wondering if the death sentence plastered across her head could be seen.

She leaned over the arm of the couch, checking the window for the fifth time to ensure the presence of Agent Derrick Roberts. Thankfully, the dark blue government car was there. Pushing her fear aside, she settled back into the couch with her father's computer keyboard.

Holding a Sutherant electronic computer card in one hand and a list of possible password combinations in the other, Tracy inserted the card into the slot and hoped for a miracle. Just like earlier in the day, a mass of encrypted garble spread across the screen.

"This is normal," she thought aloud. Stroking her fingers through Snickers' fur she reasoned, "Eric said the security card was either not in sync or that I needed some kind of encrypted disc. Either way, old girl, I can't get the program to respond."

After one futile attempt after another, she took a break – half to counter the tedium, and half out of pity for Snickers. The bundle of fur sat patiently by Tracy's side, fuzzy play toys and squeakies at the ready. Tracy tossed a mangled chew bone across the room and as she watched the pooch dart from the couch to retrieve it, she spotted her personal laptop on the kitchen table. David Frazier's comment about her dad's work routine shot through her mind: *backed up everything on his personal computer...*

"Daddy didn't have a personal computer," she reminded herself and looked at her sidekick. "What do you think, Snickerdoodle?"

She approached her laptop and powered it up.

Could he have been using mine all along?

Her cell phone rang and the sudden noise made her jump. She glanced at the screensaver and nearly dropped the phone when she saw Jared's number flashing. Reflexively, she started to disconnect, but in the loneliness of the darkened room, she could not wait to hear his voice.

"Jared—"

"T., open the back door!" Jared yelled. His voice was raspy, slightly broken.

Confused, Tracy stood and looked around the room, unsure of what he had said.

"Jared?" She asked, looking down at the screen pad of her phone.

"Open the back door! NOW!"

Tracy rushed to the kitchen and lifted the curtain. There was Jared hustling through the field, dodging knee-deep weeds and quagmire as he rushed toward the back of Lauren's complex. Under the weight of a guitar and a large duffle bag he fought his way toward her. As if in a dream, she grabbed the doorknob, wrestled the lock, and swung open the door just as Jared leapt across a barberry hedge. Breathless, he dropped his load at her feet, wrenched an arm around her, and pulled her away from the door.

"What are you..." Tracy stammered.

His kiss came with such force her knees buckled beneath her. She struggled in his arms and tried to push away, confused, shocked, and livid that he had been foolish enough to come to Newport.

"Jared..." she gasped. "Why are you here? They'll..." He swooped her up and carried her to the couch, tightening his hold to keep her from fighting. As he lowered her to the cushions, he kissed her hard, restraining her movement, overcoming her resistance. Their bodies wrestled in a tug of war – a push and pull of emotional battle until finally, Tracy surrendered, smoothing her arms around him and pulling him near. All the fear, anxiety, and confusion of the hours they had been apart faded away. His very presence gave her strength.

"Don't ever do that again," he breathed. His eyes were tired, strained, and in the dim glow of the one nightlight she had left on, she saw the teary-eyed fear gripping his face. She brushed her fingers through his sweaty hair and overcome with the sudden rush of passion, cradled his head to her chest.

"You shouldn't have come..." He pressed his finger to her lips and recoiled. She recognized that look – the pain and dejection of being left behind. She knew it first-hand.

"Don't leave me again." Jared exhaled a long, calming breath – the same breath he had held inside since awakening that morning. He sank into the couch beside her. "You scared the hell out of me, T." His eyes grew angry. "And to hear you had left with Eric Williams? What the Hell? First the asshole points a gun at me and then I find out you fly back here with him?"

"To protect you!" Tracy snapped. "It's not safe for us to be together. Do you think I wanted to leave you?" Tears filled her eyes as her body trembled in fear.

"No, it's just that I...hey, what is it? What's happened?" He looked around the room then pulled her into his arms. "And why's it so dark in here?"

"Do you remember last Thursday when Eric told us he stayed with Sutherant to finish what he and Dad had started?"

"Yes, and to find a shipment your dad had hidden."

Tracy nodded. "Until about two hours ago, I didn't fully believe him. I figured it'd take more than that to stay with such a corrupt company." She pulled her black and white copy of the golf photo from her computer bag and pushed it toward Jared. She turned on a small reading light and Jared stretched to see the photo. "Phil's part of this, Jay. These people – Phil, my uncle, and Jim Crenshaw are working together. I can't prove it, but I know Phil was at the state park..." she said. "Right before Brody Craig's body was found."

"What's that got to do with your *ex-boyfriend*?" The green-eyed monster appeared.

Tracy swallowed, took a deep breath, and recounted every gruesome detail of Dana Williams' murder.

Jared's head fell into his hands. "My God," he mumbled, cursing under his breath as he ran his fingers through his mussed hair. "That explains things. Phil's father, Robert

Murphy, heads up Internal Affairs for the FBI. He flew us to D.C. and the more he questioned me about Phil, the more I realized how wrong I've been to trust him. I found out they've been watching him for some time. Anyway, instead of heading for Savannah, Mike chartered a private plane and brought us here. He plans on taking us to a safe house. But we've got a problem. Your uncle's been spreading word about you and Lauren investigating Sutherant."

Tracy sat up and looked around the room, searching again for that safety net, but coming up empty with every turn. Her uncle, she knew, was not their only concern. Knowing the Soon family out of North Korea was behind Sutherant's corruption destroyed what was left of her hope.

As a distraction, Jared gathered the duffle bags and guitar from the kitchen. "Here, this always seems to help." He slid the guitar case onto her lap.

Tracy opened the case and positioned her guitar, strumming a perfect chord that resonated through the room. She closed her eyes and floated her fingers effortlessly through a verse of her newest melody. Jared grinned and she paused to admire him. "Even now," she waved her hand across the room, "you find a reason to smile."

"You're just so beautiful."

She draped her arms around his neck and kissed him – a long, deep kiss that in any other setting would have led right into the hot sex they remembered from the night before. *God, I love this man*, she thought as she smoothed her fingers along his stubbly face, studying his eyes. And because she did love him so much she added, "By the way, I told you I'd let you know when I was ready to marry you. Well, I am - just as soon as it's safe for us to be together."

"Tracy – we are not separating again."

She crawled from his lap and switched gears. "Did your dad call today?"

Jared narrowed his eyes at her. "He did." He stalled a moment then smiled. "Got a big old apology and everything."

"He's done the best he could, Jared. And he wants to make things right with you," she gave his shoulder a squeeze.

"He told me that, too. Even flew Mom in today so he could explain everything. I think he's finally realizing he never should have shut us out." He pushed to his feet. "I need to show you something."

Jared opened his shirt and pulled out a small daypack he had tucked inside.

"No matter how much I try and lay low, someone always seems to find me," he mused. "We happened to pull up next to Mary Luther at a stop light earlier. Before I could duck down in the seat to avoid being seen, she rolled down her window and motioned for me to follow her to the post office. Turns out your dad opened a post office box in my name – stuck me with a four year rental fee along with it," Jared chuckled. "Anyway, this was inside." He reached into his pocket and palmed a silver key. "Plus a small white card with the number 219 written on it."

Tracy opened his hand and took the key. "219?"

"Mrs. Luther had an idea - the safe deposit boxes at the bank. She got her nephew, the bank manager to come open the bank so I could try it out." He unfastened the latch of the daypack and lifted a large manila envelope from the side pocket. "She was right."

Tracy leaned closer as he dumped the contents. A stack of papers, five mini-cassette tapes and a portable player scattered across the table. She reached for her father's old security badge as it fell across the other items. Lifting it, she twisted the lanyard through her fingers.

"He opened it December 18th. – the day he was killed," Jared explained.

"And he put it in your name?"

Jared nodded.

"So it wouldn't get into the wrong hands," Tracy realized, sitting up to take a closer look.

"Right, like your uncle's. Remember last week when I met with Thad Hendricks?"

"The lawyer?"

"Yes, he was right about the power of attorney. There was no record of it ever being filed. Those papers your uncle had your dad sign were not legal documents."

Tracy pressed her temples.

"He wanted the farm, T."

"But he hates farming. Grandpa left it to Dad so it would stay in the family and…"

Jared stopped her with a raise of his hand. "I need to tell you what Hendricks shared with me."

He cupped his hand over hers and slid closer.

"I called my dad back after I opened this today." Jared lifted five cassettes from the stash. "Four of these are taped conversations between my dad and Congressional leaders, a cabinet member, and foreign diplomats from four years ago. Dad gave them to your father for safe keeping. Your dad added a fifth one just before his death. On it is a conversation that proves that your uncle was trying to blackmail him."

Tracy sucked in a breath and felt the tension in her clenched fists. "Your father told me Daddy was going to see Sheriff McClain when he crashed. Maybe he was going for help."

Jared nodded and flipped through the pages until he found one particular document – a real estate deed. "Or maybe he was trying to protect this."

Tracy lifted the papers toward the light. "A property deed? Mineral rights? What is this?"

"Did you ever wonder about that tract of land across from your house? All these years Bill Campbell made ridiculous offers and your dad never budged – even though the deal would have practically made him a millionaire." Jared chuckled under his breath. "Tracy, I didn't want to say anything until I was sure, but what I found today is going to change your life – our life."

"How?"

"Hendricks said that piece of property is sitting on one of the largest, untapped reservoirs of oil in the country. And you own all the mineral rights. Here's the will, the deed, everything. It's all yours, T. Your dad put it in my name to make sure it couldn't be taken from you."

Her brows narrowed. Lifting the contract, she skimmed it again, puzzled, excited, and overwhelmed. "*This* is what Denny's been after?"

"Probably Phil, too."

Tears gathered in her eyes and she let the deed slip from her fingers. "I can't believe it."

Before he could respond, she jumped to her feet, lifted her father's security badge from the table, and grabbed Jared's hand. "Come on, you have to help me."

She led Jared to the computer Eric had brought from Sutherant. "I've been trying most of the day and can't get in. Maybe this new security badge will work."

She inserted the badge and a sudden flash lit up the screen.

"See? That's all that happens. I can't get beyond this point."

Jared turned the monitor toward him and searched the screen. The monitor was black with the exception of one tiny scripted 'SP' at the bottom right corner of the screen. "See this icon?" Jared asked. Tracy looked over his shoulder and had he not pointed it out with the curser, she never would have noticed. "It's a security feature your dad added."

With a double-click of the mouse, the screen came alive. An animated red Sutherant Petroleum logo unveiled and beneath it a login panel appeared.

Jared typed 'F8' then the numbers '1' and '0' as he had watched Mark Sims do on many occasions. "I always thought it was one of your dad's lame jokes, but now I see why he drilled it into me. 'You have to be as quick as an F-18,'" he snickered. "I can hear him now."

With one last stroke of a key, Jared hit 'enter' and at once, a musical montage expanded across the screen revealing a program of Sutherant Petroleum financial records. Tracy watched the screen, but it was the song that took her breath away.

She recognized the tune within the first measure and could not help but smile. It was a song she had written in her early teens.

"I remember the night you finished that song. Your dad recorded it while you weren't looking," Jared explained. Tracy listened as her first original composition streamed through the small speaker. The computer screen shifted and the music faded. "And *wahlah* - your dad's program!"

Tracy moved closer.

"Looks like he has about twenty documents on here and this one alone has over two hundred pages to it," Jared estimated. "I think we just found what we're looking for." As fast as his mind would allow, he skimmed page after page of data. "Transactions, profit spread sheets, buyers, suppliers. My God, he even has a list of the covert code names they used to conceal the shipments."

"Senator Mackenzick, Congressman Davidson – even some Cabinet members. Dad's got a timeline of how they all worked together and if these buyers turn out to be foreign diplomats or business owners, this will be considered treason," Tracy added.

Jared snatched a CD from Lauren's computer desk. He popped it in the D-drive and downloaded the document. With a click of the mouse he pulled up another, scanning briefly before saving every piece of incriminating evidence that crossed the screen. Tracy stood behind him perusing her father's notations of kickbacks, money laundering and what appeared to be black market transactions - all coded to look like normal business activity. Still, this was not the incriminating evidence that she expected. To warrant murder, cross country chases, and governmental protection, there had to be more evidence than outdated financial ledgers and corporate fraud.

"Jared, Eric said that the FBI's top computer experts had tried to get into this system. What if he only *thought* they were trying? What if they never intended to get to that information?"

Jared narrowed his eyes. "To keep it concealed?"

"Even your dad said he felt like the FBI was deliberately stalling the investigation."

On impulse, Tracy walked to her personal laptop and studied the various file icons on her homepage. She recognized all of them and while many had not been opened in some time, she knew that they were her files; she had been the one to build and save them.

She flipped the laptop over to examine the USB and CD input. There was no drive designed to accept her father's security badge. Yet, Frazier's words continued to roll through her mind: *backed up everything on his personal computer.* This was the only personal computer her father would have used.

Consumed with the search, she clicked each of the file icons, briefly reviewing the documents that were stored behind each emblem. When she had taken time to explore their contents, she paused and stared at the screen. "It's got to be here*,"* she whispered under her breath. And then she wondered.

Reaching into her jeans pocket she grasped her personal flash drive – the flash drive that held every lyric, every poem, and every private thought she had safely stored away.

Surely, Dad wouldn't have...

With another glance at the homepage icons before her, she popped her flash drive into the USB port and moved the mouse toward the guitar icon, her main lyric file. But as she settled the mouse on the center of the icon, she noticed a separate design to the right of the guitar. The tiny, scripted SP icon. She had never noticed it before. With a prayer, she disconnected the flash drive. The design disappeared. She popped the flash drive in again and immediately saw the small red, design illuminate at the base of the guitar. Her heart leapt.

"What are you doing?" Jared leaned in and moved the mouse just to the right of the guitar and clicked on the scripted icon. A flash of color covered the screen. Bolting upright to get a closer look, he closed the file then re-opened it causing the same flash to jump across the screen. "It's encrypted. You need his disc to access the file. It must be with those other materials."

Tracy scrambled through the items on the table.

"Jared, there's no disc. Are you sure we need it?"

"We've got to have the disc he used when he downloaded the program on here. It's part of the security block he designed. But T., we'll still have to know the username and password to be able to decode the material. He never gave it to me."

"My God, it'll take a miracle to figure this out," she groaned.

Jared swiped his eyes. As Tracy watched the weariness spill across his face, she knew the emotional strain of the day had taken its toll on both of them. Glancing at the clock she saw it was past eight. She draped her arm around his shoulder and kissed his cheek.

"Missed you," she whispered. "And I'm sorry I scared you." As her lips brushed his, all else was forgotten. He pulled her into his lap, pushing aside the research and the discs and the people who were counting on them. He slid his hands underneath her shirt, adjusting her body to his. She kissed him again – deeply, eagerly, pressing herself into him until the slow soothing rhythm of their bodies reunited. But with a jolting shove, she pushed away and bolted to her feet.

"Where is it? Where did you move my bag?" She tossed pillows and searched under furniture until at last, she found her duffle bag.

"What?" Jared lay sprawled on his back, cursing under his breath.

"My disc! We've got to try my disc!" Before he could push himself from the couch, Tracy popped her lyric flash drive into her laptop, clicked on the small secondary icon, and inserted her personal encrypted lyric disc into the D-drive. He nestled to her side just as the gibberish on the screen began to clear.

"That's it! This is the disc he used!" Jared shouted. But just as quickly, his excitement deflated. "Dammit!"

"Username and password, just like you said," Tracy groaned.

"Okay, most passwords are very simple. Your dad would have created a password only you would understand or care about. Think along those lines. And we have to make it count. It will block us out if we try too many times."

"Any ideas?" Tracy asked.

For username, he typed in the same sequence as before: *F8 1 0 enter.* He shrugged when Tracy raised her brow. "It's the only one I ever saw him use."

Username was one thing, but finding the password would be like trying to find the proverbial needle in a haystack. Like Tracy had said - it would take a miracle. She fumbled through possible password combinations, scratching down random thoughts to see if anything made sense. Jared's words floated through her mind. *Something only she would care about.* Her head began to ache. She craned her neck in small hypnotic circles. As if someone had whispered the secret in her ear, she looked down and stroked her locket - her simple, silver music clef locket her father had clasped around her neck on her seventeenth birthday.

She wondered.

Lifting the locket from her chest, she turned it toward the glow of the lamp. She fingered the tiny music clef. It occurred to her that she had never looked inside. When she had unwrapped the gift years before, her father had suggested that she find a picture to place inside. Four days later, he died. Maybe it was superstition - or just too hard for her to face. As the years passed, looking inside faded away as something unnecessary. Now a burning urge swept through her.

Tracy unlocked the thin clasp and opened the locket. Tilting it toward the light, a tiny, paper-thin, fleck of gold floated to her hand. As she lifted it, she saw the metal was engraved.

~Keep our song in your heart~

Her lips quivered as she brushed the tiny engraving. *"Keep our song in your heart,"* she repeated as her thoughts began to swim toward a forgotten memory.

"You've had it all along." Jared grabbed the keyboard and typed the phrase. Nothing happened. "What song does he mean?" Jared backed out the letters in the password space and waited.

"*'The Family Song'* – just a song Mom used to sing at bedtime."

Tracy grabbed a pen and wrote the lyrics on the back of a magazine, reciting the words as she did. *"One plus one that's all we need. Add some love and that makes three. Together, we will always be. Family - Mommy, Daddy and Me."*

Jared lifted the keyboard to try again. He typed *The Family Song.* Nothing happened.

Tracy's mind began to blur with thoughts of her dad. She mumbled, "...used my computer...used my disc, my flash drive. He gave me that locket. *Keep our song in your heart.* It has to be the password."

And that's when it happened. A miracle. Her father's voice rang loud and clear – echoing the one phrase he had purposely overused time and time again during the weeks before he died. In answer to her many questions: Why he stayed with Sutherant for so long. Why he stayed in Newport after her mom died. Why he made her go to church every Sunday. Why she had to practice her music. Why he worked so hard to keep the farm going. His one succinct answer was the same: *For our family.*

The three words floated effortlessly from Tracy's heart, through her fingers, and onto the keyboard. When she hit the 'submit' prompt, a whirlwind of data filled the screen. Tracy felt her face flush as her chest tightened. Her mind went blank and she felt herself drift. She reached out for Jared's hand and when her breathing finally settled, she thought of her dad.

Wondering if he could feel what she felt at this minute.

Wondering if he could hear her heart pounding with joy.

Wondering if he knew how much she had always loved him.

Chapter 40

The taxi eased into Newport just before nine. Dennis Sims directed the driver to pull beside the silver quad cab pick-up truck parked in front of Milton's Market, the local grocery. It had been a helluva long day and as its end was nowhere in sight, Dennis Sims strained from the backseat, paid the driver, and approached the driver's side door of his diesel. Selena Salgado slid over, offering an inviting grin as she patted the leather seat.

"You made good time. What? Eighteen, nineteen hours?" Sims asked.

"Sixteen." Salgado pressed a kiss to his lips. "A lot of good it did me. I spent the last two hours sitting here not knowing where to look. She's laying low somewhere."

"This will help." Sims slid the small metal GPS sensor from his bag. "I must admit, my brother did have a knack for electronics."

"Is that how you knew where they were heading once they left Jacksonville?"

"Yeah, plus I got lucky and overheard their plans through a side window. They used a catering truck as a decoy then chartered a plane."

"And you?"

"Caught one of Sutherant's corporate jets out of Orlando. Didn't think airport security would like my friends very

341

much." Sims pulled his two handguns into view. He nodded toward the tracking monitor. "I guess it's time we turned that on and got down to business."

Salgado flipped the switch and their destination became clear. Sims started the truck and made his way onto Main Street. Two more miles and two more turns later, the tracking monitor's hum grew louder. Sims dimmed his lights and crept behind Lauren Mayfield's apartment complex. No one in sight. But a glance down a side street confirmed his suspicion. The blue boxy four-door sedan screamed loud and clear: *government surveillance.*

Sims lifted the half-empty bottle of Scotch from the seat and took a long swig, weighing his next option. He reached to the steering column and flicked off his headlights.

"Switch seats with me. He'll know my face." Selena climbed over his lap and took the wheel. The rumble of the diesel kept time as Sims twisted the silencer onto the Cressida .45 and slid the chamber. When their truck came to a stop beside the car, Selena waved and motioned to the driver. Innocently, the young man lowered his window. Selena smiled and offered a greeting as Sims eased his .45 toward the window. *swwipp – swwipp* Special Agent Derrick Roberts never knew what hit him. As the remaining half of his head settled against the headrest, Sims took another swig then motioned for Salgado to drive to the rear of the complex.

Chapter 41

9:02 P.M. - Sunday

On the living room floor of Lauren's apartment, Tracy sat beside Jared with the laptop balanced on their knees. With every shocking discovery of crime, Tracy scooted closer, as if their tight bond might prevent evil from approaching. Governmental financial transactions and surveillance photos of covert exchanges littered the screen and with each newly read page, she felt her body tense, sensing that Jared's forewarning of 'falling off the edge of the earth' was quickly becoming their only means of survival. There was no undoing what they had uncovered, and suddenly she felt as exposed as the criminals they were about to incriminate. These people had killed to keep the material from getting out and page by page, she realized why. The magnitude of the international corruption was clear – as was the fact that she and Jared would be their next targets.

Jared filled their shared glass with more wine, trusting it would help her escape the stressful fear of their plight. But after two tilts of the glass she passed it back to Jared, realizing it would take much more than weak merlot to ease her mind.

"Please, J... just download it all to my disc so we can forward it to Levi. I don't know where Dad found all of this, but I'm afraid to read anymore. Eric was right. The FBI never intended to let this get out." Tracy pressed numbers into her phone pad. "I'm calling Lauren to tell her what we found."

***

Lauren checked the caller ID on the first ring. "Hey, girl. Got a pen handy? You'll want to get this." Tracy grabbed a pen and leaned toward Jared. "First of all, best move you ever made was having your music agent get in touch with Levi Daniels. This guy is amazing. Let me tell you where we are: the FAA report came in from Colorado. Senator Hastings' family was murdered alright. The instrument controls of their plane had been altered. That poor pilot thought he was three thousand feet higher than he actually was."

"And you have the documentation to prove this, right?" asked Tracy.

"I've got more than that. The aircraft technician who wrote up the crash report still has a signed release from over four years ago. He got suspicious so made a back-up of his report and dubbed the videotaped footage from their security cameras before he turned the original over to the NTSB. He even remembered an FBI agent came to take possession of both items right after it happened. Care to guess who signed for it?"

"No clue."

"FBI Agent Phillip Murphy." Tracy froze. "We're checking into flight records and rental car companies to get more proof of his being there."

Tracy leaned into Jared so he could read her notes.

"But Phil wasn't the only one involved. The airport had surveillance video that shows your uncle and a guy named Louis Kincaid of Chicago. When Kincaid's face came up on the security tapes, all kinds of red flags went up. We're talking underground connections."

Tracy shook her head. "I can't believe this," she moaned. She felt a wave of nausea as the truth began to unveil.

"I don't know where you are going with this," Lauren continued, "but I found some interesting military ties. Phil Murphy and your uncle started out in basic training together in 1983, then did their first deployment in Heidelberg, Germany. They worked in different areas, but I cross-referenced their training courses and found one match. They were both sent to Fort Bragg, North Carolina for a six-week stint. But what caught my eye was the name of a Sergeant they served under – 1st Sergeant Waylon Vincent."

"You're kidding! Our very own Chief of Police." Tracy scratched down his name and underlined it.

"Strangely enough, later that same year Vincent was dishonorably discharged. My second cousin happens to be a defense attorney in the Marines and was able to do a background check on Vincent. Turns out he and some of his buddies were investigated for what they termed 'mishandling inventory and supplies' crimes. His unit suspected him of skimming weapons and ammunition off the top of shipments and selling them on the side, but it was never proven. Instead they nailed him for striking a superior officer. And I'm sure the four ounces of cocaine he had stashed in his footlocker didn't help."

"And now he's dealing through Sutherant, huh?" Tracy followed.

"While leading our town's police department," Lauren fumed. Tracy let the phone slip to her cheek. She rubbed her eyes and studied her notes as Lauren's muddled voice scratched the air. The bolded lines Tracy had sketched around Vincent's name and the words she had printed underneath stood out:

How did Vincent get appointed Chief of Police with a criminal record?

Jared scooted closer and tilted the phone to listen.

"I assume you've heard of the Green Berets?" Lauren asked. "It so happens that in 1998, the CIA Special Activities Division selected Phil Murphy to train with them."

"That explains how he could kick my ass," Jared snorted.

"Right. Guess who else was training with him. Staff Sergeant Baird Mackenzick of the 80th Airborne and the late Senator Matthew Hastings of the 12th Special Forces Group out of Fort Watson in Colorado."

"Mackenzick – the one Grant pulled over in Newport. So he, Phil Murphy, Waylon Vincent, Matthew Hastings and my uncle all served in the military together?"

"All deployed together in Afghanistan in 2001, serving as specialists in martial arts and survival tactics."

Tracy scratched their names in the margin. "And all are key suspects in the FBI investigation of Sutherant Petroleum. You're brilliant!"

"Thought you'd like it, but I also did some cross references of the units stationed in Afghanistan and came across a story about a particular mission in the Zawar Kili cave complex."

"I've heard of that – al Qaeda used the mountain tunnels as a hide out."

"Right. Two things about the article caught my interest. One was about a female soldier who got separated from her special ops unit and single-handedly ended up taking out a nest of about twenty guerrillas. She became a bit of a celebrity because before she enlisted, she was a search and rescue expert from Colorado - really into rock climbing, free-basing, and all those crazy extreme sports. Anyway, while she's out running surveillance with her unit, they get ambushed. They all scatter and she was stuck out in the caves by herself. Her instincts kick in and she starts rock climbing her way out of there. Starts getting dark and she stumbles on the enemy. Fires enough shots to draw them out of the cave, then tosses a grenade right in the center of the pack – all the while perched on a six-inch ledge three hundred feet above the ground. She turns out to be the big hero of the day."

"I can see why."

"The story was cool enough, but her name was what caught my attention. Selena Salgado."

"Never heard of her," Tracy admitted.

"Guess again. She's your uncle's girlfriend. I found that out when I was checking the Colorado airport info. The police chief there ran a check on your uncle and found out they share an apartment in Charlton, Colorado."

"The girl who was with Denny this weekend," Tracy pointed out to Jared.

"The other thing is the news story itself. I was reading it and got to the end of the story. You'll never believe who got the byline."

"Who?"

"Jim Crenshaw."

Tracy dropped her pen and fell back into the couch.

"Evidently," Lauren continued, "our favorite co-worker had a special correspondence pass that allowed him to ride along on military missions."

"So he wasn't lying about all those war stories?"

"Maybe not. But you'll love this: Levi found some holes in Jim's prize-winning story."

Tracy punched Jared and pointed to her notes. He glanced around but just as quickly turned back to his computer download.

"Remember his story was about diamond miners in South Africa?" Lauren asked.

"Yeah, who were supposedly trading slaves in exchange for their diamonds."

"Well, turns out we may have a witness who will testify that Jim's story was a lie. Jim fabricated the story to draw attention away from the real slave traders – an operation out of Eastern Europe who was in bed with some of our U.S. Congressmen. Word got out and the story got more national attention than he expected. By the time the prize nomination came down, Jim was so deep in lies he had to lay low and pretend it was true, shifting all the shame and blame to the South African company he maligned."

Tracy exhaled. "Even though they were innocent."

"Exactly. When it all became public, the South African company had no credibility and had lost all their customers. And here's the best part: Eric thinks they were the company your dad bargained with to get even with the Sutherant investors."

"What do you mean?"

"Well, Eric was pretty vague but he said your dad caught wind of a deal in the works between these Sutherant moneybags and the corrupt diamond manufacturer in Europe. Evidently, a rather large shipment of rare blue diamonds was being exchanged for some anti-aircraft weapons they had intercepted from a U.S. manufacturer. That, plus the Congressional backing for some overseas covert operations made for a pretty sweet deal for the Eastern Europeans."

"But how was my dad involved?"

"The Sutherant investors were making your dad launder the money and alter the financial records, so naturally your dad had knowledge of the time and place of the exchange. He devised a plan to clear the South African company's name and get back at the Sutherant investors by having the South African company send some worthless cubic zirconia diamonds to use as a decoy…"

"And Daddy hid the real ones." Tracy's eyes shot open. *The stolen shipment!*

"Yep, and had the feds ready and waiting to witness the exchange. The Sutherant bunch had enough Congressional pull to get out of the legal mess, but the European supplier took such a financial and legal hit it nearly wiped them out. Plus, being caught trading fake diamonds didn't do much for their reputation. I checked and it looks like they're still being blackballed because of the whole fiasco. Nobody wants to do business with them anymore."

"So Dad's intent was to help the South African company restore its reputation?" Tracy asked. Jared's attention fell to Tracy's notes and he watched as she underscored one word several times. *Diamonds.* His eyes glazed over in a daze.

"Yes. Same as Eric. He was part of the scheme so needs to find the diamonds to clear his name. Levi has worked in that area of Africa before so intends to see if he can help smooth things over with the company. He's already started an inquiry into stripping Jim of his award. Plus, Grant just started questioning Jim about the murder of that young secretary from Sutherant," Lauren continued. "Kyle Monroe, her friend running for state senate, is willing to testify that she knew about Jim's fraudulent Pulitzer story and was threatening to go public with it. Both of them had already made a statement to Arkansas's Attorney General that says she uncovered a group of military buddies who aligned themselves with Chicago mafia and the Korean underworld who contracted illegal and counterfeit trade with our U.S. Government. This small faction took over Sutherant Petroleum by way of their Congressional ties and that trickled down to our own Newport Police Department. "

Tracy watched Jared pop a new computer disc in. The screen became a blur as he searched the new documents, glancing periodically to her notepad. With Lauren talking in one ear and Jared vying for the other, Tracy fought to concentrate, determined to work the puzzle pieces from her own scribbled notes:

*December 16th – Denny comes to Newport, argues w/Dad, signs worthless power of attorney.

*Dad works deal, hides diamonds. Eric's involvement?

* Sen. Baird Mackenzick spotted near Newport; Sen. Hastings and Osteen (Sutherant lawyer) are murdered minutes apart.

* Jared taken from Newport, Dad knew this and died two days later – before they accessed his computer notes or security codes. Death was suspicious. Four years later, Jar...

"Dammit!" Jared slammed his fist to the table with such force that Tracy's pen slashed across the page.

"Hold on, Lauren," Tracy interrupted. "Jared just found something." She placed the phone on the couch and scooted closer to the computer screen.

"Congress just sat back and let this happen!" Jared fumed. Tracy's stomach turned as soon as she saw the content on the screen. A bidding war, so to speak, was in session in what looked like a hotel suite. The shakiness and poor quality of the footage made it obvious that it had been recorded covertly, but the content was clear. Whoever was taping panned to show eight barely-teen girls - naked, terrified, gagged, and apparently drugged while four unidentified men groped and purchased them.

"Sex trafficking!" Jared scowled. "And by the sound of the accents, Russian or Eastern European. If your dad saw the need to add this footage to his records that means Sutherant or at least some of their financiers are involved."

Tracy shuddered as the images changed – a girl stumbling from a chair, handcuffed and naked as two men bound her legs. "Daddy died trying to expose this."

"He probably intercepted this footage from whoever was selling it as blackmail. If the government is part of this and if they were using Sutherant to transport ..."

Pmrmp...Pmrrmp

The sound had come from outside.

Just a low guttural cough that barely scratched the silence. Heavy footsteps crunched gravel, inching closer toward the door.

Jared clenched Tracy's hand and threw his palm over her mouth. The doorknob rattled.

CRAASH!

The porch light.

Snickers bolted from the couch and skidded across the kitchen floor. Her high-pitched howl trailing close behind. Tracy lunged for her, grabbing her collar just before she attacked the door. Jared seized them both from behind, racing as one into the darkened bedroom. He stripped Snickers from Tracy's arms and shoved her into the closet, slamming the door as her grating, frantic claws dug into the wood. But the swift, pounding lunges against the back door overpowered everything.

Jared bolted to the living room, leapt across the coffee table and snatched the disc and flash drives from both computers. He stuffed them between the couch cushions and with a turn, slung the laptop beneath the couch. Tracy followed suit: seizing the strewn research notes and security badges in her arms then rushing to the bedroom.

BAM! BAM! BAM!

Jared panicked as ruthless blows pounded the back door. Wrenching the zipper of his duffle bag, he tugged and tugged, struggling to rip it free. His fingers, bloodless from the strain, tore into the fabric as Kevin's gun and clothing spilled to the floor.

Heavy, thrusting jolts hammered the patio door. *BAM! BAM! BAM!*

The back door ripped from its hinges and smashed into the cabinet.

Jared snatched the loaded 357 Magna from the floor just as a shimmer of steel flashed around the door jam. Before he could steady his aim, the barrel of Selena Salgado's gun tilted his way.

Two resounding blasts split the air.

Then all was still.

All was silent.

A faint, throaty moan rose like a wailing siren. A crescendo of pain. Salgado stumbled to the hearth, wrenching her gut as a dark, crimson stain bloomed across her chest. Jared followed her movement with a trembling aim until she collapsed to the floor. He doubled over in near panic as Death stared back at him. Dropping to his knees, he closed his eyes and exhaled a long deep breath as her deep, eerie moans slowly fell to a whisper. That's when he saw that he too had been shot.

Unconsciously, the gun slipped through Jared's fingers and without warning, his worst nightmare rounded the corner. Before Jared could flinch, the barrel of Sims' Cressida pressed into his temple. With one blur of motion Sims cocked the chamber.

Jared raised his empty hands into the air. To his right, Tracy froze in the darkened hallway. From eight feet away Sims scowled through clenched teeth when he looked - really looked – at Selena. Even in the low light, her dark, ebony eyes reflected the shock of life's end.

Sims bolted forward and thrust his booted foot into Jared's chest. "You son of a bitch!"

He plowed his fist into Jared's jaw then shifted his gun to cold-cock him with a left hook. Before Jared could adjust, Sims raised the butt of his gun and slammed it against his forehead. "You'll pay!" Sims grunted as he kicked the coffee table into Jared's chest. "Where is she?"

The one question Jared feared above all else. His breath caught and the last of his hope took a free-fall. Keeping Tracy safe was all he had left.

"*Tribune* office," Jared waved his hand around the room, "getting all this to print."

Sims choked out a laugh. He reached for his cigarettes and tapped one to the top, sneering at Jared as he gripped it between his teeth. "Don't think so." Sims lifted a stray computer disc from the couch cushion and snickered. "Hiding out in the dark won't be enough to save your ass, Frazier." He lifted his phone from his pocket, pressed a button, and placed it to his ear, all the while pinning Jared with the weight of the coffee table. Sims looked away; Jared glanced down at his leg, wincing at the sight. Blood oozed from his upper thigh.

"I've got 'em. Where are you now?" Sims barked into his phone. "You're still a couple hours out, maybe less. I'll wait." Sims crammed the cell phone into his pocket then sank his booted heel against the table thrusting harder into Jared's chest, immobilizing his arm at an angle behind his back. With every excruciating blow Jared glimpsed in Tracy's direction, shifting his eyes toward the bedroom praying that she would read his mind and escape through the window.

Sims pulled a stack of papers from his back pocket and tossed them to the table.

"Sign!"

Blood trickled into Jared's left eye as he tilted his head to read what appeared to be legal contracts. Sims kicked the table hard then lowered his foot. Jared shoved the table back, pushing himself from the floor much more quickly than Sims had expected.

"Watch it!" Sims warned with a shift of his gun.

"A signature? That's what you're after?"

Jared sensed Tracy's movement in the hallway.

"And the computer codes I know my brother gave you. Now sign!"

"There's a federal agent right out--"

Sims sucked a breath through his teeth. "Not anymore," he snickered. "He's -- gone."

Jared swiped the blood from his eye. "What damned computer codes? And what if I don't sign?"

Tracy crept from the hallway, easing into the disheveled room. Three feet away she spotted the one weapon within reach. Her guitar – solid, firm, mahogany strengthened by the test of time. She gripped the neck and hoisted it over her shoulder.

"Then you'll get to watch my friends get better acquainted with Tracy. Let's just call it payback for having to babysit her ass the past four years. But hey, the plan worked. *Daddy's* gone and now you two are all that's standing in my way of having that property. So sign!"

Tracy froze. Her uncle's words ensnared her. Had he *planned* her father's death? Her fingers tightened around the guitar frets. Years of anger pulsed through her, as did her father's voice – *Swing through! Swing through!* His unrelenting practice drills through six years of 4A softball. She raised her elbow, poised the guitar high above her shoulder and swung through, dead center into the back of her uncle's skull. Sims buckled to the ground, sprawling across the table as his gun fell free.

Tracy dropped the guitar and lunged toward Sims, lashing out in rage as her fists pounded flesh. Jared hurled her away, but Sims caught him with a right hook straight to his left temple. Jared fell head-first against the corner of the brick hearth. He was out cold.

"You bitch!" Sims fumed, clinching his brutal hands around Tracy's throat from behind. Adrenaline mounting, she dropped her head forward then with a jolt, thrust it back, forcing the brunt of the force to the bridge of his nose. She stumbled in pain but before she caught her balance, Sims grabbed her around the waist. She gripped the wine bottle from the table and thrashed it against his head, spraying wine and shattered glass across the floor. A triangular shard lodged above Sims' right eye forcing a dark stream of blood to trail from his scalp.

Tracy pushed away, but one heartless blow to her jaw sent her to her knees. Sims pinned her face-down to the floor. His fist dug into her neck and his hot, foul breath splayed across her face. Grinding his forearm into her spine, he drove the brunt of his weight into her shoulder blades. Then she heard the slide of the gun chamber.

"Should've done this years ago!" The cold steel of Sims' .45 bore into her flesh. Tracy swept the floor, searching blindly for a weapon, a distraction, anything. And like a god-send there it was – the jagged neck of the wine bottle. She gripped the glass and swung it over her head. Once, twice, three times - every thrust slashing deeper into flesh. Blood splattered across her hand with every blow, but like a demented animal Sims would not retreat. With a shove he rared his head back and laughed. Frothy, pink saliva trickled down the side of his mouth. Tracy drew strength to plunge again. But Jared was there, gripping Sims' head between violent hands.

"Get off her!" Jared raged and with a vicious -*snap* it was over. Dennis Sims' head fell listlessly to the left as his lifeless body dropped to the floor.

Silence.

Tracy collapsed. Jared knelt to her side, enfolding her into his arms as she panted and shook uncontrollably. For a moment he just held her, smoothing his hands across her body. After a moment she began to pant, crying as she turned into his chest. She brushed his hair back and warm, sticky blood tinged her fingers.

"Oh, God! You're hurt." She grabbed some napkins from the floor and pressed them to his wound. But as he swiped her hand away, she saw the blood stain on his jeans. "Jared! Your leg!"

Jared grabbed her wrists to restrain her.

"Stop! It just grazed me," he strained. "Help me get this downloaded so we can get out of here."

Jared snatched the laptop from beneath the couch. In a daze, Tracy climbed from the floor and righted the computer. She gathered the discs, flash drive and security badge from the cushions then pushed them toward Jared. Inserting each into their own slot and drive, Jared transferred the files onto Tracy's small lyric disc and flash drive, deleting each one from the hard drive as soon as each removal was complete. He grabbed the magnetic disc from his duffle bag and erased the hard drive of the computer.

"Guard these with your life," he whispered then pressed the disc and flash drive into her palm.

On pure adrenaline she started toward the bedroom. But the dark stain encircling Selena Salgado's body stopped her cold. Choking back the vomit rising in her throat, Tracy looked away only to see her uncle's broken body. The glow of his cold, malevolent eyes, even in death, haunted her. And that putrid smell – liquor, cigarettes, and deceit... made her double over as her body rejected every thought, every emotion, and every memory of her uncle's abuse. Jared stooped beside her, pulling her hair to the side and calming her until the nausea subsided. Dizzy and too weak to move, Tracy scanned the rest of the room and her heart leapt as a bigger fear paralyzed her – *Lauren's apartment.*

"God, what have I done?" she mumbled to herself. She swept her hand around the room. "They'll go after Lauren," she thought aloud. She fought to breathe, swaying as she remembered her uncle's warning: *hiding out won't be enough.* They had nowhere to run.

She kicked Sims' gun away. Collapsing to the edge of the couch, she lifted her guitar to inspect the damage. Nothing fatal - a three-inch crack in the seam of the wood that could hopefully be repaired. She rolled it over to inspect the strings and heard a rattle. Reaching her fingers into the sound hole, she felt the hanging remains of a flimsy wire. She shook the guitar and a detached piece of Velcro mounted to a small metal disc landed in her lap. *Computer chip?* Tracy stared in shock, unable to speak as a chill feathered up her spine. Her gaze drifted toward her uncle and found his cold, lifeless eyes... laughing. It was the same look from weeks before when she caught him in her bedroom, touching her guitar.

As if approaching a live bomb, she stretched her fingers into the sound hole and felt the sticky foam backing. She dug her fingernails underneath and ripped the device from the wood. *The sensor*, she realized. She grew queasy, staring down at the tiny nickel-sized gadget and then it hit her: others were out there – stalking, searching, hunting her down like a defenseless animal. To her left Jared was frantically

357

downloading the material that had made them the target. To her right, her uncle. *Two hours*, she recalled him saying. Assassins were on their way.

"What is it?" Jared snapped.

She shook her head and waved him off. When he looked away she stuffed the metal disc deep into her pocket. In a frenzy she shoved the guitar back into its case then wrenched Denny's cell phone from his pocket. Searching the history, she located the last incoming call and when Phil Murphy's name appeared, anger surged. The knot twisted in her gut as she stared at the phone screen and scrolled through Sims' recent contacts. One name crushed her – a call just ten brief minutes before the last one. She couldn't breathe. She couldn't move. The phone slipped from her hand and her vision blurred as anger churned within. She scrambled to her feet, unable to focus with the hurtful truth that was swimming in her head. Methodically, she began to grab loose pages of notes from the coffee table. A faint noise caught her ear.

"...can you hear me? Sheriff McClain is on his way..."

Tracy spotted her cell phone on the couch and placed it to her ear.

"Lauren?"

"Tracy!" Lauren shouted. "What the hell happened?"

Tracy wavered, trying to get her bearings. "You're there?"

"Hell yes, I'm here. You never disconnected! Are you okay? We heard gunshots!"

"Oh, God, Lauren," she began to cry. "We...your place is --"

"Tracy, listen to me..."

A loud crash shook the room. Sheriff McClain bolted through the door with his sidearm drawn. The beam of his flashlight aimed on her.

"Sheriff's Department! Don't move!" His voice was shaky, scared. "Tracy?"

He found a light switch beside the door. The bloody scene screamed out in horror as the ceiling light illuminated the room. McClain raised his gun, cautiously advancing toward Jared.

"Frazier?"

Tracy steadied her phone. "Lowell's here, Lauren. It's okay."

"No, Tracy!" Lauren yelled. "It's McClain!"

"I know, he's right here," Tracy agreed.

"NO! He's the fourth player." Lauren paused. "Tracy, did you hear me? Lowell McClain is in the golf photo. *He* took the picture."

Silence.

With a slow, nervous turn, Tracy faced McClain.

"He served in the same platoon as Waylon Vincent," Lauren whispered. "I missed his name. He enlisted under his first name, Alton. *Lowell* is his middle name. That's why I didn't catch it on my first search." With Lauren's every word Tracy's breathing grew heavier. "Tracy, he's part of this."

Tracy dropped the phone to the floor. She swayed and nearly fainted, but Jared was there, holding her to his side. Then, like an epiphany, it all came together. Who would her dad have gone to for help when he first discovered Denny's intentions? Who would have been on the scene of her father's crash – possibly to ensure it was fatal? Who would have hired Waylon Vincent as Chief of Police, overlooking and probably concealing his criminal record? Who would have been in position to cover up the crime ring in Newport? And who would have been the last person in the world anyone would have ever suspected? Her father's oldest and most trusted friend, Sheriff Alton Lowell McClain.

Her lips began to quiver and as her eyes filled with tears, she fought to catch her breath.

But tears welled up in McClain's eyes as well. With a shaky hand, he lowered his gun.

"Were you there?" Tracy balled her fists and inched toward McClain. "Were you there when Daddy died? Was it you, Lowell?" Her voice grew stronger. "Tell me! Did you kill him?"

"No, God no..." he rasped. "Never..." His body trembled and he clenched his chest, struggling for a breath. "I regret so much. I had to act like I was with them, but your dad is --"

A car door slammed. Jared sprang to the window. Waylon Vincent was rounding his squad car with his gun at his side. Before Jared could react, another car screeched to a halt. Two figures bolted from the car. Jared leapt across the table and grabbed the Glock.

"It's Vincent!" he warned, snatching the discs and laptop to throw them in the duffle bag. With a turn, he bolted to the bedroom closet to free Snickers and then hoisted the guitar and the duffle bag into his arms. Tracy had not moved, but stared at McClain who had collapsed to his knees, clutching his chest.

"Tracy! Come on! The back way, now!" Jared ordered as he rushed through the kitchen with their belongings balanced in his arms.

Tracy tucked Snickers under her free arm and knelt to McClain's side.

"Tell me!" she gasped, tears pooling in her eyes.

McClain gripped her arm and pulled her close. Two words crossed his lips – two barely audible, faintly spoken words. Just clear enough to crush Tracy's heart. She backed away, trembling as McClain strained to add more to the confession that would forever torture her soul.

Jared grabbed Tracy from behind, dragging her across the floor. She pushed away just long enough to grab her uncle's cell phone then lunged toward Jared as he held open the back door.

With their sights set on Denny's quad-cab parked in the distant field, they plowed through the thicket. Tracy dove in the driver's side, jarring her hip on the small metal box that was buried in the center console. She slung it to the floorboard then settled Snickers and the rest of the load.

To Tracy's left, Jared popped a panel from beneath the steering column. He fumbled through wires, sliding his knife along the plastic tubing. His hands – blood-stained and bruised - shivered as he brought the wires together. Just as the diesel rumbled to life, two shots rang out. Vincent's rage ignited as he bulldozed a path through Lauren's grill and lawn chairs to take aim. Jared shifted into gear, gunning the V-8 as the next shot shattered the rear passenger window. The pickup fishtailed away in a cloud of dust.

Tracy wrenched her gut as her stomach lurched from the forward thrust. A sharp pain shot through her as the metal box bounced across the floorboard and smacked her shin. She gripped the box, curiously flipping the switch imbedded in the side. A shrill signal blared and she nearly dropped it. But then the pitch changed and faded to a gentle hum. Before Jared noticed, she flipped the switch back and kicked the box underneath the floor mat.

Cattle trails and hayfields became their road as Jared routed an escape. Moments later when he glanced Tracy's way, she saw fresh blood streaming down the left side of his head.

"Oh, God, you're bleeding worse," she groaned. "Pull over, I'll drive."

He steered to a clearing while Tracy grabbed a shirt from her duffle bag.

"We're in too deep…"

"Shhh, it's okay. Switch places," she said, pressing the clean shirt to the bloody gash.

The truck jolted when he threw it into park. Without warning he lifted her into his lap, hugged her to his chest and held her. He was shaking.

"Shh, it's okay."

"T., we found the evidence. They'll never let us live," he breathed.

She squeezed his hand, afraid to let go, afraid to hear his next words.

She kissed him hard, gripping him so tightly she could barely breathe. She slid her lips to the leathery skin of his neck and as she did, the moisture of her tears stained his shirt. Breathless, she waited, clinging to him for hope.

"We have to die."

She swallowed hard to clear her mind, blocking out the senselessness he was uttering.

But his words remained. She reached for his face, studying his eyes to ensure this was her Jared who had spoken such words.

To die – those words pulsed as she struggled with the thought.

"Fake our deaths. Disappear. Change our names - our identities – start over as somebody else, just like you wanted," he whispered.

She drifted away, vaguely hearing him whisper about off-shore accounts, forged documents, obituaries - and as he rambled through the details, her focus darted everywhere – searching for any other solution.

"*Fall off the edge of the earth...*" she remembered aloud.

The brush of his fingers against her cheek brought her back. He was serious, she realized, and was waiting for a response.

With every pounding beat, she felt her heart race faster. And with every passing moment, her inner voice repeated the truth she hated to admit – there's no other way, there's no other way.

To die – it sounded so final, so cold. To separate from everyone and become totally alone. To completely erase their past, their identities, their lives. To deny everything that had come before and then begin again with nothing but each other. But then, as she clung to the promise in his voice, the thought blossomed into full color.

She and Jared – alone – beginning a whole new life. Safe, secure, together. Free of fear. Free of danger. Free of Sutherant Petroleum and all the pain it had created. Free to tell the truth of what she had just discovered.

The choice was clear. A single nod and tears gave way. Jared hugged her, clinging to her like a lifeline. With a new sense of urgency, he lifted her into the driver's seat. "I just have to make a stop first. Head toward the farm," he directed.

Her hand slid to her pocket and she could almost feel the sensor's hum. It felt good – knowing that she would soon be meeting her trackers face to face.

Summer Nights

Chasin' fireflies with a jar, wishin' on a distant star
Holding hands and ticklin' toes, snugglin' at the picture show
Skippin' rope and skippin' stones – talking on the phone too long
Lemonade, hammock in the shade, those summer nights and lazy days.
Fishin' holes with an old cane pole, stolen kisses on a late-night stroll
Cuttin' hay 'til way past dark, shaggin' baseballs at the park.
Swimmin' pools and broken rules, stories told the whole night through
All those summer nights we'd spend, wishin' they would never end
I remember it all like it was yesterday. That day we met, I knew right away
Of all the wishes I could choose, I'd have more summer nights with you.
Seems like only yesterday – the night I gave my heart away
And now there's nothing I wouldn't do to spend more summer nights with you

Chapter 42

While Jared unlatched the cattle gate that led to the north pasture of Bill Campbell's property, Tracy smoothed her fingers through Snicker's fur, wondering what could be so important to cause Jared to detour from their plan of getting to safety. A chill swept through the cab moving her to turn around, half-expecting Vincent or some other evil presence to appear. Nothing. Just the eerie tree-lined hayfield that bordered her family property.

"We better walk," whispered Jared, ducking his head inside the cab. "This diesel will be heard a mile away. Too dangerous."

His voice was low, distant... angry. Much too volatile for her to share her secret just yet.

"Where are we going?" she whispered as she pushed Snickers to the floorboard before shutting the door.

Jared lifted his chin to point the way. Rounding the front bumper of the truck, he led her toward the moonlit trail. Tracy twined her fingers through his and leaned down briefly to make sure the bleeding in his leg had subsided. In the distance Campbell's hay barn loomed above a tree grove. Tracy's own horses were sheltered there and she wished for the millionth time that things had turned out differently for her family's farm. Cimarron's soft whinny carried on the wind and Tracy ached for the peaceful way of life she had known just days before. But when she looked ahead to find the lights where her house had once been, the bareness taunted her, reminding her that this tainted land would never be the same again.

Jared came to her side and she sank against his shoulder. "I'll miss this place," she sighed. "It's home – *our* home."

He pressed his forehead to hers. "We'll always keep this farm, T." He brushed her hair from her face. "And we'll find a way to come back one day. Come on. I need to show you something."

A few more minutes of walking brought them to their tree. Tracy sat down to rest and hardly noticed as Jared squatted to the ground. Without a word he opened his Buck knife and slit the bark off the end of a sturdy stick. With a few more swipes of the blade, the dagger-point of the wood was honed into a chisel, ready for digging. Minutes passed. The steady scrape of his "shovel" faded into the background as Tracy sat in her own silence, trying hard to push the pain of McClain's final words from her mind. Suddenly, the grating stopped.

Tracy leaned forward. She swung her feet to the ground and squatted beside him as he brushed the loose dirt from the leather pouch he held in his hands.

"What is it?"

Jared cocked his head to the side. "Your father's shipment."

With sudden awareness, she yanked her hand to her mouth. As if led by a cosmic force, that same hand slid into the bag and the cool, smooth stones cascaded through her fingers.

"Diamonds," she mouthed. She dropped her fingers to her belly and the memory of Jared's first find made her smile. "Jared, these are…"

"Going to be returned," he interrupted, raking the diamonds back into the bag. "These are the *blue* diamonds. Since your dad died before they were found, those companies in Europe and South Africa probably think he and Eric stole them. So we need to give them back to clear their names. But for now, they stay."

"How did you know?"

"I didn't. Not until I saw your notes. That's when it hit me and I remembered finding that one." Jared pointed to Tracy's navel. He craned his neck for a quick glance then lowered his voice. "Your dad hid the stolen profits Sutherant investors had been using into off-shore, untraceable accounts – that's what Phil and some others have been waiting for us to find. But think about it - the money in those accounts was stolen. Millions of dollars, T. Those bastards can't claim it or accuse your dad of taking it without incriminating themselves."

Jared watched Tracy's expression change as the realization hit home.

"It's just sitting there, untouchable?" she asked.

"To them," he nodded. "But we know your dad's password. We can access it."

Tracy's thoughts ran wild, even as Jared's soothing voice, the voice she warmed to above all others, continued to explain his plans to use some of the money to fund their escape and to somehow compensate the girls who had been held captive by the European underground. She closed her eyes. All her mind could see was the brutal scene they had just left behind. Lauren's apartment – a blood bath of evidence that flashed like a neon sign to tell the world that Lauren was a part of this, protecting them. Tracy rubbed her cold hands together, helplessly realizing that Lauren was now a target for the assassins. That thought resurrected another scene from the apartment and her jaw tensed in anger. Seeing Phil Murphy's name on her uncle's recent call list was one thing. Seeing that other name was quite another. Pain turned to anger - a hardened distrust of everyone involved.

"Use it all," she seethed, "and I say we take down every person who is part of this."

Chapter 43

11:05 P.M. - Sunday

Driving back through town had never felt so strange. The streets were deserted. Darkened alleyways seemed to stretch on forever, concealing the honeysuckle-lined trails once so familiar. Storefronts and doorways crowded with townsfolk just hours before now stood empty. Silence weighted the air and the only home they had ever known greeted Jared and Tracy with a cold shoulder. Neither uttered a sound, yet that silence drew them closer than any words could have ever done. It spoke volumes, echoing a warning that the carefree, small-town life they had always loved in Newport was no longer theirs to claim.

Jared squeezed Tracy's hand and as his warmth channeled through her, she longed to keep driving – far away from all the lies and heartache that had taken root. But another, much stronger desire reigned. Until the truth of all that had taken place under the disguise of Sutherant was exposed, she knew there could never be real peace. So as Jared turned south onto 2nd Street and pulled to a stop in the rear parking lot of Hendricks-Bates Attorneys-at-Law, Tracy took a deep breath to clear her mind.

"Hendricks is already here," Jared said. "We need to make some decisions about the farm."

"Can you amend the land deed and appoint someone to take care of things around the farm?" she asked.

"Sure. Maybe Eric or Bill Cam…"

"No! Someone else," Tracy shot back. She swallowed. "I'd rather it be somebody different."

Jared hesitated, reading her carefully. "Okay, Hendricks will know someone. We'll name an executor to oversee the land and oil production, the maintenance, and security. We can have him add a clause that says that the property cannot be sold. Wish we didn't even have to leave."

At the moment Tracy wished a lot of things. She wished she could have all the years back that Jared had been gone. She wished her dad had never left home that night. She wished Lauren was a million miles away from the danger that was closing in. She wished Te Lei Soon would find Phil Murphy in one of those dark alleys.

And she wished she had never learned the truth of her father's death.

* * *

Five minutes later Jared and Tracy were sitting in Thad Hendricks' office - bandaging wounds and discussing the legal documents Jared had requested.

"Okay, Tracy, just to get you updated on what Jared and I discussed earlier this week, Agent Mike Richardson has approached Jared with plans to enter the two of you into the federal witness protection program. But Jared wants to take a different path." Tracy shifted in her seat to have a better view of their file. "This morning Jared called me to get me started on drawing up new legal documents and identification for the two of you. Now, of course, this is all strictly confidential."

He opened the file folder, fanning the papers out for Tracy to see. "What I have is the land deed, two marriage license applications, two marriage certificates – one pair in the names of Jared Frazier and Tracy Sims, the other in your new identities."

"Marriage certificates?" Tracy glanced at Jared.

"Jared thought, and I agree, that it would be easier to get married before you change identities, that way, changing a maiden name a second time can be avoided. I also have legal identification, social security numbers, passports, and an unlimited joint credit card. Does that cover what we had talked about, Jared?" Hendricks paused.

Jared nodded. "But I also need to make a revision to the land deed."

"That's easy." Hendricks chuckled as he selected some papers from the pile. "Marriage certificates and passports in one day? That's another story. You're just lucky Oklahoma doesn't require a blood test. And having a lawyer with a friend in the U.S. Marshall Service doesn't hurt either. I just need some signatures – your given names on one set of marriage documents and your permanent names on the other. Then you can finalize it when you're ready."

"Finalize it?" asked Tracy.

"Get married." Hendricks winked.

Tracy snatched the marriage certificate. "But we're ready now." She turned to Jared. "Aren't we?"

Jared's mouth dropped. "You mean right now? Tonight?"

She leaned into Jared and lifted the marriage license. "J., if what we just went through is any indication of what it's going to be like for us, I think we need to get married as soon as we can. We may not get another chance once we leave Newport."

Hendricks cleared his throat. "I, uh, am licensed by the state of Oklahoma to perform marriages as the Justice of the Peace in Brevard County if you need me to officiate."

Tracy reached for the second set of marriage certificates to read them for herself. "James Shannon and Teresa Smith?"

She smiled and fell back into the chair. "*James and Teresa Shannon.* Mom would have loved that." She grasped Jared's knee and massaged it.

"That way she can always be with you...even in our new life."

Tracy did not hesitate. She took a pen from Hendricks' desk, signed both licenses – one with her current name and one as *Teresa Smith*. Sliding the documents to her right. Jared sat up, staring at her with his dark, captivating eyes.

She pulled the brim of his ball cap playfully. "Ready?"

"So we're actually doing this?" Jared beamed. "The low-key, no frills wedding package?"

Tracy slapped at his arm. "There's no such thing as a 'no frills' wedding. Besides, it's not the ceremony that matters. Plus, you know Jodie will make us do this all again when it's safe for us to all get together. She's been saving my mom's wedding dress for me all these years so you know she'll plan something big. Can I text Lauren?"

Jared nodded and swiped the tip of her nose. He pushed the marriage certificate across the desk then pulled the land deed and will from the file. Hendricks thumbed through the papers and exhaled a long breath.

"Jared, do you even know what that place is worth?" Hendricks asked.

"Thad, I've fished every pond, rode every trail, and cut and baled hay from just about every acre of that place. From the time we were eight years old, Tracy and I ran those fields. So yeah, I know what it's worth." Jared shifted and faced him more directly. "But financially?" he asked. "You tell me because honestly, I have no idea."

"Tracy, your dad had fourteen hundred acres. That alone is worth a fortune," Hendricks stated. "And with the mineral rights and the potential profits once the oil is pumped and refined, we're talking several million."

Tracy patted Jared's knee and sat up. "That's unbelievable. Really, thank you, Thad. But right now I just want to marry this guy."

Hendricks smiled and backed his chair away from his desk. "Soon as we get two witnesses."

"Lauren Mayfield is on her way..." Tracy looked up from her phone. "But we need two?"

Hendricks smiled. "My son's home from college. He'd be glad to help."

Moments later there was a light tap at the door.

Hendricks opened the door and Lauren bolted toward Tracy without a word. They fell into each other's arms, succumbing to the emotional strain of the night.

"I'm so sorry about all of this," Tracy said. "Your apartment is..."

Lauren waved her off. "Mike Richardson heard what happened and said his team would take care of things. Do you know how much you scared me?" she fumed. "What was I thinking leaving you there alone?"

That's when she spotted Jared and rushed his way. Grabbing him by the sleeve, she yanked him into her arms and held him, slowly swaying in his hold.

"God, it's good to see you." She pushed back to really look at him. "I can't believe it's you." Tears welled in her eyes as she kissed his cheek and pressed closer to his ear. "She never stopped looking for you," she whispered. "Never."

Hendricks excused himself to make the document changes. Tracy and Jared led Lauren to the desk and updated her on what had happened at the apartment. Reaching into her duffle bag, Tracy retrieved the downloaded computer discs.

"I don't have time to explain it all now, but we're counting on you to get this to print," Tracy said.

Jared grabbed the disc from Tracy's hand and waved it toward Lauren. "But you've got to understand - this information is dangerous." He lowered his voice. "Te Lei Soon – you ever heard of him?" Lauren shook her head. "Korean mafia. These files show all his deals with the European and Asian financial markets – the agreements, the trades, the investments…all based on the counterfeit money he printed. Billions! Just imagine what it would do to the economy if this gets out."

"Mmm…makes it tricky for the sucker who gets the by-line," Lauren chuckled.

"I'm serious! Too many people have already died because of what's here," Jared swore.

"Okay, okay. I'll take care of it." She and Jared locked into a stare and after a long moment she added, "Trust me. And I understand how delicate the financial issue is."

"You and I are going to write a teaser and run it as the cover for tomorrow's early edition," Tracy explained. "We'll forward it to all our affiliates and see what happens." She grabbed the marriage certificates with her free hand and handed them to Lauren. "But first I need you to sign these."

"A marriage license?" Lauren's eyes volleyed between the two tentatively. "Now?"

Tracy nodded. "You know how long we've waited for this."

Lauren cocked her thumb at Jared. "As long as you're sure about this goofball," she teased as she pulled them both into a hug. "And what was with your text? Why didn't you want Eric --" Before Lauren could finish, Tracy jerked her toward the door.

"Come with me. We need to walk Snickers and I need to get something from your car. You did bring it, right?" Tracy rushed her outside and shut the door behind them.

Once alone, Lauren yanked Tracy to a stop. "What's going on? First that text about Eric and now you're obviously keeping something from Jared."

"Get in the car," Tracy stressed as she reached for the passenger door.

Lauren's hands-on-hips refusal stopped her fast. She did not take orders.

"Please... get in the car before someone sees us," Tracy softened.

They both climbed in.

"So talk," Lauren locked her arms across her chest.

Tracy eyes became teary. Lauren noticed and leaned nearer.

"Hey, what is it, Trace?" She patted her hand.

"I love you, Lauren," Tracy sniffled. "You're my best friend and you know I trust you with my life. But right now I need you to do something for me without asking any questions."

"Anything." Lauren pulled Tracy's hand into her lap.

"From this point on...you, me, Jared, and Levi. That's it. No one else can be trusted."

Their eyes met and for a moment Lauren's thoughts ricocheted through scenes from the past few days: the unnerving car chase and Eric's aimed gun, his nervous confession at the coffee shop, and his constant insistence that he *stay close* for her protection. Not to mention Mike Richardson's constant insistence that she relay every text message and every phone conversation that took place with Tracy or Jared. All week her gut feeling was one of mistrust.

Suddenly, Tracy's reasoning was clear. With a gentle squeeze of Tracy's hand, Lauren nodded.

After walking Snickers around the front lot, they retrieved a dress from Lauren's car and then returned to Hendricks' office. Lauren ushered Tracy toward the hallway and found a small conference area and adjoining restroom where Tracy could change and freshen up. Jared stood waiting in the front of the law firm's conference room dressed in a clean pullover and sport coat, compliments of Thad Hendricks.

"Hey, Spiffy," Lauren teased. "Fair warning, Tracy had me go pick up something from my mom's attic so act surprised when you see it," Lauren said, taking Jared's hand to emphasize the importance. "She wanted this to be special, okay?"

Jared smiled. "Got it. Now," he tugged at his coat sleeve, "do I look alright?"

Lauren straightened his hair and patted his chest. "I'd marry you." She hugged him and swallowed the lump in her throat. "You know I'll go crazy if I can't at least talk to her every couple of days."

"I know. We'll work it out. But I'm worried about you, Lauren. They've heard about your research; they know that was your apartment. You can't stay here. You and your mom need to go somewhere safe."

"Mike's arranging a safe house for us and --" Jared shook his head and cut her off.

"No. Change of plans." Jared grabbed a notepad from Hendricks' desk and scratched down his father's contact information. "Grant can get into your apartment. Have him pack enough for the next couple of weeks and we'll get you settled with my parents. Tell him to put everything else in storage for now. Just leave the FBI out of this," he insisted, waiting for Lauren to agree. "What will you do about the *Tribune*?"

"I don't know. I'm hoping this story will open some doors for me. Levi Daniels mentioned a position in Nashville so I may start there."

"Hmm, making a move for a guy? Sounds serious," he chuckled.

"He is pretty hot," she teased, taking the note from him. "Seriously though, he is quite impressive. You never know, I may settle down and surprise you one day."

"Tracy got the feeling you and Williams were an item."

"Mmm..." Lauren fought for the words and remembered Tracy's concern. "We're not really from the same mold."

Jared brushed his finger down her cheek. "Well, one day you're going to make some lucky man very happy. Go check on Tracy. I'll give my mom and dad a call."

In the back conference room Lauren put the final touches to Tracy's hair, which was pulled into a loose bun with a blue hair tie. Hendricks' happened to have a vase of fresh flowers on the small kitchenette table, so Lauren twirled them into a bouquet and placed them in Tracy's hands. She slipped her own Pandora bracelet from her wrist and clasped it to Tracy's.

"A blue hair tie, a borrowed bracelet and dress, some new flowers, what else?" Lauren asked.

"Something old," Tracy remembered, scanning the room for anything that might fulfill the wedding custom. Nothing seemed appropriate. Then she saw Lauren. "Wait! You! You're my oldest friend. That will work. Walk me down the aisle, Old Friend."

Moments later, Jared followed Thad Hendricks and his son, Scott, to the front of the room. Jared pulled the wedding bands from his pocket and handed them to Scott, rambling nervously about their recent shopping spree at the mall in Little Rock. The back door opened and as they turned, they both fell silent. They were not prepared for the vision.

Like an angel spun in God's light, Tracy glowed as she appeared in a lacy white dress. That youthful, innocent beauty that had always taken Jared's breath, shown from her face as she clung to Lauren's arm. And as Jared watched them enter, his breath caught again, amazed that the girl he loved more than life itself was about to become his wife.

At Jared's signal, Scott pushed play on the CD-player. Tracy immediately recognized the music. *Now and Forever*, a very rough rendition of the song she had written just days before while in Memphis. She blushed, knowing that Jared had somehow recorded it without her knowledge. She drew closer, her heart pounding in excitement at the sight of him – the love of her life, her everything. Still, as sacred as the moment was, she could not concentrate on anything but the plan she and Jared had devised earlier in the night.

Glancing to her left, she saw Lauren and knew how hard it would be for her to write the two articles that would announce their fate. The first, a wedding announcement detailing the marriage of life-long residents Tracy Sims and Jared Frazier, and the second, an obituary which would run two days later detailing that Mr. and Mrs. Jared Frazier had died in a plane crash off the coast of Galveston while on their way to Cancun for their honeymoon. It would state that Frazier was piloting the rented plane, that they were the only passengers on board, and that while all personal belongings and identification had been scattered among the debris of the wreckage, the newlyweds' bodies were never recovered. Lauren would ensure that the story would get national coverage and would irrefutably seal the news of their tragic deaths. Once that story was published, Lauren would construct her life's masterpiece - the investigative report bringing international attention to the multi-government corruption tied to Sutherant Petroleum. Lauren, Tracy knew, had that kind of talent and determination. She would get the truth out and leave no survivors.

Tracy thought of the blue diamonds and the illegal money Jared had discovered hidden in the accounts her dad had set up. She was so proud that Jared was honest enough to return the diamonds and generous enough to have shuffled most of the money into untraceable accounts – enough to afford reparation to the victims of those harmed under the pretense of "Sutherant Petroleum business" and to compensate his father and Lauren for all they had done to help restore justice. Thad Hendricks would be compensated for overseeing the farm, oil production, and Tracy's horses, and what was left would be more than enough to fully fund the after-life Jared and Tracy were about to face. That thought drew her eyes back to him just in time to hear the breathy "Wow!" escape from his lips as he watched her approach.

Tracy took his hand as Scott Hendricks and Lauren gathered beside them. The ceremony was short, simple and as they repeated the vows she and Jared had hurriedly written, the words *commitment, loyalty, patience,* and *love* defined all they had been through in the past years. Their love story had endured hardships and separation few could survive. When Thad announced them "Mr. and Mrs. Jared Frazier," Tracy smiled, knowing the name she had dreamed of sharing forever would only be hers for a moment.

Jared leaned down to kiss his bride but hesitated, taking her face in his hands to whisper one small word. "Thanks."

No one else heard and would not have understood if they had. But Tracy did. In that one simple word, Jared acknowledged all that she meant to him. *Thanks* – for being my best friend since we were kids, for being my first and only girlfriend, my first kiss, my first love, for waiting for me and never giving up, for protecting me, for writing songs about me, for marrying me and for leaving your life behind to be with me.

As they kissed, she remembered all the years of their past and felt all the love that had grown between them. She brushed the stubble of his cheek and smiled.

Lauren snapped pictures of the happy couple while Thad popped the cork from a bottle of champagne he had stashed away. But all too soon, the celebration took a turn.

Jared's phone rang first. Before he could answer, Tracy received a text message. Another vibration alerted Lauren as the same message flashed across her screen.

Jared's smile faded as he listened to Mike's voice.

"We've got to move!" Mike rushed. "Senator Baird Mackenzick was spotted leaving Chicago an hour ago. An aviation ground crew recognized one of his passengers - Eduardo Odelis, a drug lord out of Central America. He's a bounty hunter the DEA's been monitoring - most recently in Eastern Europe." He paused and in the silence, Tracy and Jared locked eyes. "An FBI informant said your name popped up in the conversation, Jared. I'm not taking any chances; I've got a car coming to take you to the airport. Where are you now?"

In a sudden panic, Jared waved an alert to Tracy and Lauren, mouthing "NO!" as he rushed toward his duffle bag to secure the computer discs and paperwork he and Tracy had collected.

"Mike, here's Lauren. Fill her in on what you've found out." Jared covered the phone as he passed it to Lauren. "Stall him! Do not tell him where we are or what has happened."

He pulled Tracy aside. "T., you know my gut feelings are hardly ever wrong," he whispered. "I say we get changed and finish up with Thad – and then get out of here."

Ten minutes later they had changed and in the whirr of commotion that followed, Tracy caught bits and pieces as Lauren relayed Mike's report.

"They're going to track Mackenzick and bring him in for questioning for the murders of Leonard Osteen and Senator Matthew Hastings," Lauren explained. "Grant is willing to testify that he saw him near Shiloh at the time of the murders so the FBI wants to review the home security video to see if it matches. And Jim Crenshaw?" Lauren turned toward Tracy. "Mike said that Bill Campbell came forward because he saw Jim walking from the hayfield near the area they found Larry Nelson's body. He said he was carrying a crowbar which according to the medical examiner may have been the murder weapon. He got a search warrant to check your barn and Jim's car trunk for prints."

A cold chill swept down Tracy's spine. She pulled her denim jacket closer and snuggled into Jared's side. As detached as she had been from the investigation, she knew for a fact that details of Larry Nelson's murder had not been released to the media. How could Bill Campbell have known Larry Nelson was killed? Without knowing about Nelson's death, why would Campbell have been suspicious of Crenshaw carrying a crowbar? And why would Mike tell Lauren this key detail in the first place when the FBI is still gathering sensitive evidence?

She glanced down the darkened street and shuddered. Goose bumps spread across her arms as she realized how wide-spread the corruption had grown. She narrowed her eyes and focused on the *Tribune* building just down the street.

Jim Crenshaw. Sure, the man was known for stealing leads and had probably plagiarized everything he'd ever signed his name to, but would he ever physically hurt anyone? Then again, those odd times when she was the last to leave the office, it wasn't unusual to see Jim waiting in the darkened parking lot watching her from a distance. Could "Creepy Crenshaw" really be involved in murder? Or is Bill Campbell looking for some way to draw attention away from himself? He may have known about the oil. Could he have fallen into corruption like so many others in the town?

Lauren's voice brought her back.

"But right now Mike's fear is that you're a threat to their counterfeit operation. If it's exposed it could make the stock market take a nosedive. Nobody, especially Te Lei Soon, will let that happen, so Mike wants to get you both back to D.C. tonight," Lauren urged. "And Jared, your mom and dad were scheduled for a deposition, but Mike hasn't seen them since dinner. He was hoping they had contacted you."

Jared chuckled and tugged on the brim of his ball cap. "Knowing my dad, they're long gone. I'm sure he had a reason for bailing on Mike. You and your mom will be safe with them."

"Tracy, Grant said to tell you it looks like Sheriff McClain died of natural causes, possibly a heart attack. Neighbors heard three gunshots and Mrs. Leonard saw four men running through the field behind the complex shortly after the shots were fired. They're getting descriptions as we speak."

The three stood in silence while the update settled. Tracy thought back to the first time she met Mike – his sincere smile, his warm hug. What reason would he have to deceive them? There was only one way to find out.

Tracy reached into the pockets of her jeans and withdrew Denny's cell phone. She saw the confusion in Jared's eyes as she lifted it into view.

"Denny's phone." She offered it to Jared explaining that the last call to Sims before he died was from Phil Murphy. "Sounds like he's on his way here to *assist* Denny."

Jared stared at the phone and pursed his lips, processing.

"Seven minutes before that Denny received a call from Mike Richardson. Mike's call sounded more like a taunt – daring Denny to show his face. It was weird." Tracy considered the other name she saw on Denny's call list – the call three minutes before Mike's. For the moment she chose not to disclose that name. Instead, she took Jared's free hand and pressed the tracking sensor into the center of his palm. "This is how they've been following us," she explained. "It was hidden inside my guitar. Came loose when I nailed Denny."

Jared tossed the sensor in the air and caught it.

"Since we left the apartment," Tracy continued, "Denny has received three calls and four text messages – two calls from Phil, one from Jim Crenshaw, and the four texts from Baird Mackenzick, trying to make plans for meeting up in Newport. They obviously don't know Denny is dead."

He stepped away and studied the phone and the sensor. Turning back, he pushed the sensor deep into his pocket. "Lauren, we may need your help with this."

He pressed the cell phone back into Tracy's hand. "Send them all a text. Make it sound like it's your uncle responding. Tell them your uncle forced me to open your dad's files. Explain that he has us at gunpoint and then say he'll be in touch, or whatever." Jared's eyes narrowed. "Whoever's been placing those calls will be after us, you know."

"I'm counting on it." She especially wanted to confront the one caller she had not mentioned.

***

The next few minutes became a blur. Tracy strode through the office gathering Mrs. Mayfield's wedding dress and the few materials she and Jared had managed to salvage before leaving the apartment. As she made her way to the truck, she overheard the tail end of Lauren and Jared's conversation.

"It's too dangerous to try it alone. Grant and I are helping you and that's all there is to it. Now tell me about your plan for what happens after that."

"Simple. We finish things here in Newport, we fly south, refuel outside of Galveston, stow our things in a locker and then head out over the Gulf. We ditch the plane, meet up with her uncle, Kevin, who's picking us up in his friend's Baystream yacht, and once we get back to shore, we disappear – new names, disguises, and no paper trails."

Lauren glanced at Tracy and then back to Jared. The silence became awkward until Jared grabbed the bags from Tracy and lifted them into the truck cab.

"For how long?" Lauren's voice was nothing but a whisper.

Tracy stepped closer. "As soon as things are secure – after the story runs – then we can contact you." She squeezed Lauren's arm and forced a smile. "We'll send you a phone that can't be traced. And later we can meet somewhere…a safe place."

Lauren nodded and as much as she strained not to, Tracy knew she was fighting back tears.

Jared stepped between them. "Lauren, four years ago I got my first glimpse at the kind of power these guys have," he said. "My family went into hiding, changed our names, changed our identity, changed everything – a new background, new routines, new hobbies, and new personalities. We cut ties with every person from our old life." He glanced at Tracy. "Had to move every time something seemed suspicious or any time someone looked at us too closely."

From south of town a train whistle blew. Jared paused to let the noise pass. "I always thought it was my dad they were after, but now I see why Tracy and I are such a threat to them. We can prove their guilt so they want us dead, but at the same time we're the only chance they have in getting that money out so they need our help. Either way, once they find us, we're dead. And now that they know you are connected to us, you're in as much danger as we are. So you've got to trust me. I only wish I had a plane so we could all get out of here without being noticed."

Tracy was surprised Jared had not mentioned this before. "I know where we can get a plane." She went on to detail the location of Eric's Cresta, confiding that not only had she seen Eric leave the key under the passenger seat, but that she had also seen the security code to the airport gate when he had punched it in. "He even had it refueled for his dad," Tracy added with a wink.

"A Cresta, huh? Perfect. Then I'll square-up with Hendricks and go over what needs to be done on the farm."

***

Within fifteen minutes, Jared had made arrangements for Hendricks to oversee the farm, horses, and oil production and had given Kevin and Jodie Mason power of attorney over the farm and property.

"Copies of these documents and your new identification papers will be forwarded to Tracy's relatives in Jacksonville," Hendricks confirmed. "That will prevent you from having to come back here and will help me keep things more -- *confidential*."

Once Tracy was settled in the cab of the truck, Jared tossed a wave in Lauren's direction. With a back road detour through Lucerne, the town west of Newport, Jared pushed the diesel to its limit, searching the darkness for any movement.

Jared steered his thoughts from the cold night that had surrounded them. Yet one thought warmed him like no other. *Mr. and Mrs. Jared Frazier.* Nothing would ever come between them again.

"Will you do something for me?" Jared asked as he stretched his arm around her.

"Anything," she promised. He buried his face into her hair and breathed in her scent.

"Sing to me. That song you were working on at the cabin."

Tracy smiled and slid closer, nestling her head against his chest as she began to hum.

"When you take me by the hand - in my heart I understand - how loving you comes naturally. It's when I feel you touching me... a gentle brush against your skin - like a cool and gentle wind, loving you so easily, anytime you're touching me..."

He slowed the truck and coasted to a stop on the side of the road. For a moment they simply looked into each other's eyes. Leaning in, Tracy kissed him. She pressed against him and whispered, "Our first and last night as Mr. and Mrs. Jared Frazier."

He lifted her left hand and smoothed his thumb across her wedding ring. "I wish things could have been different."

A sudden flash of light reflected in the rear view mirror and splayed across Tracy's face. Jared glanced up then pushed her away. "Company!"

That all-familiar strain twisted Tracy's stomach. She held on tight as Jared gunned the engine. She was thrown against the door as the truck tires spun, slinging dusty gravel behind them. Pressing the heel of her shoe against the metal box in the floorboard, she could feel its evil lure drawing the enemy closer.

"Right according to plan," she breathed. "Should *Denny* text them our destination?"

Jared pulled Kevin's 357 Magna from his bag. "Definitely. The west pasture, near the tree. Say he has us at gunpoint."

Chapter 44

Jared powered the diesel – dangling the carrot just enough to keep his trackers on the chase. The cat and mouse tussle intensified with every passing mile as they coaxed their stalker down one dirt road after another toward the remoteness of Tracy's farm. Jared slowed to a crawl at the cattle gate, threw the gear into park and shoved the driver's door open.

Tracy followed Jared's lead and scrambled from the truck cab. Wasting no time to unlock the gate, they scaled the split rail fence and broke into a run down the old familiar path that lined the pasture. Side by side they rushed deeper into the darkness. Tracy's heart pounded in her ears – half from fear of the pursuers who were close behind and half from that sickening *deja vu* of running for cover after leaving the cabin. That same ominous dread weighed her down, screaming at her to *GET OUT!*

"Whew! Not the kind of exertion I had hoped for on our wedding night," Jared gasped as he skidded to a stop just shy of the brook at the base of their tree.

Tracy caught her breath and collapsed to her knees. "Night's not over," she grinned.

Spinning tires and the grind of brakes sounded from the main road. Then came the heavy slam of a truck door and the rattle of the cattle gate chain. A hard thud and quick footsteps followed.

"Here, tie my hands," Jared's voice broke her thoughts. He tossed her a loop of rope he had been carrying then mussed his hair and tore the front of his shirt. "Not too tight. Smear some dirt on your face and shirt. Take your hair down and remember, whoever shows, we need a confession."

They positioned themselves at the edge of the hayfield, just beyond the cottonwood tree. Tracy secured the gun in the back waistband of Jared's jeans then looped a length of rope around her own hands. Together, they enacted pained expressions to make their captivity believable.

The crunch of twigs put them on alert.

Tracy stole a glance toward Jared and peered behind him into the darkness, trying to recollect the plan, trying to remember what they had rehearsed, trying to recall what she was and was not supposed to say. Suddenly, a figure appeared. Tracy turned and in the faint moonlight and glow of the tracker's flashlight saw all she needed to see - the other contact on her uncle's phone. His presence proved his guilt and erased the one last sliver of doubt she had been clinging to. She so wanted to be wrong but as she looked into his ocean blue eyes for what seemed the thousandth time, she felt her stomach drop and felt Brutus' sharp blade of betrayal rip through her heart. *Lies,* she realized. *Nothing but lies.*

"Eric!"

Williams slowed his pace, cautiously advancing as he scanned the adjacent tree line. He looked tired, strained. And by the looks of his wrinkled jeans and shirt and his mussed hair, Tracy reasoned he had spent a stressful night hunting innocent newlyweds. Her entire body tensed. It took all her strength not to blurt out all the blame, accusations, and distrust streaming through her mind. But she stayed quiet…waiting for the truth and the confession she so dreaded to hear.

"Where's Sims?" Eric asked as he squinted behind them into the darkness.

"You're the one working with him. You tell us." Tracy snapped, bitterly dismissing every smile, every conversation, every shared kiss, and every single memory ever wasted on the man who stood before her. *I TRUSTED YOU!* – The accusation screamed from her glare.

"*Working* with him? That computer work I did for him?" Eric pressed. "All I know is that Lauren said he was giving you some trouble earlier, so I called him and threatened him to back off. Then I got this text saying he's got you at gunpoint here at the farm. So where the Hell is he?" Eric stooped down to untie them but hesitated when he saw the confusion in Tracy's eyes.

"What's going on?" His focus shifted to Jared then to the tree line in the distance.

"Oh, God, he's telling the truth, Jay," Tracy realized. Panic set in and she began to tremble.

"What the hell is this?" Eric mumbled, unaware of the snake pit he had wandered into.

"Eric...just leave. Now!" Tracy whispered. "You're not part of this."

"I'm not leaving' you here." He reached to pull Tracy to her feet but Jared kicked at him.

"This has nothing to do with you. Get out of here!" Jared's voice was a strained whisper but was convincing enough to make Eric back away.

"What's wrong with you, Frazier? I'm trying to help."

"Leave!" Jared snapped.

Eric eased backward, never breaking the worried gaze he shared with Tracy. Then he saw it - a movement from the bushes a few yards behind them – just enough to let him know they were not alone. He froze, lost somewhere between the *smart* thing to do and the *right* thing to do, needing to escape the obvious danger but wanting to help his friends. His body seemed to sidle behind Tracy and Jared on its own accord, becoming a barrier of protection between them and whatever threat lurked in the distance.

"Please Eric, get out of here. It's not what you think." Tracy turned and started to rise, begging him to leave. Eric never heard the pleas as he scrambled to untie the already loosened ropes before those behind them attacked. But he never expected danger to appear in front of them.

"Stop right there!" A harsh, grating voice sparked an explosion of chaos as a covey of dove scattered from the treetops. All eyes shot forward to the front tree line where feathers and leaves rained down like confetti. Phil Murphy entered the clearing. Gun drawn and seemingly dressed for business in hunting camo, he moved with military precision, centering his aim on Eric Williams. "Back away!"

"Is this FBI protocol, Phil? Finding innocent people being held captive and shouting orders at the one person who's trying to help them?" Jared sneered, shifting his now unbound hands to steady the gun Eric had just maneuvered into his hand.

"And while you're here why not explain what you were doing in the state park when Brody Craig was killed?" Tracy pushed, bent on getting the confession she knew they needed.

Phil chuckled. "Knew you'd bring that up sooner or later. Lucky you didn't end up like him. But I can do it now just as easily. No one will ever know." He waved the gun in her direction but kept his eye on Eric Williams. "I told *you* to back up!"

"Mike Richardson knows," Tracy interjected. "By the look on his face when I told him you were at the park, he guessed right away that you were the one who killed Brody."

"That rookie had it coming. The way he bounced around that hotel lobby it's a wonder Mike got any surveillance done. No great loss."

"He had a wife and kid!" Jared said, having managed to slide the chamber on his gun while they kept him talking. "That's the thing about you, Phil. It's always been about you. You never gave a damn about my dad – even lied about him wanting to get me out of the way when he was just protecting me from guys like you."

"Yeah well, Daddy's not here, is he? And you're right, I *don't* give a damn about him 'cause you're about to make me a very rich man. Now get up. It's taken me four years to finally corner you so it's time to access those computer files."

"And me? What are your plans for me?" Tracy could barely contain her excitement over getting his confession on record.

"Tracy Sims, your family's been a thorn in my side long enough. Between your dad drawing up that last-minute will and you hanging around Newport the last four years, we've never been able to get our hands on that oil. Not to mention the millions we know your dad has stashed in those hidden accounts. After tonight all that changes. If it was up to me, I'd take care of you right now." He flashed a grin. "But Mackenzick and Te Lei Soon convinced me that a sweet little country girl like you will make them a lot of money on the market."

"You son-of-a-bitch!" Jared shouted as he bolted to his feet. But Eric had moved faster and before anyone saw him aim, he had fired a shot into Phil Murphy's thigh.

"You'll die for what you did to my sister, you bastard! Made her crawl and beg for mercy." Eric's voice was level and eerily calm. "Made sure she'd feel every severed nerve. Made sure she would have to suffer and choke on her own blood. Did you stay and watch her after you crammed that knife in her throat?"

Even in the darkness Phil Murphy's face shown ghostly white as Eric's words and image brought a buried memory to life. He had not come prepared to face his past. But now here he was, kneeling in the dirt with both hands gripped to his leg, panting like the cornered animal he was with nowhere to hide. He looked behind him for help but saw no one.

A glimmer of steel flashed as Eric shifted his gun's aim on Phil's heart and walked slowly toward him "My dad's a Baptist preacher down in Texas. Big believer in "turning the other cheek" and all that. But I think in this case he'd go with "an eye for an eye" and call it justice. I've seen you get away with deceiving, cheating, and killing way too many people in the last four years." He raised his right arm and tightened his grip on the handle of the ten-inch Bowie knife he was eager to use. "And knowing how you stole my sister from us and left her there like a skinned animal, my dad would more than support what I'm about to…"

Swipp – Swipp

Two flashes sparked from the tree line. Tracy sat oblivious until Jared tackled her to the ground. Phil Murphy fell face-down and motionless. To his side, Eric stumbled to the ground.

"Noooo!" Lauren wailed as she scrambled from the tree line, blowing her cover as she struggled to reach Eric. Grant was on her heels pulling her to the ground and shouting commands.

"Sheriff's Department! Stay down! Jared, talk to me."

"Two shots from the trees. Phil's down, Eric's been shot. Shooter's still out there!" Jared yelled.

"Eric…God, no…" Tracy moaned as she shoved from the ground, crawling toward Eric. But in a blur of movement, Jared was there to block her path.

"Tracy, get down!" His look of terror forced her back. Robert Murphy appeared from the tree line, gun drawn as he eased toward his son's body.

"FBI! Nobody move!" Director Robert Murphy stooped to the ground and retrieved Phil's gun, sliding it securely inside his own waistband. With his hand pressed to his son's back, he leaned in and whispered what must have been parting words before addressing Eric Williams who was struggling in pain just two feet away. Robert Murphy picked up Eric's gun, slid it into his shoulder holster, and then knelt to the ground at his side.

"I could never replace what my son has taken from you, Mr. Williams," Robert Murphy began. "But from the very deepest part of my heart, I am truly sorry for all the hurt and pain he has caused you and your family." He helped Eric to his feet and checked his shoulder. "You caught a stray." He paused at Phil's lifeless body then looked toward Jared and Grant, "I trust you got the confession you needed. I'll get with Mike Richardson and tie up the loose ends on the investigation. Now get this man some medical help. I'll clean this up."

There would be no calls for back-up. There'd be no media crews, EMTs, or witnesses to question. No coroner would be called to confirm the time of death and certainly no clergy would be enlisted to offer last prayers. Instead, Director Murphy threw his sport coat over his son's body then pulled Grant and Jared aside.

"This will be handled internally," he directed as he acknowledged the scene. "This kind of attention would blow the investigation. My team will take care of it."

Robert Murphy glanced to the scene playing out ten feet away and saw Lauren and Tracy hovering at Eric's side. He pulled Eric's gun from his holster, flipped the safety, and handed it to Jared. "Officer Reynolds, none of you were ever here and this is not connected to Sutherant in any way. All of this is strictly off the record. Understand?"

"Yes, Sir. I'll stay and help with --"

"No! Not necessary," Murphy barked as he scanned the ground. "Frazier, I need to meet with you to see those computer files. It's time to put this investigation to a close and the sooner we prosecute, the sooner this whole thing will be over." He threw his attention back to Grant. "Follow my instructions: tomorrow morning I want you to call a press conference and make a statement on behalf of the Newport Police Department. Say that you had a report that someone heard gunfire out here during the night. When you arrived you found Agent Phil Murphy, dead from a gunshot wound. Call it a hunting accident, call it a prowler, call it whatever you need as long as the case gets closed and the shooter is never found. Is that clear?"

"You want me to cover it up," Grant nodded.

"I want you to *protect* our investigation," Director Murphy corrected as he lifted his phone to make a call.

Grant Reynolds had grown accustomed to spreading lies in order to keep the Sutherant investigation intact. But Jared was not so prepared. He turned away with a sudden urge to vomit – not so much from the queasiness roiling in his gut but from wanting to rid himself of the filth that had so infiltrated his life. One thing was for sure: Jared had no intention of sitting down to any computer with Robert Murphy. Instead, he sauntered away unnoticed, then hurried Lauren, Tracy and Eric into the cover of trees.

"Eric, they'll take you as far as the hospital, but you'll have to go in on your own. Make up some reason you were shot but not a word about any of this." Jared stuck his hand out and gripped Eric's. "I won't see you after this, but I want you to know how much I appreciate all you've done. Be expecting a small package in the mail in the next few days. You'll know what to do with it." Jared's brown eyes were so intense Tracy knew not to question anything he said or did. So when he told her to drop Eric at the hospital and then to wait in the back parking lot of the *Tribune* office, she didn't hesitate.

Chapter 45

The downtown streets of Newport were veiled in a thin fog – just the added touch to create more fear during an attempt to slink away from the *Tribune* offices before daylight. Jared balanced a box of files and documents on his thigh, while Tracy and Lauren fumbled to re-set the alarm on the back door. With a harsh thud, the deadbolt set and the familiar all-clear hum sounded. With a collective sigh of relief, they raced alongside Jared toward the dark shelter of the Longwood Pharmacy's dumpsters.

Hours before, Jared had ditched Denny's truck and had caught a ride back into town with Grant Reynolds. Lauren and Tracy had parted with Eric's truck at the hospital just after procuring Mrs. Mayfield's minivan. As Jared opened the sliding door, Tracy slipped around him and allowed him to take the front seat. What she needed more than anything was to close her eyes and process all that had taken place in the last four hours. The caffeine kick she had nursed throughout the night was wearing thin and her concentration was pushing its limits. Four days. Had it only been four days since Jared's return had caused such a whirlwind of change? She glanced to the front seat and saw that Snickers had roused from Lauren's side and was heading her way. Tracy laced her fingers through the cocker's silky fur and smiled at Jared as he looked on.

"It's Monday, old girl," she crooned. "Deadline day at the *Tribune*." A glance at the console clock confirmed the time – 4:58. "Stan's probably piling eggs on his plate right about now. He'll be pulling in the lot in an hour," she mumbled under her breath.

In her mind she could see Stan Dothan's whole morning routine play out. He'd sit down to his desk, tear into a new cigar and pick up the first layout of the Tuesday edition expecting to read the planned headline – a two-column spread announcing the ground-breaking ceremony for the new town library. Instead, he would discover that someone had come in after hours to replace that story with a full-page split-column feature. Stan would smile and read with pride as on one side was an over-line caption announcing the marriage of Tracy Sims and Jared Frazier, with the photo Lauren had taken just after the ceremony.

Then his smile would fade because just beneath the matrimonial spread, Lauren had run the breaking news lead.

The layout was still fresh in Tracy's mind:

Tornado Alley:
Oklahoma's Sutherant Petroleum in Stormy Path
of Congressional Corruption Cover-up
~ An exclusive report by Jim Crenshaw,
Independent freelance reporter for the Newport *Tribune*

Tracy smirked and wondered what was going to happen to Jim Crenshaw when the news broke in less than an hour. She didn't care. He deserved to feel the same terror she had felt in knowing assassins were on her trail. She imagined what it would be like on Thursday, the *Tribune's* other weekly publication day when Lauren's other article headlined. How would Stan react when he found out right along with the rest of the world that she and Jared had been killed just as their honeymoon began when they crashed into the Gulf shortly after taking off from Galveston?

Tracy's mind wandered to the long, arduous hours of the night, recounting all that had happened since leaving Eric's side: relocating Lauren's mother to the safety of a small motel in a neighboring town; finalizing arrangements for Lauren and her mother to stay with Jared's parents in a safe house near Nashville until arrests were made; coordinating the packing and storage of Lauren's furniture and belongings with Grant Reynolds; and finally, sneaking into the *Tribune* office, writing and setting the new layout for the Tuesday edition; and then waiting in fear while Jared had returned to the farm to unearth the diamonds. She grinned as she pictured what it would be like when Eric opened the package of those rare, blue African diamonds. He would finally be able to return them to the Pretoria Diamond Corporation and clear his and her father's name of wrongdoing. Of course, Jared had enclosed an account number and instructions for Eric to access his share of the Sutherant money. She hoped the compensation would in some way make up for the sacrifices he had made – not to mention payback for the plane they were about to crash.

"Stan's got a long day ahead of him," Lauren shared with Jared. "The international press will be waking up to one heckuva story tomorrow."

"We held nothing back," Tracy added. "The takeover of Sutherant, the assassinations, the blackmail, the Congressional ties, the counterfeit-ring and Te Lei Soon…it's all there. And the best part," she drum-rolled on the back of the seat, "Lauren gave Jim Crenshaw the byline."

Jared threw his head back and laughed.

Lauren half-grinned. "Stan may know it was us, but as far as the rest of the world, Jim Crenshaw will forever be known as the one who squealed on the Sutherant Petroleum scumbags. But," pointing to the backseat, "she promised that I get to write the follow-up that will incriminate the CEOs and members of Congress. Levi and I get that byline."

"And this first story hits the stands tomorrow?" Jared asked.

Lauren nodded. "Cover story in twenty-two affiliate publications."

***

Sunrise took them by surprise and after stopping by a 24-hour Price-Smart to pick up snacks, water, and a twelve-pack of beer, Jared grabbed the keys from Lauren and drove toward the old railway bridge overlooking the South Canadian River. It was obvious where they were heading – the Landing, a small secluded inlet where they had spent many a summer day relaxing in the sun.

"Since we've got to wait until dark to take that plane," Jared explained, "we can swim a little, get some sleep...maybe be the last chance we get to spend some time together."

***

Lauren was the first to rouse from the two-hour nap after their post-lunch swim. She rubbed the kink in her neck and sat up, scanning camp for other signs of life. No such luck, other than Snickers who was tugging on her leash as she stretched to capture a chew toy just out of reach. Tracy, whose left thigh had made a pretty fair pillow, was still tangled in Jared's arms and by the sound of her steady breathing, had no intention of waking. And Jared? He had never looked so peaceful. She smiled and could not help but snap a quick picture to remember her friends just as they were – safe, happy, and right there beside her.

The late afternoon heat had begun to ease and Lauren shivered as a cloud shaded the last of the sun's rays. She checked her phone for messages and felt her heart sink as she saw the names Mike Richardson and Grant Reynolds light up her screen. The story she and Tracy had compiled must have started spreading sooner than expected. If the numerous phone messages were any indication, the impact of the publicity was sure to be momentous to say the least. A surge of fear shot through her, and the healthy glow she had gained from her day in the sun faded. The cold, lonely night began to close in. But then a new message came through and when she read the name of the sender, a wave of calm embraced her. Levi Daniels, her new writing partner.

Hearing rumors of tomorrow's story. Just tell me you're okay...

Her reply came quickly: *For now. Still on for next week?*

Levi's next entry took her breath away.

Unless I can convince you to come tonight. Can't wait to see you again.

"Oh, my God..." she sighed.

"Good news?" Tracy asked as she stretched her arms.

"Levi." Lauren tilted her phone so Tracy could view the message.

"'Come tonight' as in come stay the night?" Tracy questioned.

"Who knows?" Lauren pushed her playfully. "At least I'll have a place to go since it looks like news of our *wicked* little town is spreading more quickly than we anticipated. I think I need to get my mom out of here tonight."

"Good. Fly with us as far as Galveston and I'll have Kevin arrange for a car. Drive your mom to Nashville. She can stay with Jared's parents while you and Levi... *finish your report*," Tracy grinned.

"One thing still has me stumped," Lauren reflected. "We know how your uncle and Phil have been tracking you, but how did Robert Murphy know where to find you last night? Did he follow Phil? And why wasn't Mike there to help? Aren't they kind of partners now?"

Jared and Tracy both sat up, considering her questions. Jared slowly exhaled. His brow tensed and he had that nervous twitch in his jaw that Tracy had seen so many times in the last few days. Tracy's mind flashed through scenes of their involvement with the FBI. Every encounter struck her mind like a bad note.

In a daze she leaned into Jared's side. "I'm a little afraid to mention this because I was totally wrong about Eric, but can we trust Mike? The coffee shop in Nashville...he checked out the older lady and the computer guy, but remember how cool he acted when we asked about the girl – the *same* girl who turned out to be Denny's accomplice?"

Jared nodded. "And the hotel in Nashville - just before you bolted for the door, he was huddled around a bunch of business execs. He never did say who they were."

Tracy gripped his arm. "That night at the state park, he said he was planning to relieve Brody at ten the next morning, but he returned two hours earlier. Why the change in plans?"

"One thing's for sure. Whenever Phil turns up, Mike usually does, too. Or is that just an FBI team kind of thing?" Lauren laughed.

Her input silenced the group. All eyes fell uncomfortably on Lauren whose banter had not intended to cause so much attention.

A team – the word had rolled off Lauren's tongue with ease but had left Tracy and Jared with a very bad taste. And with the vision of Robert Murphy shooing Grant away from the crime scene still drumming in her mind, Tracy was at a loss for words.

"Oh, Jesus!" Jared's face flushed and before his next breath he grabbed Tracy's arm. "A vest! He was wearing a damned vest."

"Who?" both girls intoned.

"Phil Murphy! He's not dead!" Jared shouted as he pushed them toward the van.

"What are you talking about?"

"It just hit me! Robert Murphy could have taken a clean shot through the head if he really wanted to kill Phil. Instead he aimed right in his chest area – the place most covered by a vest. Then Murphy threw his coat over Phil's body, not to hide the blood but to hide that there *was* no blood."

"They faked it?" Tracy's eyes widened.

"Yes, like you said, Lauren, Phil and his father were working as a team. They must have planned that whole thing. Thank God, Eric screwed it up. They were probably there for me and who the hell knows what they would have done to you, Tracy."

"That's what it meant," Lauren mumbled under her breath. Jared and Tracy both looked her way. "When Robert Murphy bent down to Phil's body, Eric said he thought he heard him say 'stay down' or 'lay down' or something."

"Robert Murphy shot Phil to save him from Eric. Then he shot Eric in the arm, saying it was a stray bullet," Tracy realized. "He kept Eric from killing Phil."

"Murphy brought me here to Newport under the pretense of it being safer than going to Savannah," Jared reasoned. "It wasn't to keep me safe; he was planning to turn me over to Phil! Maybe Mike is just as clueless and we were about Robert Murphy. Maybe he's as innocent as we are. I'd like to be able to trust him; he's a nice guy when you get right down to it."

"Doesn't really matter. Even if Mike is innocent, he can't do much to help us at this point. Now that the Murphy's have failed, they will try again. And if Mackenzick and this Soon guy are on their way…" Tracy warned.

"You're right. We're leaving now. Lauren, tell your mom we'll pick her up in fifteen minutes. Then call Grant. He needs to know Robert Murphy cannot be trusted."

"And that Phil Murphy isn't dead," Tracy added.

Chapter 46

Tuesday 12:37 A.M.

The steady, hypnotic whir of the small twin-engine aircraft was enough to cause Tracy to drift off to sleep. Cuddling in the warmth of the flannel blanket, she had kept her eyes glued to Jared for the past hour of the flight as he maneuvered the Cresta 414 south of Galveston. She studied his strained eyes, the soft dimple in his chin, the scruffy whiskers that lined his jaw, and as he raised his left hand to swipe the unruly hair from his forehead, she saw a flash of gold – his wedding band.

"What?" His question interrupted her thoughts.

"Hmm?"

"You're smiling. What's up?"

Tracy smoothed her hand along his thigh and sighed, inching closer to his side. "Just enjoying the scenery." Jared was so gorgeous and with all the turmoil of the past week she had not had time to relish that fact.

He tapped on a couple of switches on the control panel. "But you're worried."

Tracy nodded then turned away. "How long?"

The question had hovered in her mind for the past hour, since the moment she watched Lauren and her mom exit the La Porte Municipal Airport just north of Galveston. Between the frantic departure from Newport, the rush to download the remaining computer files, and the scramble to assemble a make-shift disguise to shield Lauren's identity, the flight had not given them time to say a proper goodbye. Instead, a gentle squeeze of hands, a knowing glance, and a last embrace were exchanged while Jared spewed out final directions on concealing IDs and not using credit cards or public transportation. She had watched him stuff an envelope full of cash and a disposable cell phone into Lauren's bag as he made her promise not to make contact with anyone until she met up with his mom and dad near Nashville. With a turn, she and her mother had climbed from the plane and hurried to the tinted SUV Kevin had arranged. And then she was gone – driving away into the darkness.

Tracy pushed her attention to the present to take in her current surroundings – Eric's cramped Cresta 414 miles from shore with nothing but darkness in every direction. If Jared's plan worked, they would never be found again. Every detail of their escape ensured that fact. The meticulous manner of refueling at La Porte Municipal Airport: flashing their credentials as they introduced themselves as Mr. and Mrs. Jared Frazier, facing directly into the security camera so the world would know they had been there, making small talk with the airport manager and mentioning their hometown, her employer and lyric credits, their affiliation with Sutherant Petroleum, and their destination in Cancun. There would be no mistake of being identified when the flight was reported as missing. Jared had even detailed their plans of having a nice dinner in town while the plane was being serviced and refueled so he and Tracy could covertly drive the airport loaner car to Galveston East Beach to rent a storage locker to store their personal belongings. Upon return to La Porte Municipal, Tracy even phoned Mike Richardson, apologizing for the late call and explaining they had suddenly decided to get married so had not been able to meet him. The plan had been calculated to ensure one thing: that he and Tracy were not on the run, but were in fact, excitedly happy to be en route to Cancun for their honeymoon.

Tracy glanced at Jared and suddenly felt so strange. A week ago he was not even part of her life and now they were married and ensnared in a lethal governmental conspiracy. It was so surreal to know that in a few short minutes their identities of Jared and Tracy Frazier would be buried forever. She felt her heart clinch and closed her eyes.

"I never should have come back to Newport." His voice was barely audible in the noisy cockpit. "You've had to give up everything..."

"It's all replaceable – the house, the jeep, the job...even my music if I had to give it up. Except you. You're the one thing I can't live without."

She pulled a duffle bag from the floor and sifted through driver's licenses, passports, credit cards, prescription bottles, a few vials of insulin, and car keys, reciting the name of each as if saying a final goodbye. She placed their marriage license on top.

"So all of this will be found in the wreckage?"

"And this," Jared added, patting the suitcase just behind her seat.

Tracy opened the larger suitcase which they had filled with purchases made at a truck stop on their way back to La Porte. After removing the price tags from the swimsuits, flip flops, and vacation attire for the Cancun honeymoon they would never have, she closed it and pushed it to the back of the plane.

Secured with a small chain and pushed deep inside the pocket of her jeans, Tracy carried a small key which would later open the oversized storage locker they had rented in Galveston's East Beach. Stashed inside were the items they would keep after meeting up with Kevin: two duffle bags filled with clothes, toiletries, and diabetic supplies; Tracy's locket, lyric disc and flash drive; her collection of writing journals, photos, and personal items she had taken from home; enough cash to last several months, and their new marriage license bearing their new permanent names. Deep in the locker, tucked behind the duffle bags stood Tracy's guitar - worn, bruised, and ever faithful. The tracking device had been stripped away and was now buried inside the pocket of Jared's jeans, still active and still being monitored by the unknown.

"Hey, our new name is perfect," Tracy whispered. "Mr. and Mrs. James and Teresa Shannon," she beamed. "So where to, once we get back to shore?"

Jared paused. "The edge of the earth." His face had lost its smile and Tracy could see his muscles tense. He was scared, just like back at the farm where they had witnessed so much evil. His jaw twitched and her heart felt heavy knowing their future was so uncertain. She listened to the soft hum of the engines and soon gave way to sleep. Minutes later Jared brushed her cheek.

"We're about five minutes out. Time to suit up."

Jared flipped a switch and unbuckled his seat harness. He yanked the handle of the bulkhead compartment to release the tandem pack Grant Reynolds had procured from the National Guard armory. Jared noticed Tracy grow pale as she stared at the packs. He knelt beside her. "You're shaking."

"I'm terrified," she mouthed. A nauseating fear had gripped her.

"We'll be just shy of 15,000 feet so should have an easy jump. Check your blood sugar."

Tracy's stomach churned again. She pulled her knees to her chest and fought to breathe.

"T, we're jumping together so you won't have to do a thing."

With a groan she pricked her finger to test her levels. "128. It's fine."

Jared strapped her into the chute. Her head lolled limply from side to side. He detached her insulin pump and slid it and her glucose monitor into a double-lined waterproof bag then began to strap it underneath his shirt.

"Wait!" Tracy slid her phone from her pocket and held it out for him. "This is my recording of everything last night. It's all there. Phil's confession, Eric's accusations, Robert Murphy's attack...everything. Lauren and Grant got it all on tape, too."

A grin spread across his face and he slid it into the waterproof bag. "Okay, two minutes," he announced as he disengaged the automatic pilot and set the plane's course to make a fast descent. "As soon as we hit the water, we blow this whistle here on your vest; the emergency lights come on automatically. I'll pull the release to detach the chute then we'll drag it in."

"No evidence?"

"Right." Jared pointed to the faint glow of a spotlight. "Kevin has us in sight."

He braced his upper body to unlatch the door. With a hefty push the door jolted open and he slid the rod to prop it open. He strapped into the tandem harness and grasped Tracy's straps.

"Okay, T., I've got you. Now, just close your eyes and think of something good – like that big comfy bed at Jodie's."

The corners of her mouth curled into a smile.

"Remember how nice it was with that breeze blowing in from the river?" Jared's strong arms went completely around her. He backed out and pulled her weight into him as he moved through the doorway. "Remember the soft rain? The cool night air? That kiss we couldn't end?" He tightened his grip and secured her against his chest. His voice was intoxicating and the more she concentrated on him, the more she began to float away into that magical place lovers go when the world closes its eyes and leaves them totally alone.

Enraptured in sweet memories of love, Tracy felt him lift her from the floor and slide toward the wing. A rush of wind slapped her hard, but his voice held her steady. "That night you said you wished it could be like that forever. It will be, T. I promise." There was a sudden jerk as he gripped her arms. She closed her eyes then felt a frigid chill as her body fell free – weightless through the air. She felt her arms jerk free, felt the rush of gravity claw at her flesh, felt a tighter squeeze, a cold violent wind, a brisk catapult through the air, and as she held her breath…

felt herself slowly…

lose consciousness.

And then…

Rapture.

As if God placed His hand beneath her, a soft cushion of air rose up to greet her. She felt the strength of Jared's arms and tasted the salty dryness of her lips. She wanted to turn around, wanted to hold him and kiss him and thank him for this – one of the most sensual experiences she had ever known. Then Jared tugged her ear and at once, her heart surged. She gripped his hand to her cheek and felt the thrusting power of his pulse against hers. Flesh to flesh. At that moment, she understood the real virtue of marriage. God had truly made them one – forever.

She opened her eyes and peered up into the dark, boundless sky. Like that empty plane disappearing into the darkness, her old life was being left behind – fading further and further away in the vast distance. In that death-like quiet she drew a breath of fresh sea air then slowly exhaled, releasing all the fear, the sadness, and the pain that had come before.

They had made it – *the edge of the earth.*

Tears stung her eyes as she looked toward Heaven – so thankful for the new life God had given them. From behind, Jared brushed her cheek and his light-hearted cackle filled the air. She looked to her right and dangling between his fingers was the wire that held the tracking sensor. His fingers spread and the final link to their predators shot into the night air. She and the love of her life were alive and safe and free. And suddenly her own small laugh pricked the air as she floated fearless to the dark waters below.

Chapter 47

A light morning mist coated the docks with a cold, gloomy haze. The soothing lull of the tide dampened the mood; its low, steady rhythm stifled only by the distant rumble of boat engines revving up for a late morning launch. Gone were the sunrays, the pastel pullovers, baggy board shorts, and sunbathers that usually dotted the Galveston Yacht Club pier. In their place hobbled Santiago's twin, drifting along the weathered planks of the boardwalk straight from the pages of Hemingway's tale. A grungy dampened raincoat hid the leathery, sunbaked skin clinging to the shell of the man who used to be - a nomad of the sea who now faced life from behind the brim of a faded fedora. Unshaven, unkempt and alone, he wandered the deserted walkway hindered only by the grocery cart leftovers of his life. A reel-less rod, a rusted can of day-old bait, the sea-green thermos of lukewarm coffee, and a box of stale saltines were all that were left under the protective cover of a stained stadium blanket. His *catch*, too, had withered away and only the burdens of his past remained.

Climbing from the deck of the *Renegade*, the 47' Baystream yacht Kevin Mason had docked just an hour before, Jared shouldered two duffle bags and stepped ashore. Tracy turned and followed him down the ladder and once her foot hit the last rung, he embraced her from behind, holding on so tightly she could feel his indecision. He too was nervous about the next leg of their getaway. She turned in his arms and held him, just as she had done throughout the night after being pulled from the Gulf. Kevin had retrieved them a hundred miles out with warm blankets, sandwiches, and a bottle of Cristal champagne - a heartfelt welcome as they arrived for their first night as Mr. and Mrs. James and Teresa Shannon.

Tracy noticed the wanderer, smiled, and watched him advance as he pushed his rickety cart along the battered planks. For a moment the man paused and lifted his weary eyes. Sadness swelled deep inside Tracy as his gaze settled on her. His frailty, or the way he shuffled aimlessly under the weight of his load, triggered a wave of fear – a premonition of what she and Jared were heading toward. Homelessness. Isolation. Nameless faces.

Jared whispered, "Kevin said he'd meet us at the locker."

Tracy swept the blonde hair extensions from her face and adjusted the coral hoodie more securely around her halter top. She ran her fingers through Jared's newly dyed sun-bleached hair. Kevin's contribution of facial hair, temporary tattoos, a faded visor, and well-worn flops rounded out the convincing disguise.

Drifting her hands into the back pockets of his board shorts, she inched closer, filling all the empty space that separated her from her new husband. Still basking in the euphoric bliss of the first night of their honeymoon, she playfully traced her finger across his bottom lip. "Sooo...level with me. Why are you and Kevin so interested in the lockers? That's the third time you've mentioned it."

He shrugged. "Just a hunch."

Tracy squinted, wondering why he did not elaborate. "So we get our things, rent a car, and then lay low for a while?"

Although Jared had just confirmed this moments before, Tracy repeated the plan again to make her new life seem more real.

"And after we've had some time for ourselves..." he brushed the tip of her nose, "and *if* it's safe, we'll meet up with Kevin to help with the Sweet Escape camps down in the islands."

She tugged the cords of his hoodie and pressed a kiss to his firm, bare chest. "Life in the Caribbean," she purred. "With my scruffy, beach-bum husband."

Jared threw his head back and laughed. "Come on. Let's get our stuff."

Chapter 48

Wednesday – 9:45 A.M.

Nashville

The hallways of the Southern Tradition Production Studio pulsed with commotion – a din of paparazzi, ego-laden artists, synthesizers, and upwardly mobile snakeskin boots and high heels. In spite of sleep deprivation from the all-night drive and a morning of tweaking the final draft of the feature that would run front page of twenty-two national newspapers the following morning, Lauren strode toward Dale Saunders' office with a confidence that made others step back and take notice. With Levi Daniels by her side, she carried herself more gracefully than most of the rich and famous who were rushing through the same hallways. She tightened her grip of the padded shipping envelope containing Tracy's latest instrumental track, downloads of Mark Sims' computer files and Grant Reynolds' recording of the attack scene at the farm, then grasped Levi's extended hand and smiled. His warmth had welcomed her to Nashville just hours before, and just as in the last time they were together, that instant attraction had ignited and had drawn them closer more quickly than either had imagined possible. After helping to get her mother and Snickers settled with Jared's parents, she and Levi had spent the rest of the morning scrutinizing the horrific evidence Jared had downloaded from Mark Sims' computer files - information that was certain to seal the prosecution of several sitting members of Congress, high-ranking government officials, and international traders affiliated with Sutherant Petroleum.

"You look beautiful, by the way," Levi whispered as he reached to open Dale's door.

Lauren paused, taken by his charm and the way his muscles flexed beneath his tailored shirt and blazer. "And you look..." she allowed her eyes to roam freely, "well, I know *I'd* never grow tired of looking at you," she grinned.

Levi's face brightened. But he couldn't hide the hunger in his eyes – an intensity that Lauren fully understood. She felt it too.

Dale Saunders was everything she had expected based on Tracy's narratives over the past two years. Professional, confident, focused... a total contrast to Levi's relaxed, down-home, seat-of-the-pants approach to sniffing out a story. But as Dale listened to their plan and made suggestions for their journalistic approach, she could tell he added the needed balance to Levi's "hit 'em where it hurts" plan. What's more, Dale knew money. Based on the figures he was currently discussing on the phone with the owners of two television networks and a major newspaper affiliate, she and Levi were in line for a hefty commission.

"Two things," Dale began as he ended his call. "We get a safe location for you two to complete the investigation. Plus, any future book deals, movie rights, or additional journalistic opportunities related to Sutherant Petroleum go through me. I want to make sure you don't get screwed when this thing spikes the interest of the global markets. If you can agree to that, HR will set you up with a retainer, expense accounts, travel..." Dale slid a piece of paper across his desk. "And this compensation for an eight-story exclusive."

Lauren read the six-digit figure and nearly fainted. She looked to her side and saw Levi's calm expression.

Impassively, he checked his cell messages while she silently freaked out inside. Had he not seen Dale's offer? That's when she remembered who she was sitting beside – the legend, Levi Daniels. He was used to this kind of deal. And now they were working together. Just as she was about to speak up, Levi winked at her and responded to Dale.

"Add one clause to the contract." He cocked his head toward Lauren. "Her name will be listed first in the byline and she gets an open-ended contract to work as my partner once the eighth story is published. Now where do we sign?" Lauren's heart pounded until she felt Levi's warm hand cover hers. As he gave a gentle squeeze, she knew this was the start of a whole new life for her.

Chapter 49

The parking area of the Galveston Yacht Club was nearly vacant. The light drizzle had dampened the asphalt and by the looks of the ominous clouds, had set in for the morning. Tracy stepped from the boardwalk into the parking lot and turned toward the low hum of a fog horn sounding in the distance. That's when she detected the security camera high above the light post adjoining the bathhouse. The camera had been smashed - as if it had imploded into a mangled, heap of wire fragments. She had not noticed it before; her curiosity slid down its pole to the ground littered with shards of glass and metal.

"Jay," she mouthed, drawing his attention toward the scene.

Jared nodded once, his eyes on alert - dark pools of defiance searching the area. "I saw it last night when we stored our stuff. Kevin came ahead of us to...*disable* it - just in case."

"In case what?" Her question went unanswered. Jared pulled a pair of Kevin's gloves from his pocket and tugged them over his hands. He gripped her elbow and led her toward the bank of lockers beside the bathhouse. And then it hit her: the gloves, the "disabled" security camera, the very fact that they were here so early in the morning – Jared was ensuring there would be no witnesses or evidence of them having been there. He had to create the appearance of having flown straight from La Porte before crashing into the Gulf so there would be no evidence of them ever having been to the Galveston Port. *That's why he signed a fake name to the locker rental agreement*, she realized. No record of us at all.

"In case they're still following us!" he answered. "In case I'm right about there being more than one tracking sensor."

Tracy stalled. She opened the locker and eyed the few belongings that were left inside. "Where? We searched everything."

Jared leaned closer. "It's something Eric said." He lifted the locket from the hook on the back wall. "A comment he made about making this with your dad." He flipped it over to show her the backing. The inscription was engraved on a small silver disc – similar to the one hidden in her guitar.

Tracy's face drained.

"I think your dad had this made so he could keep track of you... to keep you safe."

In a strange way it made sense to Tracy. Before his death her father knew the danger they were in. Maybe he simply feared that their plan to turn state evidence had been leaked. That alone would have spurred him to get his only child to safety. No doubt he would have wanted to track her whereabouts.

Tracy thought of all the terror she had seen in the past week and all the heinous evidence she and Lauren and Jared had uncovered in their research. How could she question her father's need to watch over her? How could she question his reason for driving away in anger that night? In light of all that was taking place with the company, how could she question any of his actions?

Things are not always as they seem. Frazier's words ran through her mind. As did the promise she made to her Aunt Jodie: not to let anything she found out change the way she remembered her dad. Like Jodie had said, he was a good man. Unanswered questions would not change that.

Just feet away, someone cleared their throat.

Jared grabbed Tracy's hand, but she did not need the vice grip of his strength to keep her from turning around. She knew who was there. Her sixth sense had anticipated his return all along and as she caught wind of his dime-store cologne, all doubt was erased as to who had arrived. The stabbing pressure of the FBI-issued 9mm against her spine made it certain that Phil Murphy had found them.

"Nice trick - spreading that story across the front page of yesterday's paper and signing Jim Crenshaw's name to it. Probably saved your life. 'Course Jim wasn't so lucky. Heard he went into the office early this morning and put a bullet down his throat before those Koreans could find him."

Tracy gasped and steadied herself against the locker. That vision made her queasy and with the feel of the gun barrel against her skin, she began to panic. But like a cornered animal her instincts said *escape!* She scanned the locker in search of the 357 Magna they had borrowed from Kevin.

It wasn't there.

Phil thrust Jared against the locker. "The diamonds and the discs now!"

From beneath the crushing weight of Phil's braced arm, Jared allowed the music clef necklace to slip through his fingers and into Tracy's hand. She glanced down and read the inscription. *Keep our song in your heart.* Six simple words - a message so personal no one else would ever detect that it was the key to unlock her father's computer files. But to her, that sentiment was a precious reminder of her father's undying love. His way of protecting her.

"They're not here!" Jared fought for position. "It's all been turned over as evidence right along with signed confessions from Grant Reynolds and Eric Williams who will swear that you were murdered in that field."

"I'm obviously not dead," Phil sneered.

"Well, we have proof that you are," Tracy countered. "Video footage of everything that happened and everything you and Eric said."

"Sorry, Doll Face," he mocked. "Your friends made the mistake of showing that footage to my old man. Let's just say it was confiscated. So I'm living proof I'm not dead." Phil's frat boy retort shimmied between them until a God-sent gust of gritty sand stung his face. A fog horn moaned in the distance, and as if on cue, David Frazier rounded a grove of fronds steadying Kevin's 357 Magna in his gloved hand.

The shocked look on Jared's face made it clear to Tracy that the rendezvous was not part of his plan. Part of her wanted to reach out and hug her new father-in-law; another part wanted to reach out and slap the hell out of him. She had dreaded this moment since hearing his name in Sheriff McClain's final words as he was confessing who was responsible for Mark Sims' death. Now she could barely stand to look at the traitor.

"You're right, Murphy," Frazier senior's deep timbre resonated through the somber air. "If you were to suddenly show up alive, your father, Robert Murphy, couldn't be pinned with the crime. So to make sure your dad gets the death sentence he deserves, I'm here to guarantee nobody ever finds your body."

Murphy's wrist flinched but Jared was there to wrestle the 9mm from his hand. In one flowing motion, Jared pinned him to the ground.

Phil raged and struggled. "I will track – you – down!"

Tracy jammed her foot into Phil's spine, bending to cram the locket into his back pocket.

"No – you – won't! You are dead! And *we* just died in a plane crash, you idiot. This is the last time you will ever see us."

David Frazier took her place and drilled a knee into Phil's thigh. He yanked the length of rope he had snatched from a tie-off piling and bound Murphy's hands.

A misty gust whisked through the sea oats. The hypnotic *whirr* of the rising wind and the steady *ppusshh* of cresting waves heightened the tension and made Tracy more anxious than ever to leave the scene far behind. But something made her want to stay. Maybe witnessing Phil Murphy's demise would bring closure to the curse that seemed to plague her in the deepest sleep of the night. Seeing the faces of the victims and hearing the cries of the ones they left behind...Matthew and Clair Hastings and their three children, Leo Osteen, Clint Burris, Hank Tisdale, Officer Everett Hadley, Cynthia Latham, Sheriff McClain, Derrick Roberts, Brody Craig, Dana Williams. And when she thought of her own father, she knew that for Jared's sake she would have to take the truth of her father's killer to her grave. Phil Murphy, on the other hand, had been a major reason her dad had crawled into that truck that fateful night. Plus, he had deceived Jared. When she heard his cursing and whining just feet away, she wanted only to –

BBRRUMPH!

David Frazier evidently felt the same way. After connecting with Phil's face, he wiped the trace of blood from his fist and stood, pushing the Magna 357 into the pocket of his windbreaker. Murphy would be out cold for some time.

Padunk, padunk, padunk, padunk... the steady rhythm of the drifter's grocery cart rolling along the boardwalk set a new rhythm for the scene. The drone of the steady cadence captivated her and when she lifted her face, *Santiago* seemed to smile. Curious, she watched as the lonely wanderer stepped from the pier, nodded toward Frazier, and let his weary, dismal eyes lift from beneath his fedora. He pointed toward the western sky as a break in the clouds and a warm ray of sun bled through, unveiling a double rainbow spanning across the horizon.

"Promising," *Santiago* reflected.

Tracy looked at the sky and then closed her eyes to absorb the warmth of the bright blue patch of Heaven. She reached for Jared's outstretched hand, but a faint, ominous sound made her flinch.

Chut-Chuc! Sliding the chamber of the Magna 357, Frazier wasted no time in attaching a silencer. But it was the drifter who had stolen Tracy's attention. Their brief gaze sparked a kaleidoscope of memories and as her heart began to race, she released Jared's hand, swiped her eyes, and studied the nomad's familiar gait.

"Oh, God..." she breathed.

Peeling away the raincoat, the frayed fedora, the meager spoils and the façade of added years, she saw the wanderer through new eyes. *Things are not always as they seem.* Frazier's words danced across her mind, thrusting reality into a tailspin – free-falling through years of lies. Tears began to well in her eyes as the truth started to unfold.

David Frazier stepped to her side. "He had no choice – there was no other way to draw them away from you."

She pressed forward, shaken and confused. Jared placed his hand to her back as the drifter released the cart and moved toward her. Years of doubt and grief crumbled from her mind and as she stepped closer, the strong arms she had so missed embraced her and sweet memories of her father came alive.

The voice she had long imagined wrapped around her again as through soft tears, he whispered her name. "Tracy... Tracy...my sweet, sweet girl," he breathed.

But their reunion, he explained, would be short-lived. Being seen and identified would negate all the precautions that had been taken. A true reunion would have to wait for a safer time, a safer place. So as Frazier tugged the grocery cart closer, Tracy and Jared stepped back and allowed their fathers to complete the plan Kevin had helped them devise.

Every movement was precise and deliberate. Frazier passed the Magna 357 to Mark Sims who secured it in the pocket of his raincoat. Sims yanked the stadium blanket away to reveal a blue plastic tarp which had been draped inside the grocery cart. Frazier unfolded the tarp allowing the edges to overlap the sides of the cart. Wrenching his hands underneath Phil's shoulders, he nodded for Sims to grab the legs and together, they lifted him into the cart.

Phil started to stir. His eye was swollen and as he pried it open, he flinched on seeing the drifter. In his next breath his face lost color, his lips began to tremble and all he could manage was, "You..." Without saying a word Mark Sims slammed the butt of the Magna against his temple.

Frazier folded Phil's limbs into the cart and tugged the tarp over his body. Sims snapped open the stadium blanket and let it drape the cart. As Tracy watched the methodical movements, she saw her assumption was correct: their fathers had planned on Phil tracking them here, and now they were ensuring that his body would never be found.

Kevin approached from the boardwalk. As if in rhythm to some silent music, he snatched the Jaguars ball cap from his head and flipped it around – cramming it into place backwards - the precise motion he routinely performed just before he set sail.

"Tracy, Jared, you'll one day see it had to be this way," Kevin said. "I will be the contact and when things get secured with the investigation, we'll arrange a location for a real reunion."

"You've known?" Tracy asked, turning from Kevin to Frazier.

"They knew," her father nodded. "And Lowell McClain, who never revealed the truth even when he had to pose as the enemy. But that's it, not your Aunt Jodie and not your mother, Jared. That staged wreck, the power of attorney...I had to somehow convince them I was dead so that they would need you both to live. But we're all safe now. And with all you and Lauren have done, Agent Richardson will have plenty to incriminate those involved."

"Mike Richardson? We can trust him?" She glanced around the group.

Frazier shrugged. "Doesn't matter." He waved a finger around the group. "None of us exist anymore, right?"

Tracy felt weak and as she had so many times in her past, looked to her father's arms for support. This time, he was there. It felt as warm and as loving as she had always remembered. That was enough until they could meet again.

She felt Jared tug her hoodie from behind – the sign that they needed to leave. Blank stares and pursed lips to hold back the tears were all she could manage as she and Jared silently said their goodbyes to her uncle, her father-in-law, and her father. *Santiago* placed his fedora back snuggly over his brow, but from beneath she could see tears well up in his eyes.

"I love you, Daddy," she mouthed as her own tears began to fall. Jared gripped her hand to make the short walk to the marina so they could catch a bus into town. From there...no clue.

The rhythmic *padunk, padunk, padunk* cadence echoed through the chilly air. Through a thin, almost bare opening of the fronds, Tracy could just make out slip #9 where Kevin waited. As if on cue the rumbling motor of the *Renegade* stirred to life.

Charuunnggggggggggggg...

Tracy paused. "Where are they going?"

"About ten miles out," Jared crooned.

Just then she saw *Santiago* and David Frazier roll the grocery cart from the dock to the hoist of the *Renegade*. The two men pulled straps and pulleys and within seconds, the blue tarp was lifted over the bow and into Kevin's hold. The realization sank in. They were making sure Phil Murphy's body would never be seen again.

Tracy turned away, wanting the warm embrace she had just shared with her two fathers to be the way she remembered them. Phil's demise no longer mattered. Neither did the counterfeit ring, or the Soon family, or Baird Mackenzick. None of it mattered. Eric would heal and return the diamonds. Lauren would get her big story, start a new career in Nashville, and one day meet up with her again. Mike Richardson would bring indictments. Kevin and Jodie would watch over the farm until one day, maybe, she and Jared could return to make it their home again. The only certainty? Jared would never leave her again.

Tracy lifted her guitar case and felt the all familiar comfort in the way the old heirloom settled against her back.

She reached for Jared's hand. Facing into the breeze she felt her mind clear of all that had happened. So much had been left unsaid, so many questions left unanswered. For now it would have to do.

Teresa and James Shannon had a life to live.

THE END

Acknowledgments

I have moved a total of thirteen times. Sometimes out of desire, sometimes out of necessity. But the hardest move I ever had to make was when my family left Oklahoma. I love Oklahoma. I love the people. I love the down-home feel. I love the endless fields of wheat, the herds of cattle, the red dirt, and yes, the unyielding wind. I've been away for years, but sometimes I still catch myself calling it home. When a place leaves such an impression, it naturally becomes the setting for any story you want to tell. So when I started kicking around ideas for that one thing that could test a love more than anything, I knew that love story would have its beginning in Oklahoma.

So first and foremost, a big thanks goes out to all my family and friends back in the heartland. After all these years I have not forgotten you – as evident in the personalities of some of the more favorable characters.

Writing can be quite grueling at times, so I'd be amiss if I didn't thank Sugar, my faithful, loving cocker spaniel that never left my side. And yes, she earned her cameo.

For all the times you never complained about my laptop being in the way, the infernal clicking from the keypad, my inability to drive on long trips so I could sit in the back and write, late dinners, no dinners, inattentive moments, and yes, neglect at times – I sincerely thank my biggest fans,

Ethan and Erin.

You kids are my life and I never would have finished without your motivation. Your teasing "just get it done already" words of inspiration kept me on track more than you know.

Erin, you'll always be my favorite editor-in-chief.

Ethan, kudos to you for creating the title!

May you both find that one thing in life that gives you the kind of joy writing brings to me.

And because he is my everything, I thank my husband, Jim. Your constant patience, your firearm, aviation, and legal expertise (sometimes in the middle of the night), your gentle hugs when I didn't deserve them, your understanding when creative juices flowed right over our conversations, and your undying support in allowing me to pass up jobs in order to stay home and write have proven time and time again that you are the better person in this relationship. Thank you for the love story we continue to share.

You'll always be my Jared!

Lastly, but more importantly than all others, I must thank God. Without His direction in my life, I would never have been blessed with my wonderful family and all the daily joys I have in life.

CPSIA information can be obtained at www.ICGtesting.com
Printed in the USA
BVOW08s1122190816

459034BV00003B/1/P